I0810362

IMAGES
of America

GARDEN STATE PARKWAY

On the Cover: The rolling topography of Monmouth County displays the open nature of the Garden State Parkway, separated from nearby development and offering a pleasant travelling experience. (Courtesy of the New Jersey Turnpike Authority.)

IMAGES
of America

GARDEN STATE PARKWAY

The New Jersey Turnpike Authority

ARCADIA
PUBLISHING

ISBN 978-0-7385-9844-4

Published by Arcadia Publishing
Charleston, South Carolina

Printed in the United States of America

Library of Congress Control Number: 2012949469

For all general information, please contact Arcadia Publishing:
Telephone 843-853-2070
Fax 843-853-0044
E-mail sales@arcadiapublishing.com
For customer service and orders:
Toll-Free 1-888-313-2665

Visit us on the Internet at www.arcadiapublishing.com

To the employees of the New Jersey Highway Authority and the New Jersey Turnpike Authority for keeping the Garden State Parkway special.

Contents

ACKNOWLEDGMENTS

The Garden State Parkway was designated as an eligible historic district in 2001. This publication was developed as a result of the cultural resources requirement for one of the largest improvement projects on the Garden State Parkway since its original construction in the 1950s, the widening from Interchange 30 to 80. It took nearly a decade to get this project from concept to construction, which was due to the leadership of the executive staff currently under the direction of executive director Veronique Hakim and the tireless efforts of many of her departments, including individuals of the New Jersey Turnpike Authority's engineering department headed up by chief engineer Richard J. Raczynski and his deputy chief engineers Robert J. Fischer and J. Lawrence Williams and their consultants. While this aspect of the massive project represented a very small portion of the effort, development of this publication was a rewarding experience, an opportunity to work across departments and relive some of the former New Jersey Highway Authority's greatest moments.

After the retirement of G. Bruce Connor, Lamis T. Malak, senior highway engineer, took over management responsibility of the Parkway widening project, which included overseeing the development of the book. However, the greatest contributors to this book are former New Jersey Highway Authority employees, now New Jersey Turnpike Authority employees, who shared their own experiences and body of knowledge for the benefit of this book. John T. Withers, who started with the New Jersey Highway Authority and is now the New Jersey Turnpike Authority's supervising engineer of Highways and Building Design, shared his knowledge of the history and workings of the Parkway and New Jersey Highway Authority, which greatly enhanced the quality of this book. His longtime coworkers, Denise deSante, customer service manager, and Bridget Harrington Ernst, engineering administrator, also freely shared their knowledge of the New Jersey Highway Authority's administration and social activities as well their fondest memories of the New Jersey Highway Authority. Denise deSante maintains the extensive archives from which all of the historic material was drawn and continues to maintain the archives of the New Jersey Turnpike Authority's latest accomplishments.

Gannett Fleming has a long history with the Parkway as it was the designer of record for some southern sections of the original roadway and was integral in the image and text assembly of this book. Led by John W. Martin, he shared writing duties with Mark Brosnan and Carrie Bonano, also of Gannett Fleming, as well as the selection of images and organization.

All images in this publication are courtesy of the New Jersey Turnpike Authority.

INTRODUCTION

The Garden State Parkway traverses New Jersey from the New York state line south to Cape May in what has been important real estate throughout history. The first inhabitants were Native Americans who have occupied the area from perhaps as early as 12,000 B.C. Early populations of Native Americans in New Jersey were small groups focused on hunting and gathering who moved with the seasons and the availability of food and raw material resources. The groups likely populated river floodplains, streams, and marshes and utilized waterways and trails for movements across the area. By around 4,000 B.C., the natural vegetation and climate in New Jersey was the same as today and the forest offered food sources, such as seeds, nuts, and game. Shellfish were abundant at the shore, and regular, seasonal movements were part of the lifeways of New Jersey's Native American populations. The arrival of Europeans permanently altered local societies and a combination of disease, conflict, and competition for resources led to the dispersal of many of the remaining Native Americans west to the northern Susquehanna River or western Pennsylvania, Ohio, and beyond, or north into Canada.

The Swedes, Dutch, French, and English settled parts of New Jersey during the 1700s and established whaling, fishing, and oyster industries along the outer coastal plain. Villages and fortifications were built along the Delaware River as European enterprises struggled for control of the area. They built sawmills and furnaces and mined bog iron and transported their products on sand roads, creeks, and rivers via ferries and barges. Settlement was centered near resources, and waterways were the primary means to send goods to market.

During the late 1700s, pleasure travel became more prevalent, especially to the New Jersey shores. Stage roads allowed stagecoaches to travel from Camden to Tuckerton in one and a half days. By the mid-1800s, railroads opened New Jersey to more travel and industrialization as transportation became more affordable and easily available. Industrial towns and cities developed near railroad terminals as people moved there to be close to employers. With time, the cities grew big enough that employees could no longer walk to work. Soon trolleys and commuter trains transported both workers and consumers in and around cities. The workforce and consumers were becoming more mobile but still reliant upon transportation lines. Population growth was fueled by multiple waves of immigration.

After World War I, the automobile reversed the trend in which trains and trolleys created a concentration of goods, services, and workplaces at various locations. The automobile allowed for population dispersal. People could live farther from both work and resources, as they were no longer dependent upon the rails. Industries could be housed farther away from the railroad as trucks began to transport goods to consumers, resulting in the demise of trolleys and the loss of railroad dominance in commercial and passenger transportation.

However, the road network, or lack thereof, became a pressing issue. In 1919, the War Department conducted a much-publicized training exercise known as the Transcontinental Army Motor Convoy. The expedition was to travel along the route of the Lincoln Highway from Washington, DC, to San

Francisco, operating as if they were traveling through enemy territory during a fictional conflict. The journey took 62 days to complete, mainly because large portions of the highway consisted of dirt roads; sections that crossed western deserts were often little more than unimproved tracks. Complicating matters, few of the participating enlisted men had any experience driving motorized vehicles. Among the military personnel was Lt. Col. Dwight D. Eisenhower, who would later champion the construction of an integrated national highway system following this experience and his observations of the German autobahns during World War II.

At the time, very few states had highway departments and roads were the primary responsibility of the local municipality or rural communities who often could not afford to build new roads. In 1921, Congress passed the Federal Highway Act, which provided funding for states with established highway departments. This gave states an incentive to create highway departments. The Federal Highway Act helped to double the number of paved roads across the country within a decade. As roads were built, automobile and truck use proliferated. However, these roads were not designed for such a dramatic increase in traffic and high load capacity truck use. Highway departments recognized that new roads designed for the increased capacity and load were needed. By World War II, many New Jersey highways transported nearly twice the amount of traffic they were designed to carry. In the urban areas, commuters jammed local roads while vying with trucks for space. In southern New Jersey, vacationers sat snarled in traffic on local roads as they attempted to reach the shore. Officials feared that resort towns would begin to die as people, exasperated by the effort to drive to the shore, decided to travel elsewhere.

In 1945, the New Jersey Legislature recognized the need to alleviate the immense overcrowding on the roadways from population increases. That year, Gov. Walter E. Edge signed legislation that authorized the Garden State Parkway project, which would be a modern facility that connected the urban areas of the north with the shore points. The Garden State Parkway was originally Route 4 and a project of the New Jersey State Highway Department. Ground broke on the Route 4 project in November 1946. Between 1946 and 1953, three short sections of Route 4 were constructed in Cape May, Ocean, Middlesex, Union, and Essex Counties, totalling a mere 22 miles. Progress was slow and limited because the state legislature was required to allocate the funds for the construction and maintenance of the roadway. The Garden State Parkway project did not receive the funding it required from the legislature and, consequently, the design, property acquisition, and construction efforts remained spotty.

From the outset of his administration, Gov. Alfred E. Driscoll (1947–1953) was concerned with the inadequacy of the road network in New Jersey. By 1952, Governor Driscoll was frustrated by a lack of progress in the project and feared that Route 4 would never be finished if it relied completely on state funds. He proposed that a new agency, the New Jersey Highway Authority, be created to manage the project, creating a toll road from Cape May in the south to Paramus in the north. The idea for the Garden State Parkway was born. The agency needed large amounts of funding in a short period of time, so Governor Driscoll argued that the New Jersey Highway Authority be allowed to pay for construction through state-supported bonds. It was calculated that toll revenues would be sufficient to repay the bonds and cover maintenance and operational costs. The New Jersey Highway Authority would use the Route 4 sections already completed and then add roughly another 153 miles to create the Garden State Parkway. By January 1952, he urged the legislature to allow creation of the new road, and by April 14, he signed the New Jersey Highway Act into law, thus unleashing a herculean effort to build the Garden State Parkway.

One

The Origin of the New Jersey Highway Authority

Many people, especially businessmen and politicians, realized that there was a great need for the Garden State Parkway, but the lack of both funding and an organization to manage the effort were major hindrances. With the passage of the New Jersey Highway Authority Act in 1952, both issues were addressed. The act authorized the sale of bonds to be repaid with future toll revenue and established a board of three unpaid commissioners to be appointed by Governor Driscoll and approved by the New Jersey State Senate. The commissioners would manage the New Jersey Highway Authority and shape the development and construction of the Garden State Parkway. While commissioner terms were set at nine years, the initial appointments were for staggered lengths of three, six, and nine years, so as to keep from having all positions up for appointment at the same time. The New Jersey Highway Authority commissioners developed and set policy and bore a great deal of responsibility for the Garden State Parkway project. Experience, competency, and drive were obvious assets necessary for the positions, but so was a desire to accomplish this state-altering task.

During the summer of 1952, the State Highway Department completed comprehensive engineering reports and consultants were brought on board to help manage the project. The firm of Parsons, Brinkerhoff, Hall, and MacDonald was retained as the general engineering consultant, Coverdale and Colpitts was retained to perform additional traffic and revenue studies, and Clarke and Ramaupo was employed for landscape architecture. The New Jersey Highway Authority chief engineer was Harold W. Giffin, borrowed from the State Highway Department, with Oliver W. Deakin assisting him as design engineer. With many of the crucial elements in place, the project was set to move into high gear.

However, the consultant teams were only responsible for the design and construction of the project, leaving the operation to the New Jersey Highway Authority. Therefore, in addition to the commissioners, the New Jersey Highway Authority required the leadership of an executive director who would be responsible for the day-to-day operation and the initial task of completing the Garden State Parkway. Eventually, the executive director would be in charge of a 1,148-person force that operated and maintained the Garden State Parkway.

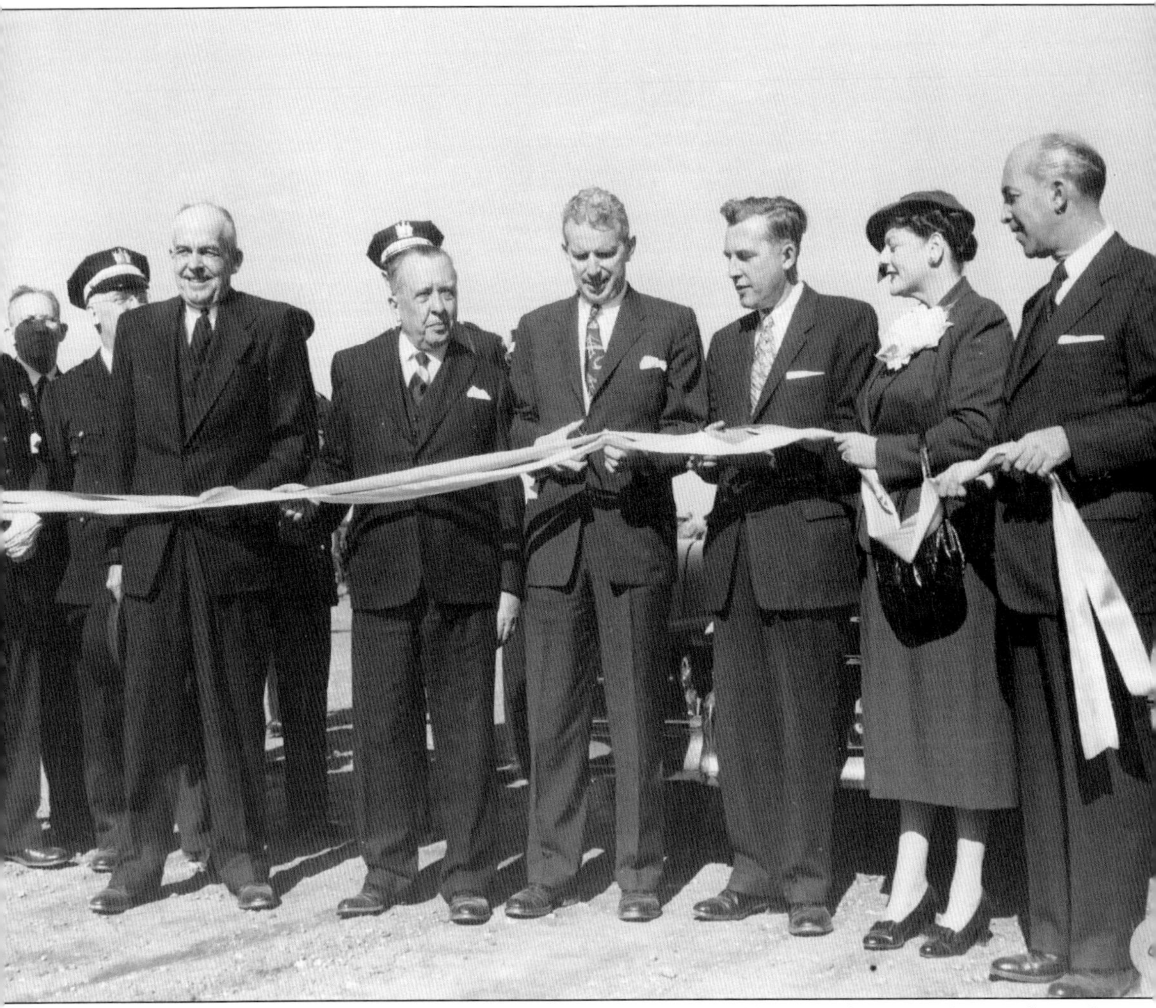

The official grand opening of the Garden State Parkway was held on October 23, 1954, at Telegraph Hill Park in Holmdel. Those participating included, from left to right, New Jersey Highway Authority executive director Ransford J. Abbott, New Jersey Highway Authority chairman Orrie de Nooyer, former governor Alfred E. Driscoll, Gov. Robert B. Meyner, and Commissioners Katharine E. White and Bayard L. England. Although the construction of the Garden State Parkway was accomplished in short order, it still spanned across administrations and appointees, requiring a cooperative effort from many important individuals. Ransford J. Abbott was a state highway commissioner when he was appointed as the first chairman of the New Jersey Highway Authority in 1952. He resigned after two years when he became its executive director, a position he held until the end of 1954. The Garden State Parkway was considered "the road of tomorrow" and was built in several sections, ultimately resulting in 173 miles of road.

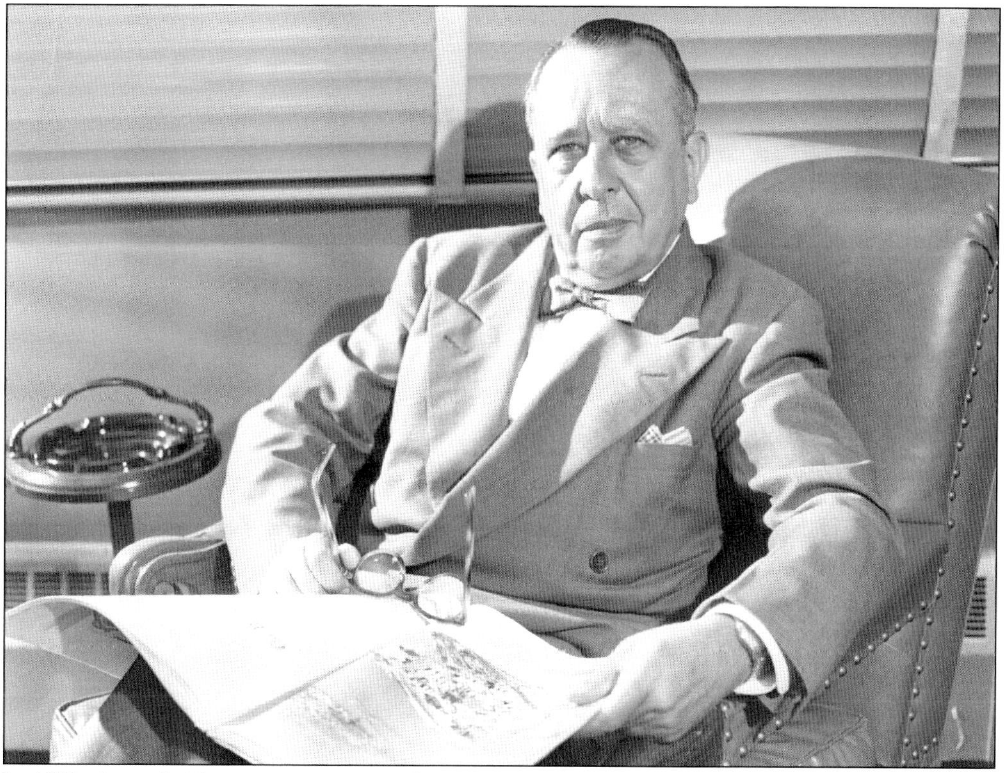

In 1952, Orrie de Nooyer was appointed to the Board of Commissioners for the New Jersey Highway Authority by Gov. Alfred Driscoll. At the time, he was the vice president for purchasing at Julius Forstmann & Company, a woolen manufacturer located in Paterson, New Jersey. Gov. Robert B. Meyner appointed him as chairman to succeed Ransford J. Abbott in 1954, a position he held until his term expired in 1955.

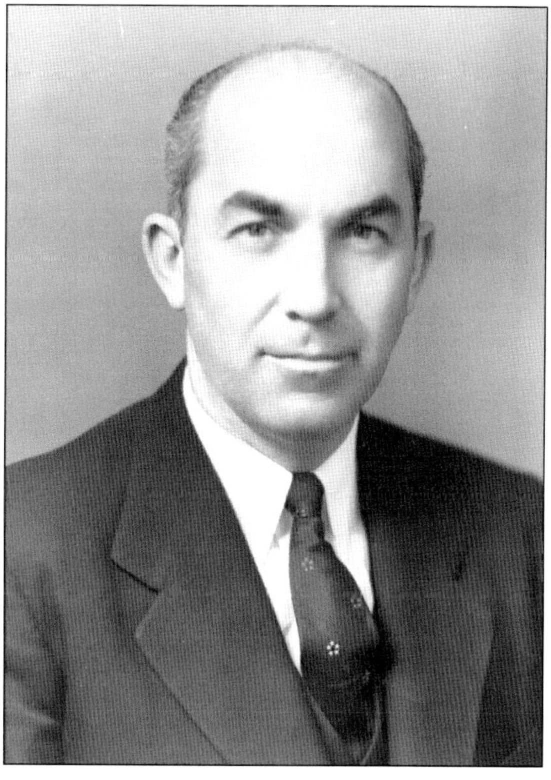

Bayard England was the president of the Atlantic City Electric Company when he was selected for the New Jersey Highway Authority commission on June 26, 1952, by Governor Driscoll. He was reappointed as vice chairman in 1954 by Governor Meyner and continued to serve as a commissioner until resigning in 1955. Bayard England was keenly aware of the benefit for easier travel to places at the shore, such as Atlantic City.

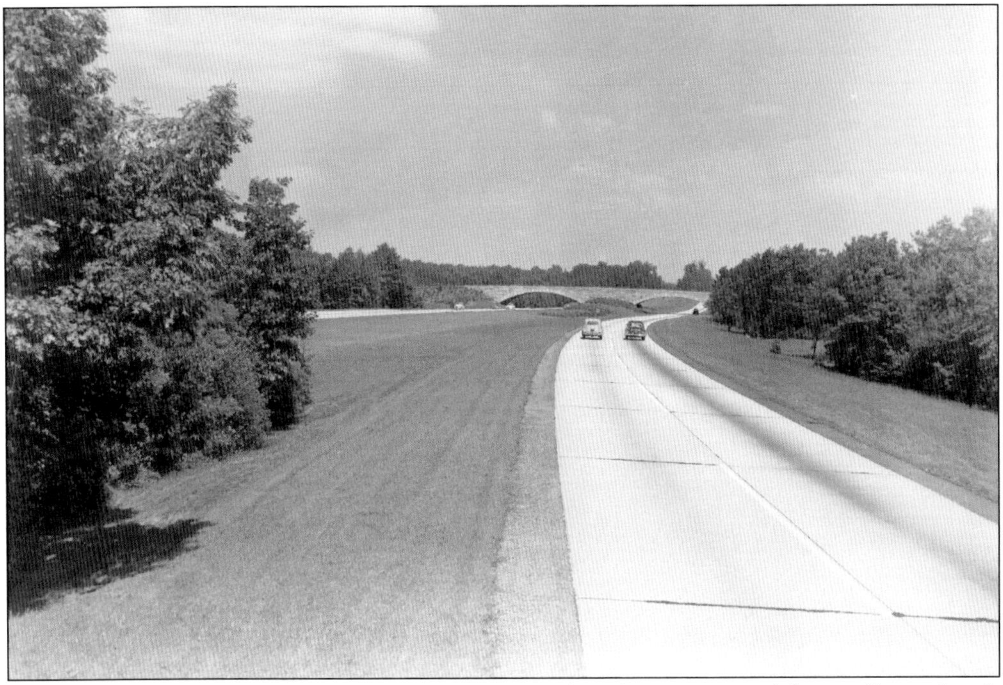

The State Highway Department constructed 25 reinforced concrete rigid-frame elliptical arch bridges in the first 20 miles of Route 4 prior to the creation of the New Jersey Highway Authority. The one here in Middlesex County was faced in stone, as were all of the northern county structures built in the state section in order to blend in with the nature of the landscape.

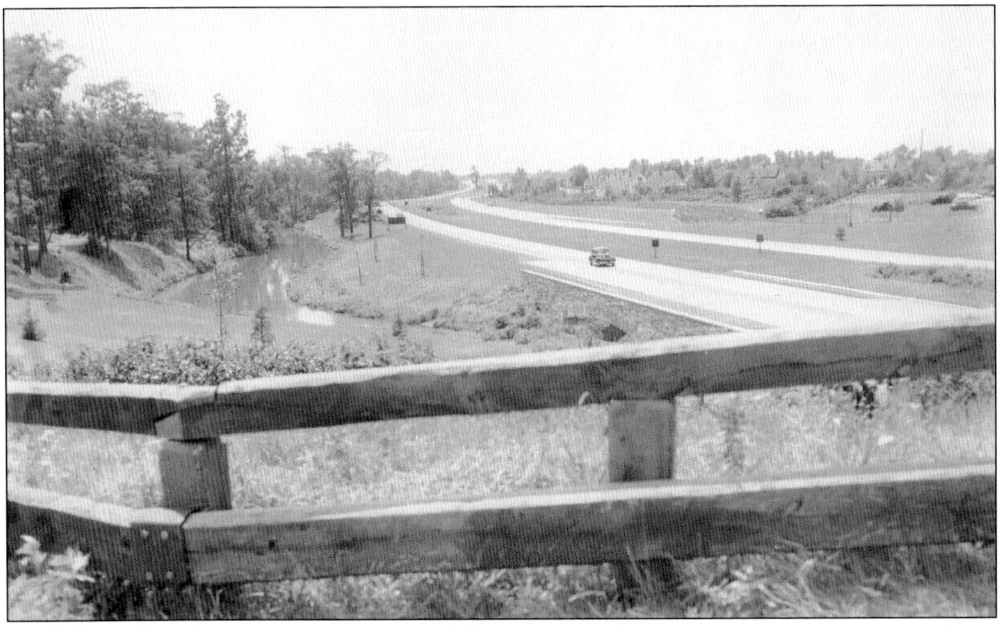

In this 1953 view of the state section in Middlesex County, drivers were treated to a scenic drive. Tolls were not charged on the portions of the Garden State Parkway constructed with funds from the state legislature, only those funded with bonds. Motorists could hop on and off this section without paying because there were no tolls on the exits.

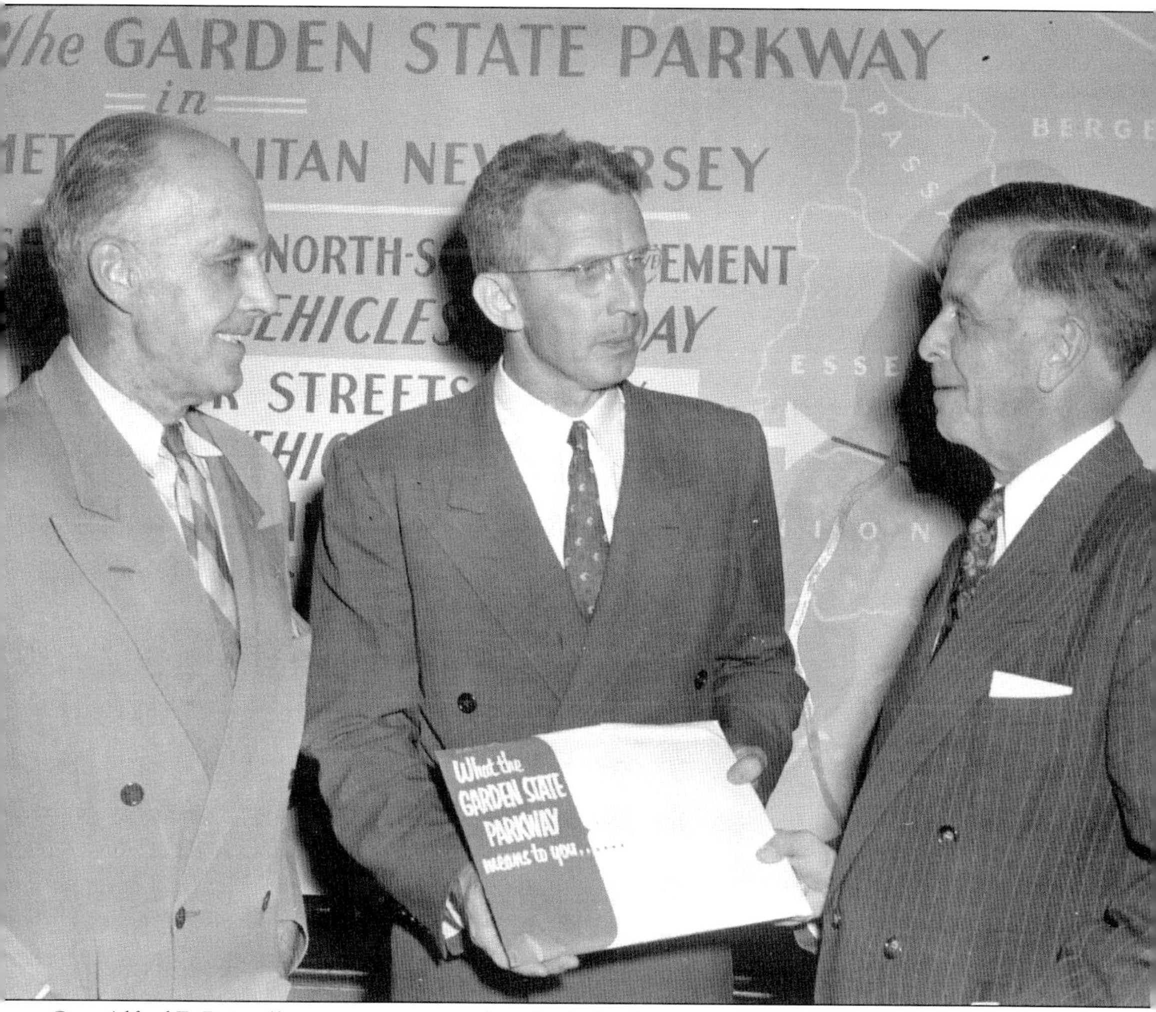

Gov. Alfred E. Driscoll, center, campaigned tirelessly for the creation of the Garden State Parkway and even appeared in a film extolling the benefits of its construction. Here, with Commissioner Ransford J. Abbott (left), he explains the expected benefits and provides an information packet titled "What the Garden State Parkway Means to You" to an unidentified man. Governor Driscoll was responsible for the two most well-known roads in New Jersey: the Garden State Parkway and the New Jersey Turnpike. The New Jersey Turnpike was seen to be important for the movement of commercial goods through the state and was designed to be efficient and utilitarian. The Garden State Parkway, however, was important for the people of New Jersey commuting to work or vacationing at the shore. There was a serious need for easier access to the resort towns along the shore that were in danger of being bypassed because of traffic-clogged local roads. From its conception, the Garden State Parkway was to provide a safe and pleasurable experience for the motoring public.

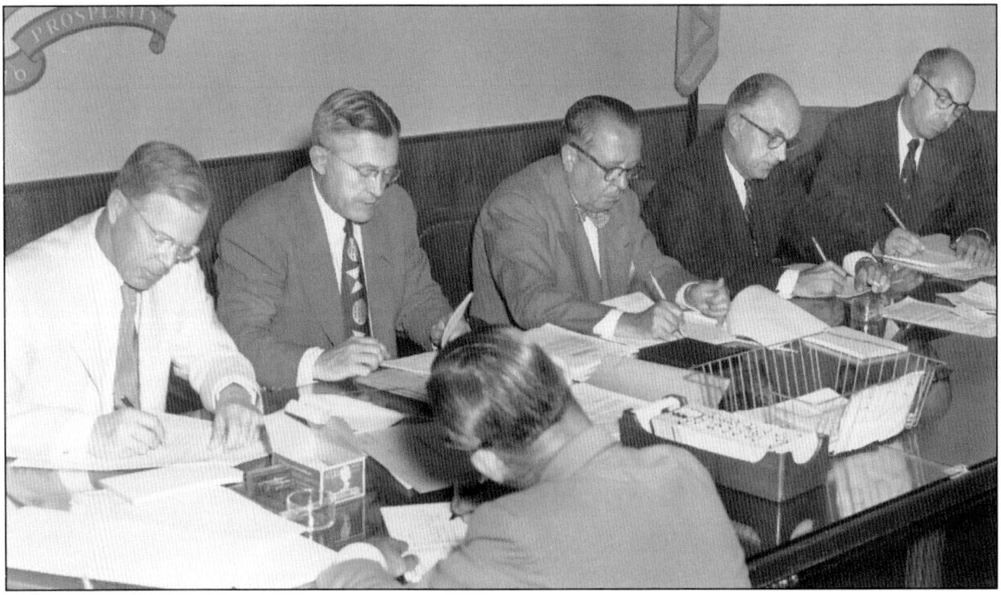

Chief engineer Harold W. Giffin (left) participates in a bid opening in 1952. Harold Giffin is credited with inventing reflective curbs and "singing shoulders." He was also an authority on the traffic circle, once a characteristic of the state roads of New Jersey. On the Garden State Parkway, Harold Giffin employed cloverleaf designs for interchanges because of the need for grade separation between roadways.

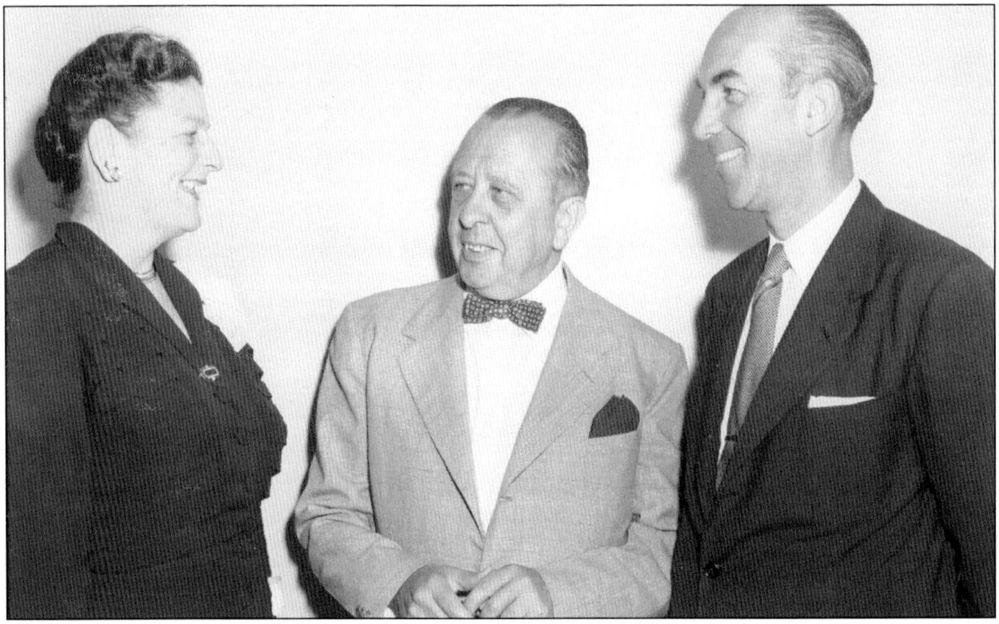

The New Jersey Highway Authority commissioners who oversaw the completion of the original portion of the Garden State Parkway comprised Commissioner Katharine E. White, chairman Orrie de Nooyer, and Commissioner Bayard L. England. Commissioners de Nooyer and England were two of the original three appointed by Governor Driscoll. The New Jersey Highway Authority was responsible for the planning, design, construction, maintenance, and operation of the Garden State Parkway. The bulk of its 173-mile corridor was completed between 1952 and 1956.

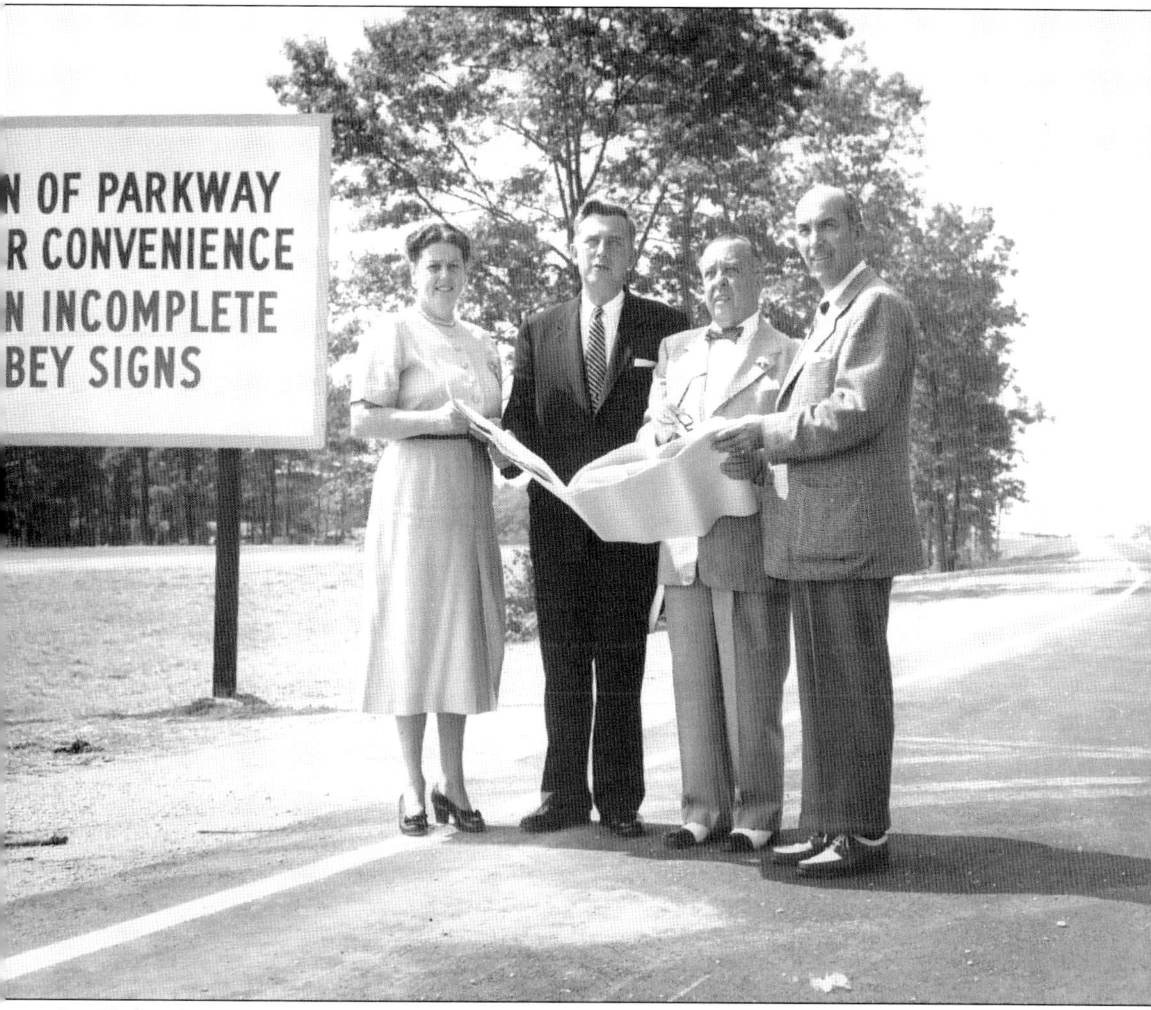

Gov. Robert B. Meyner (second from left) succeeded Governor Driscoll and oversaw the completion of the Garden State Parkway, including the appointment of the second set of commissioners. Governor Meyner (1954–1962) was a Democrat but carried on with the Garden State Parkway plans of his Republican predecessors. A gifted orator, Governor Meyner could help sell the idea of the project and ensure its completion and connection to the New York State Thruway. Due to a change in state law, Governor Meyner was allowed to serve two consecutive terms, providing a stay in office that was not afforded to Governor Driscoll. However, the importance of the Garden State Parkway was understood by most in state government. Governor Meyner is also responsible for New Jersey's Green Acres program, which provides state funding for the preservation of open space and is still an important program for the state.

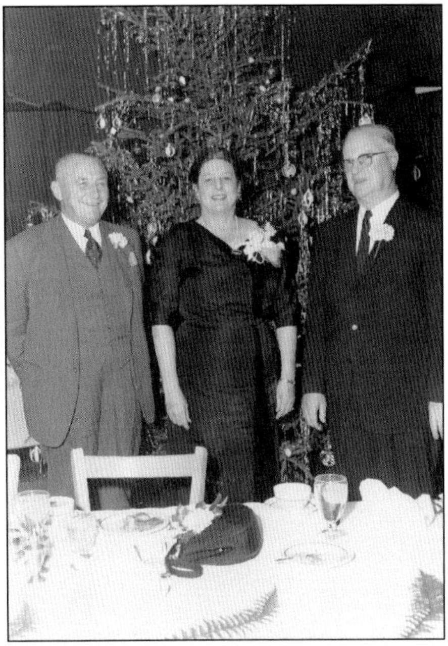

Commissioners Sylvester C. Smith Jr. (left) and Dr. John B. Townsend flank chairman Katharine E. White at the 1961 Christmas party. Sylvester C. Smith Jr. was the general counsel for the Prudential Insurance Company of America when appointed by Governor Meyner in 1955 to succeed Orrie de Nooyer. A resident of West Orange, he was elected treasurer following his appointment. Dr. Townsend was a physician in Ocean City when he was appointed to replace Bayard L. England in 1955. He was elected secretary of the commission and was appointed vice chairman later that year, following the elevation of Katharine E. White to chairman. He continued to serve as secretary until 1959. Both men would go on to serve over 20 years as commissioners, a testament to the importance placed on the New Jersey Highway Authority and Garden State Parkway. During their tenure, the Parkway was completed and expanded, demonstrating the importance of the road and the growth it fostered.

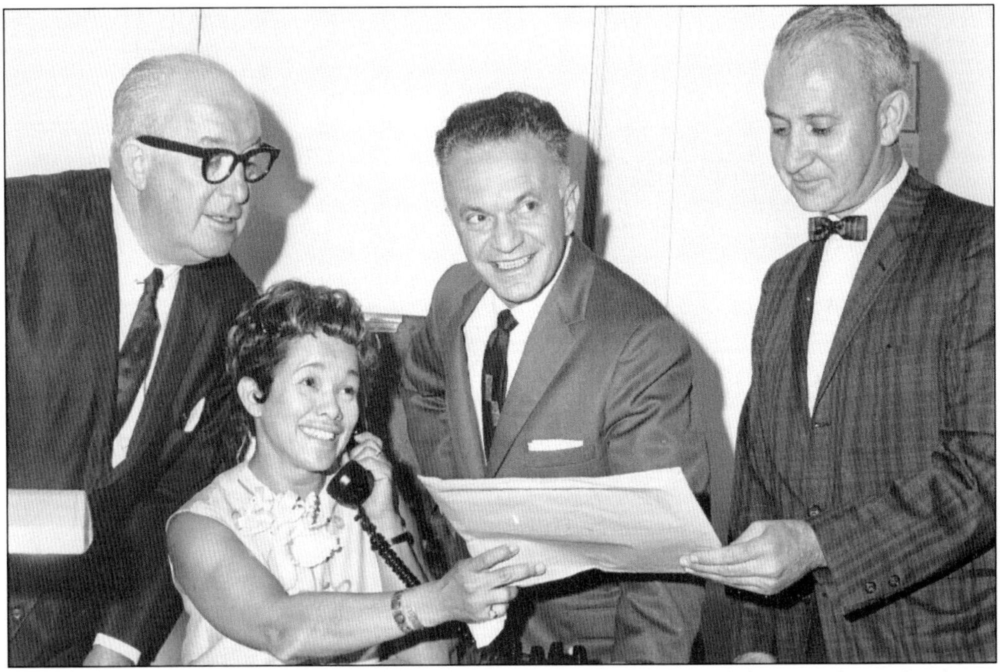

D. Louis Tonti (standing, center) served as the executive director of the New Jersey Highway Authority for 16 years following the resignation of Ransford J. Abbott at the end of 1954. Here, he is flanked by East Orange mayor James Kelly (left) and New Jersey Highway Authority public relations director Milton Levy (right) in 1964. Secretary J. Brown is on the phone at the information center for the Interchange 145 construction project. Under Tonti's leadership, the Garden State Parkway was completed and portions expanded from the original design. He was a driving force behind the creation of the Garden State Arts Center (now the PNC Arts Center). Tonti stepped down as executive director to run for the governor's office in 1969.

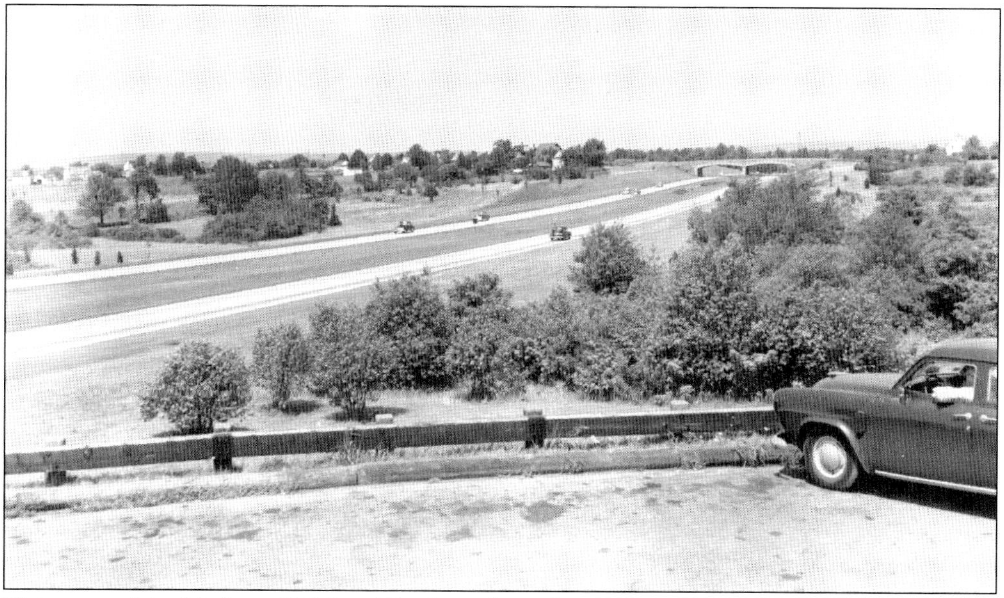

This view of the Madison Hill Road Bridge is from the Madison Hill rest stop in a state-owned section of the Garden State Parkway in Clark Township, Union County. The photograph illustrates the country feel landscape architects designed. Despite the fact that the Garden State Parkway in this section runs through a heavily developed portion of the state, the encroaching built environment would not be apparent to motorists.

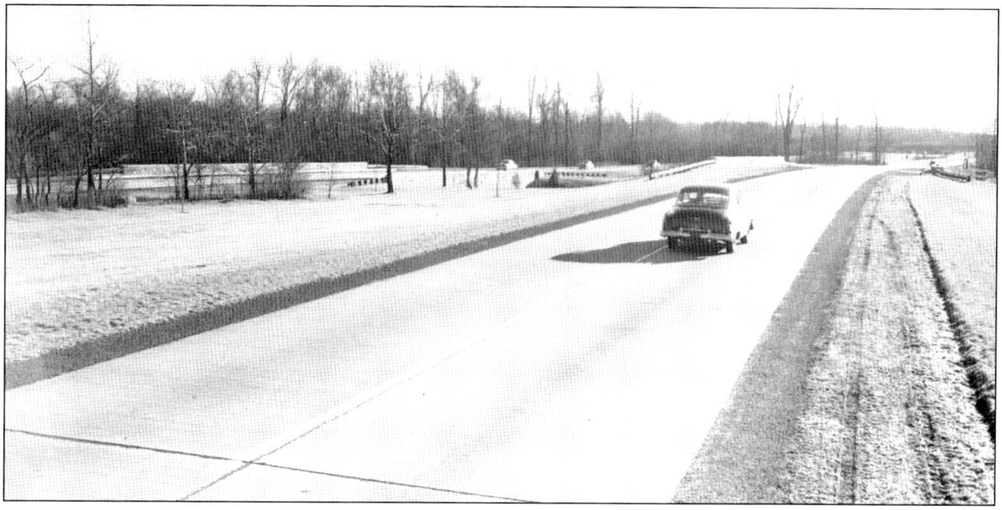

This portion of the Garden State Parkway in Middlesex County was part of Route 4, originally constructed by the State Highway Department. Because it was built with taxpayer money, exit tolls along this section were not installed. However, the absence of exit tolls for these four sections created funding issues for the new Garden State Parkway. Drivers soon realized that exiting from the toll-free sections saved in their costs at the expense of the New Jersey Highway Authority since the Parkway maintenance was funded through toll collection. The results of a traffic survey in 1958 predicted that the road would face a deficit by 1964 under the existing operation due to the prevalence of toll-avoiding drivers in the heavily used northern section. Barrier tolls were added in part to prevent the avoidance of tolls and to increase revenue to sustainable levels. Their presence also reduced the traffic on local roads, a primary objective of the Garden State Parkway.

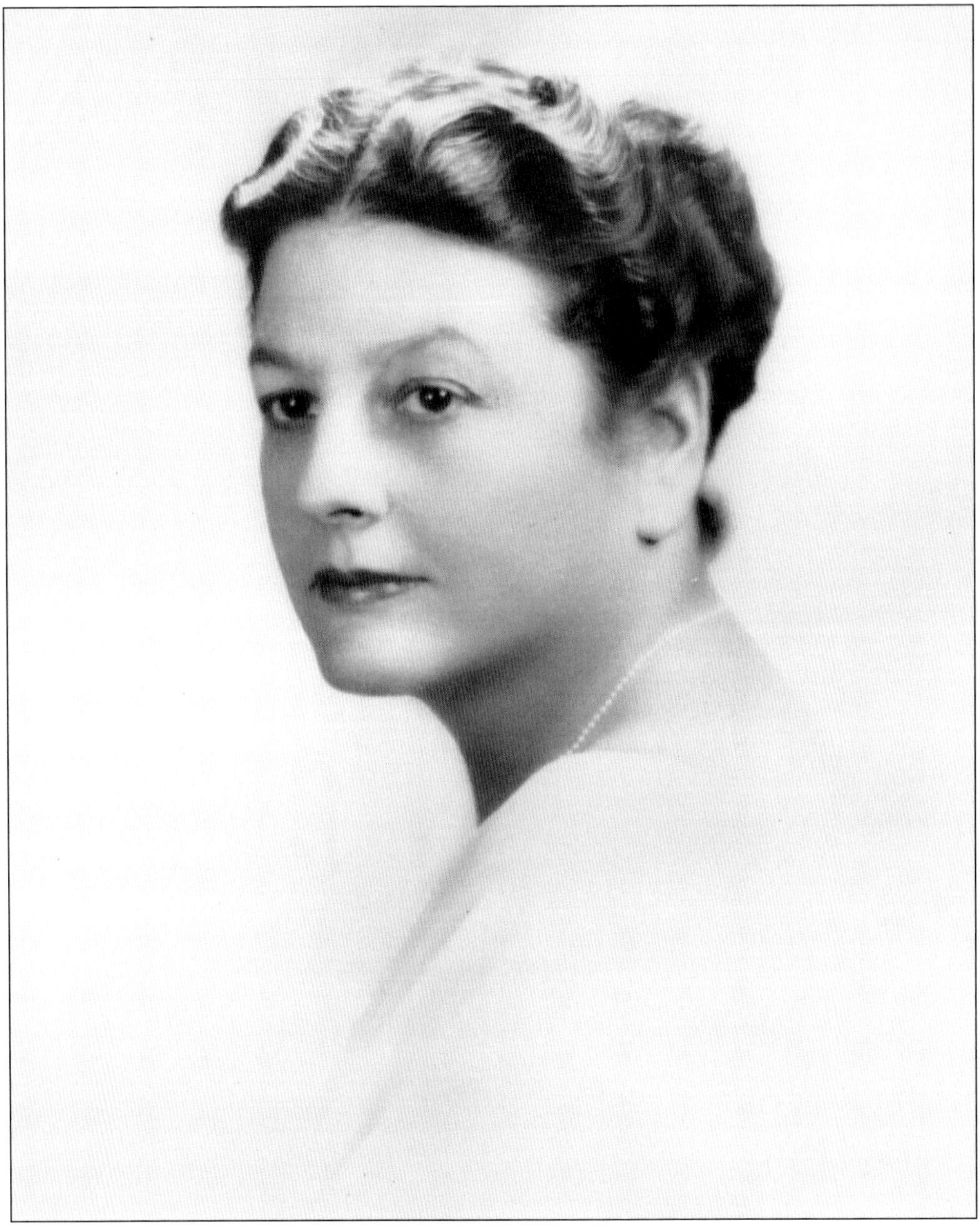

Katharine E. White was appointed chairman of the New Jersey Highway Authority commission in 1955 and held the position until 1964. She was an impressive leader, elected mayor of Red Bank three times, and then appointed by Gov. Robert B. Meyner to finish Ransford J. Abbott's nine-year term in 1954; she initially served as secretary. She later succeeded Bayard L. England as vice chairman and was elected treasurer one day later. She replaced Orrie de Nooyer as chairman in 1955, following the completion of his term, thus becoming the first woman leader of a state transportation bureau. She was an overachiever during a time when few women held political office in the United States and positions in business and government were dominated by men. Following her tenure at the New Jersey Highway Authority, Katharine White was appointed US ambassador to Denmark by Pres. Lyndon Johnson in 1964.

Two

Building the Garden State Parkway

The goal of the New Jersey Highway Authority was to create a parkway that was uninterrupted, safe, fast, and scenic. While it was intended to be a recreational drive, the New Jersey Highway Authority also planned for the Garden State Parkway to perform a vital role in statewide transportation. Harold Giffin, called a "visionary and innovator," served in the State Highway Department as the chief designer of the original 20 miles of Route 4. The New Jersey Highway Authority borrowed him from the State Highway Department where he was secretary and appointed him as chief engineer for the Garden State Parkway. He worked with a large team to ensure the Parkway was a modern highway with a scenic, country feel, created by shrubs and trees within medians plus wooded buffers alongside the travel lanes.

Harold Giffin was assisted by Oliver W. Deakin as design engineer. Parsons, Brinkerhoff, Hall, and MacDonald functioned as the general engineering consultant and oversaw the group of engineering consultants. Cloverdale and Colpitts performed revenue and traffic studies while Clarke and Rampaupo designed the landscape architecture. Gilmore Clarke was already a well-known New York landscape architect who worked on the 1939 New York World's Fair and Bronx River Parkway. Demolition experts, bridge specialists, and paving contractors rounded out the team.

The result was an innovative highway constructed in a way that had not been attempted until the 1950s. Before then, modern highways were straight, parallel lanes of traffic with narrow medians or barriers separating the different directions of traffic. Studies of the Pennsylvania Turnpike, which was traditionally constructed, found that drivers experienced fatigue on long, straight stretches. Garden State Parkway engineers took this information to heart and designed a highway where the opposing lanes of traffic were separated from one another by wide medians when possible, followed their own alignment, and introduced curves into the plan to help reduce driver fatigue.

The 173 miles of the Garden State Parkway opened from the New York Thruway to Cape May, or the top to bottom of the entire state of New Jersey, within five years of the creation of the New Jersey Highway Authority. It is doubtful that this feat could be replicated today.

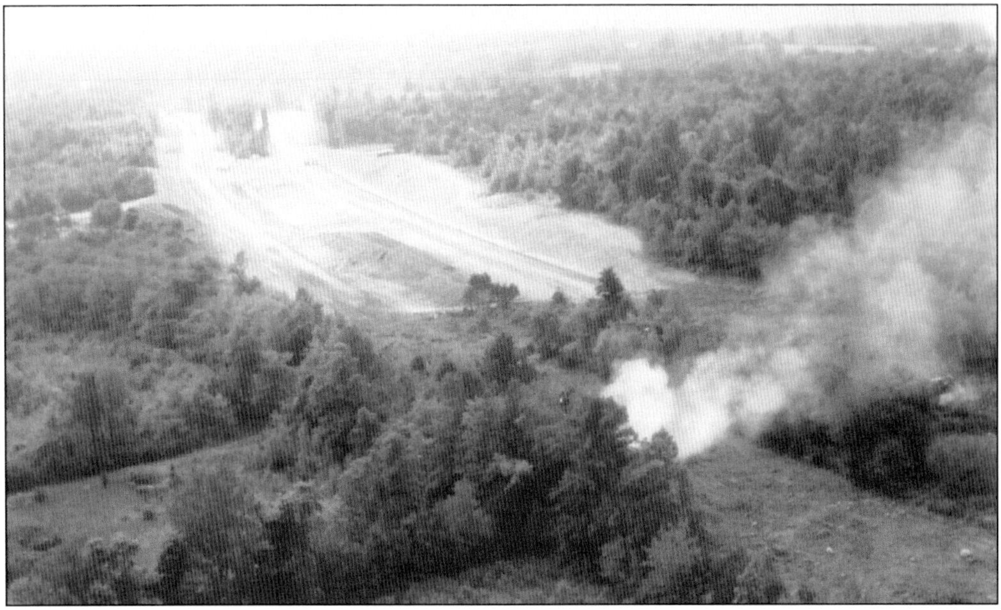

The Garden State Parkway was constructed in forested areas throughout much of its southern portion. Although extensive swaths of land were cleared for the construction of the Parkway, portions of forest such as the median here were preserved. This section in Wall Township, Monmouth County, was undeveloped prior to the construction of the Parkway, which changed the landscape of New Jersey, both in terms of transportation and growth.

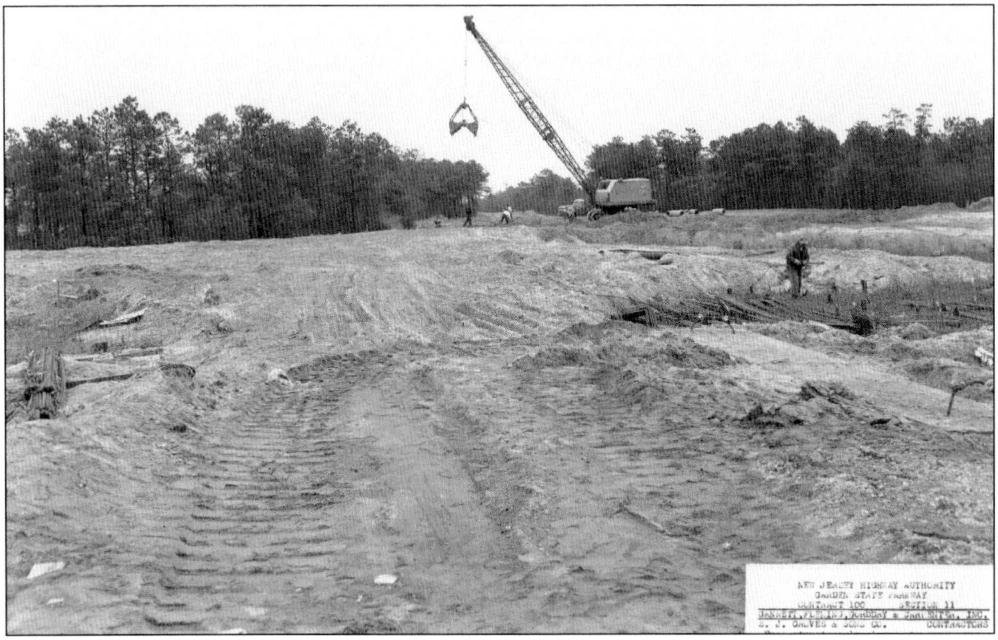

The construction of the Garden State Parkway included the excavation of nearly 53,250,000 cubic yards of earth. Construction in Atlantic County in 1953 illustrates the enormous amount of earthmoving required to construct the Parkway. Contractors cleared land equivalent to a third of the area of Manhattan, or about 4,300 acres, and excavated enough soil to fill the Atlantic City Convention Hall 94 times.

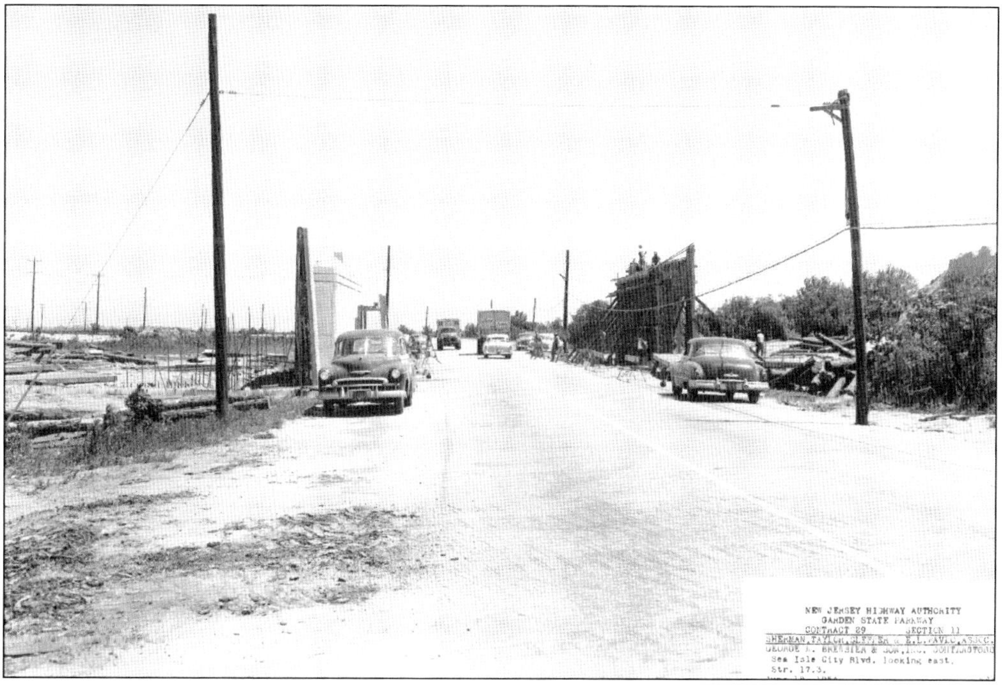

A work crew places concrete into a form for a bridge support over Sea Isle City Boulevard in Dennis Township, Cape May County. The opposite abutment to the left of the roadway is already complete. In all, 25,665 tons of reinforcing steel was used during construction of the Garden State Parkway.

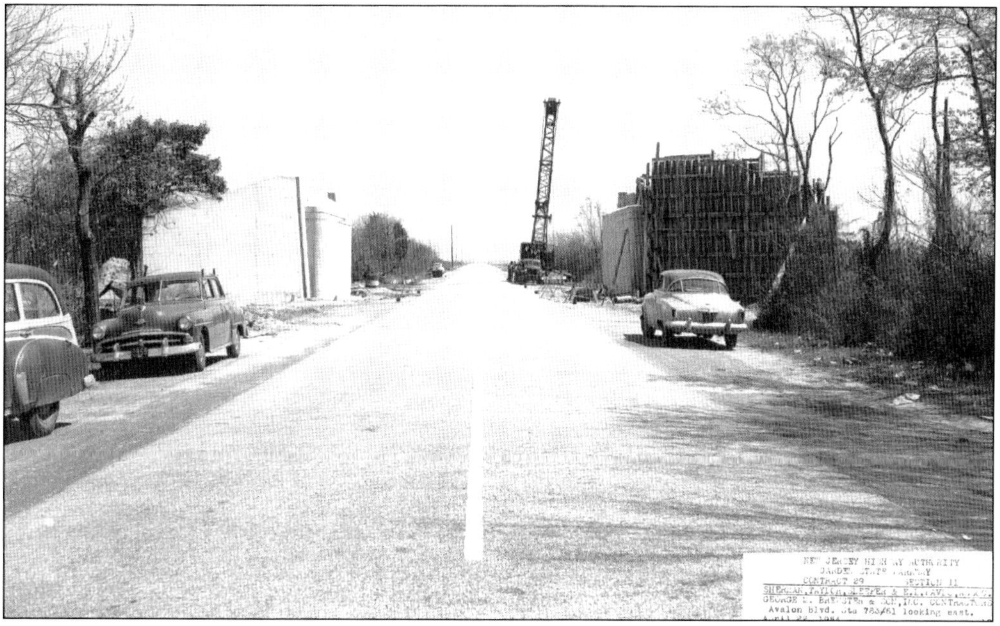

When the Garden State Parkway was completed, this bridge carried one direction of traffic for the Parkway over Avalon Boulevard in Middle Township, Cape May County. In order to expedite the opening of the roadway to traffic, this span and others carried both northbound and southbound traffic until both roadways were finished.

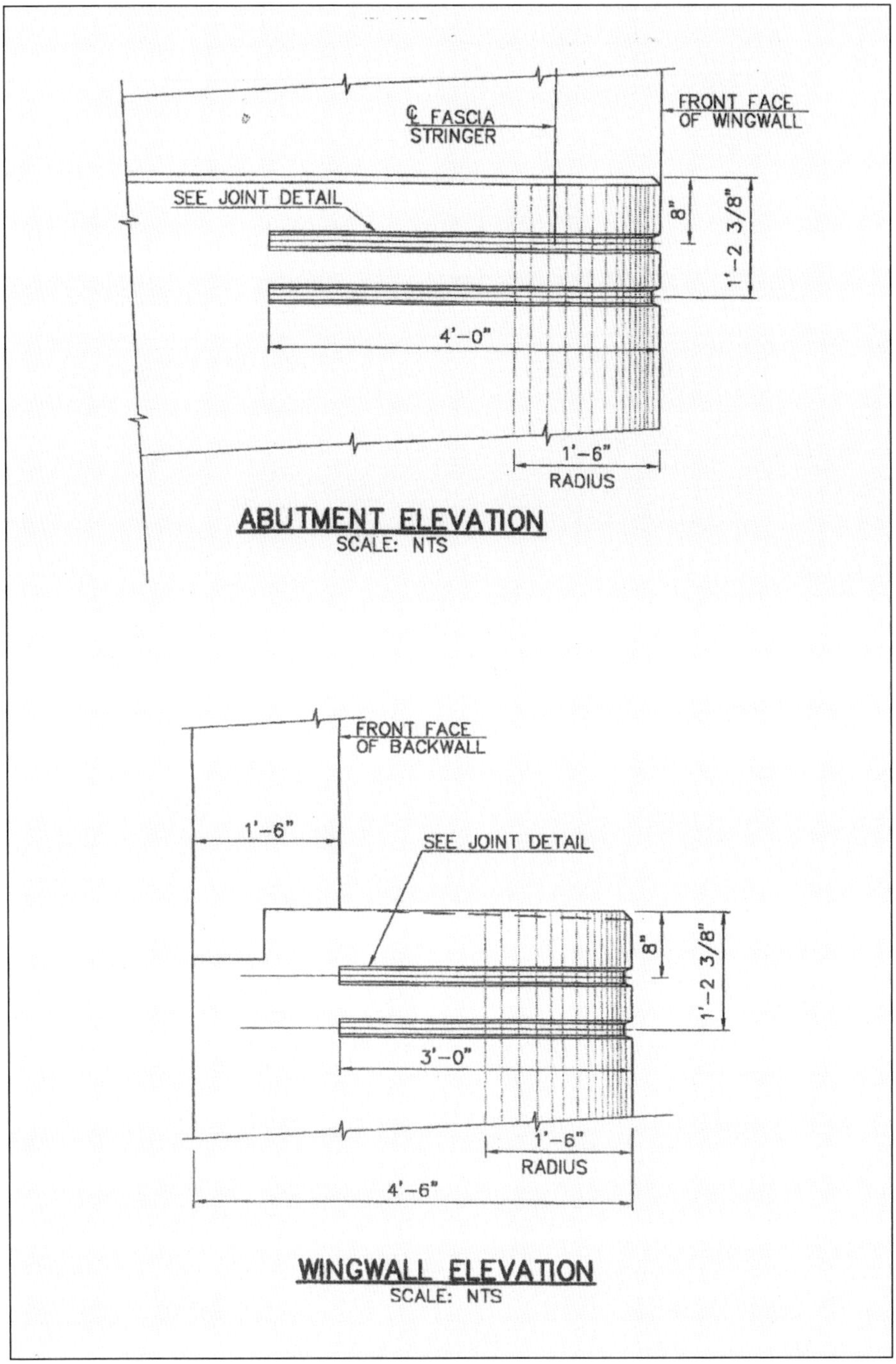

The bridge supports of the Garden State Parkway were constructed of reinforced concrete and featured two or three indented bands or reveals. This stylish feature not only gave the structures a consistent look, but also a sleek Art Moderne appearance. The Parkway, while providing a relaxing journey free from adjacent development along much of its route, was built for the future. The stylistic design cues of the structures and their consistent themes provide a harmonious and subtle feel. Such attention to detail helped to separate the Parkway from other, more utilitarian roads.

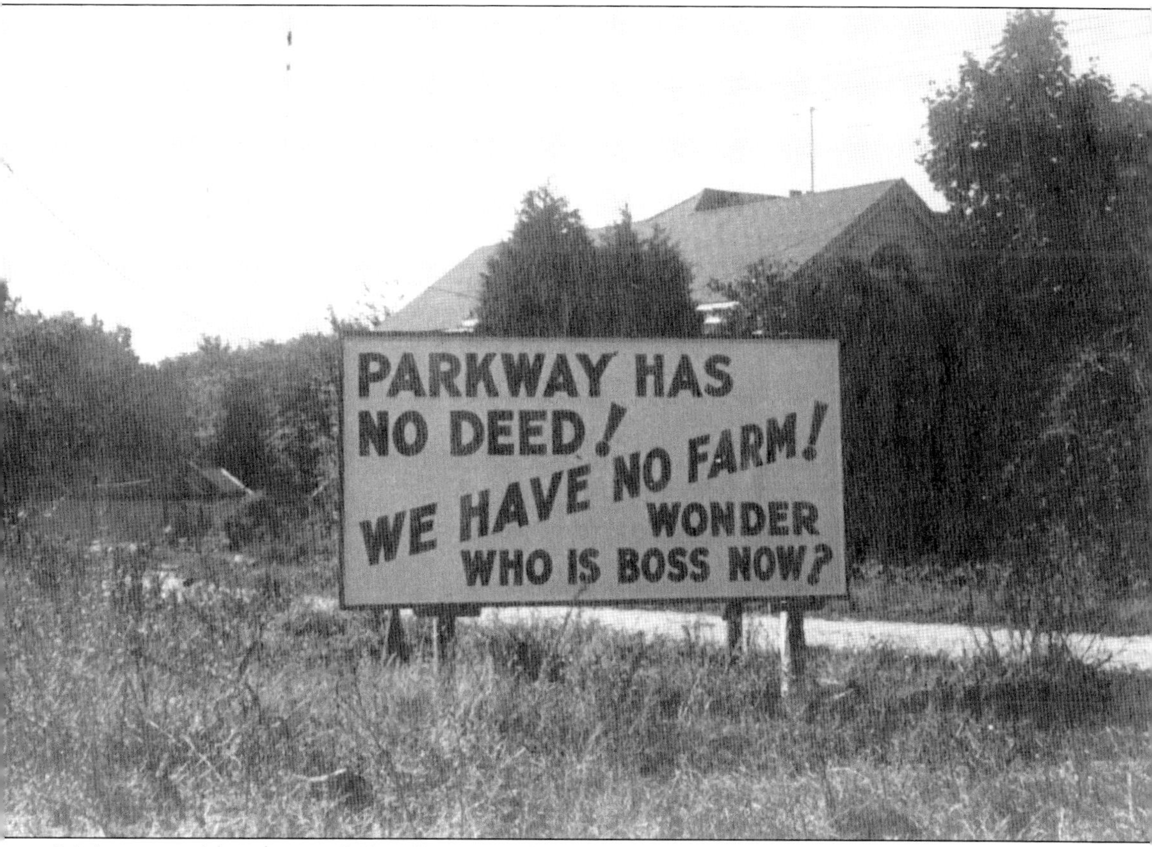

Of the original bond issue, $41 million was allotted for the acquisition of land for the Garden State Parkway right-of-way. A local paper, the *Bergen Evening Record*, characterized the property transactions as "the largest real estate deal of its kind east of the Mississippi." However, there were many landowners who were reluctant to sell their property for the road, even though a nearly two-to-one passage of the bond referendum signalled support for the project across the state. In the end, the removal of over 2,000 homes was necessary for the project. Not all land acquisition went smoothly, as this sign in Middletown, Monmouth County, attests. Other challenges were also mounted against the project. A lawsuit was filed against the New Jersey Highway Authority over the legality of the financial backing for the bonds that funded the Parkway. The Supreme Court of New Jersey ruled that the state guarantee of the bonds was constitutional in May 1953, removing the last major hurdle for construction of the Parkway.

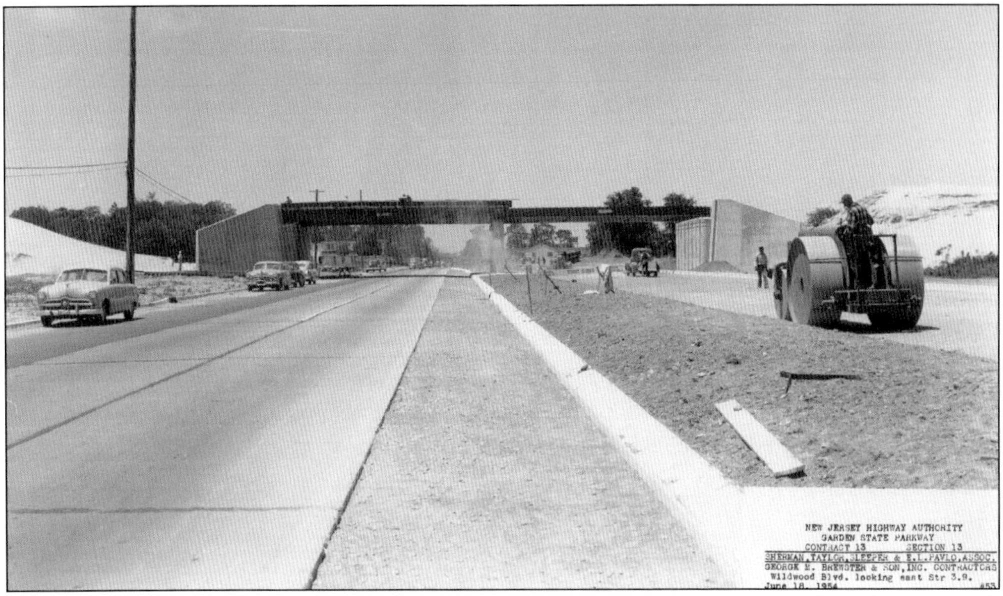

The Garden State Parkway utilized 37,100 tons of structural steel. Here, rolled steel girders will carry the Parkway over Wildwood Boulevard in Middle Township, Cape May County. This is the most common type of bridge on the Parkway, with 271 examples. In the northern urban sections or locations where the geography was constrained, single bridges with narrow concrete medians carried both northbound and southbound traffic. In locations where large medians separated the different directions of traffic, one bridge accommodated northbound lanes and a second carried southbound traffic.

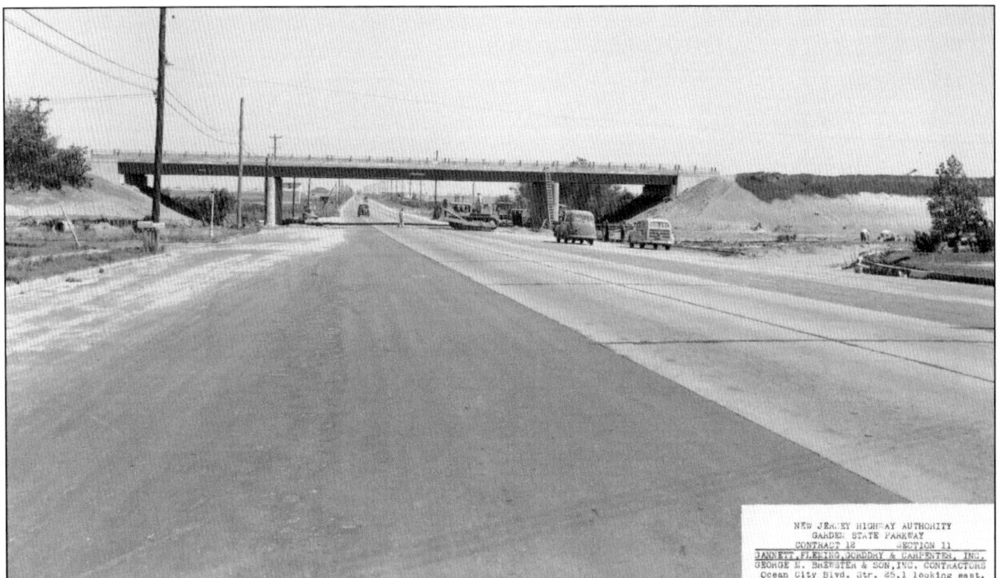

Nearing completion in 1954, the three-span rolled steel girder includes the distinctive tri-rail railing on top. The long center span would allow for the widening of Roosevelt Boulevard in Upper Township, Cape May County. This streamlined form would become fairly typical for later roads, such as the interstate system. The girders carry a concrete slab roadway for the Garden State Parkway.

The rapid construction pace of the Garden State Parkway involved dozens of contractors and engineering firms, all managed by the New Jersey Highway Authority and their general engineering consultant, Parsons, Brinkerhoff, Hall, and MacDonald. Both local and out of state firms were needed to complete the project on schedule. While each section may have had different designers and contractors who worked separately, they were not working independently.

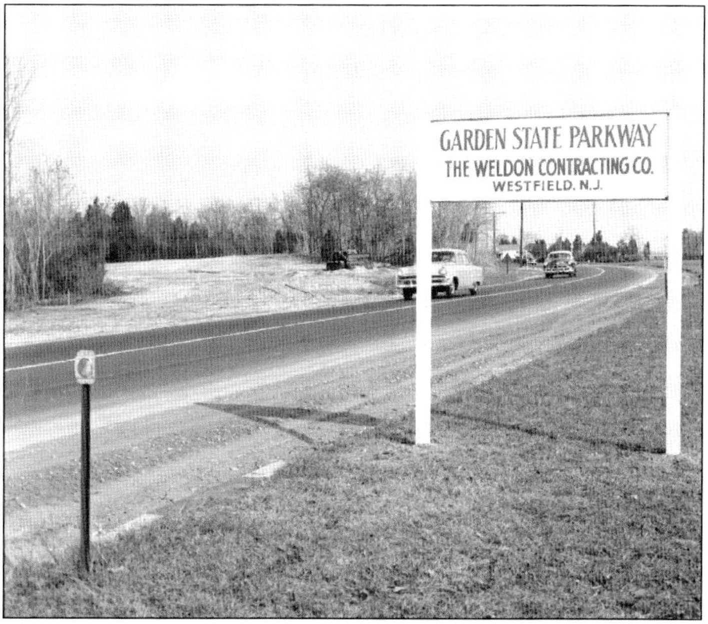

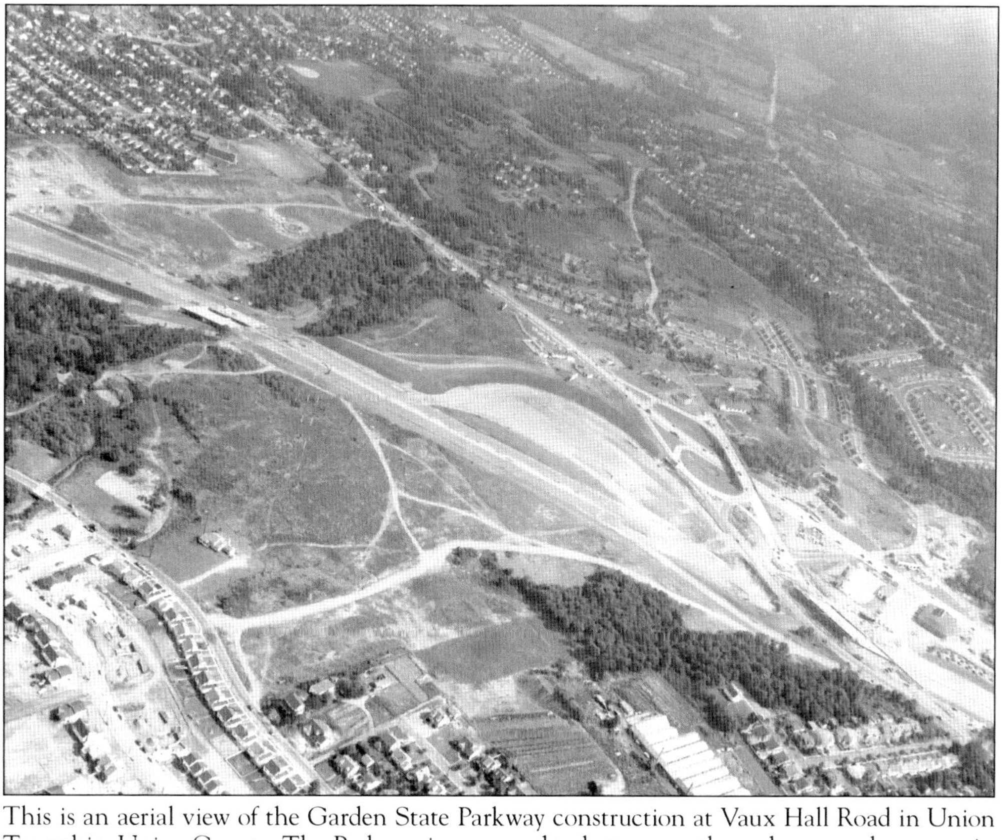

This is an aerial view of the Garden State Parkway construction at Vaux Hall Road in Union Township, Union County. The Parkway is narrowed to better pass through more urban areas in such locations. The cleared area would become the Vaux Hall Service Area, one of eight service areas constructed along the Parkway and operated by the New Jersey Highway Authority.

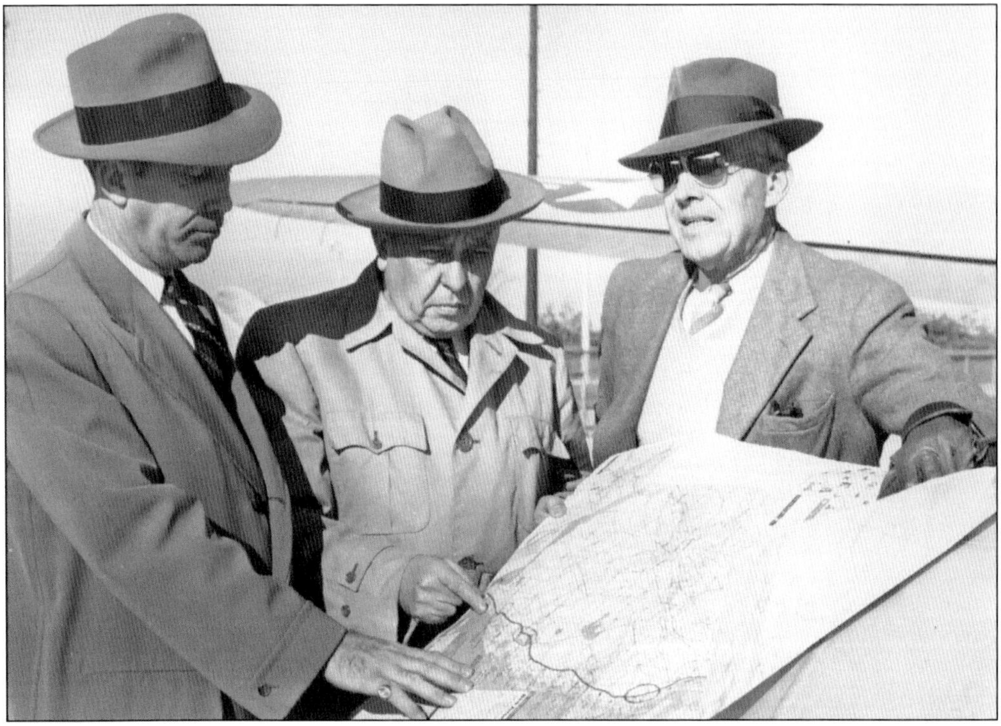

Early in the life of the New Jersey Highway Authority, from left to right, Commissioners Bayard L. England and Orrie de Nooyer and chairman Ransford J. Abbott surveyed the Garden State Parkway's progress by plane in 1952. The massive undertaking required coverage throughout the state, efficiently accomplished through the air. The scale of the project required that many sections be under way at once, and coordination and management were key.

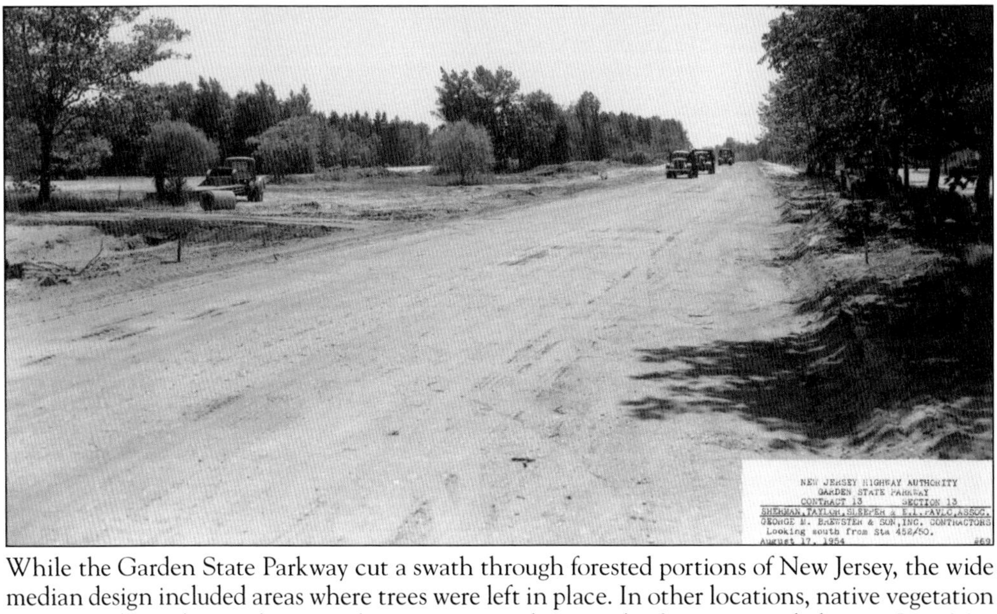

While the Garden State Parkway cut a swath through forested portions of New Jersey, the wide median design included areas where trees were left in place. In other locations, native vegetation was planted to enhance the naturalistic setting. In this stretch of outer coastal plain in Cape May County, the median trees enhanced the parklike setting for both roadways.

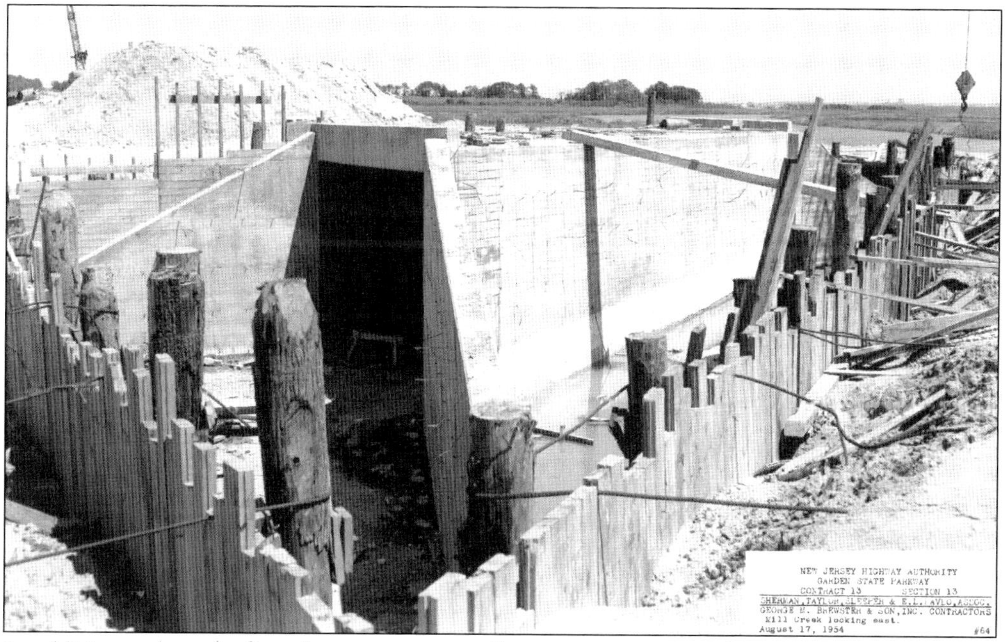

In addition to large bodies of water, many smaller watercourses are also crossed by the Garden State Parkway. Mill Creek in Lower Township, Cape May County, would flow under the Parkway through a concrete box culvert. A cofferdam has been built around the area to allow for the excavation of the area and construction of forms for the culvert and wing walls.

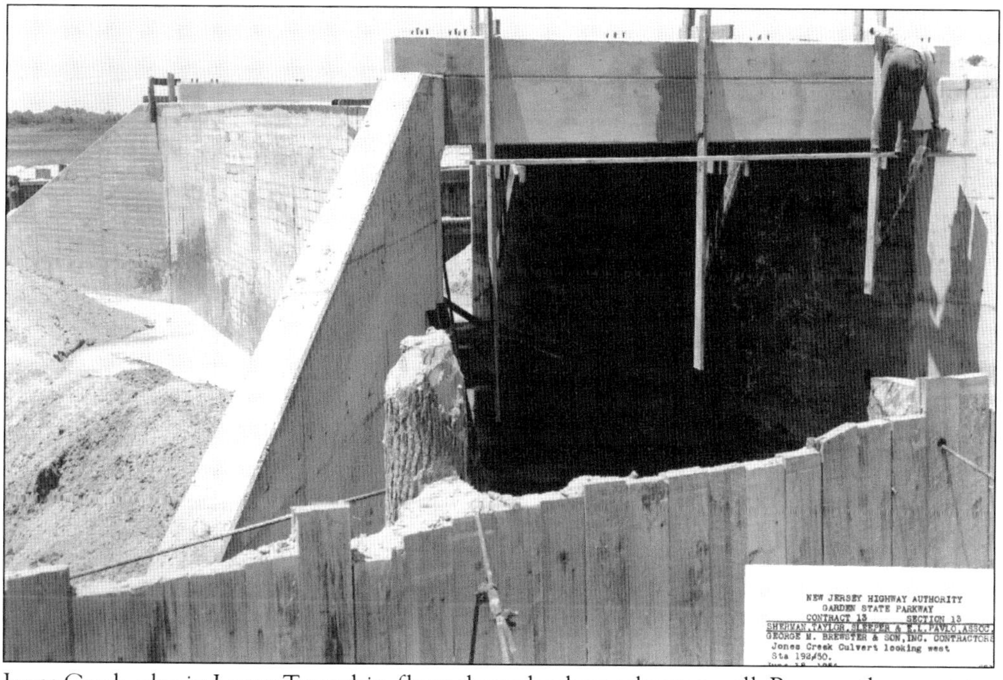

Jones Creek, also in Lower Township, flows through a box culvert as well. Because these cast-in-place structures were not nearly as visible as those with roads or navigable waterways, they did not include the reveals or other design elements. Instead, they stuck to a utilitarian appearance that can be found on any roadway.

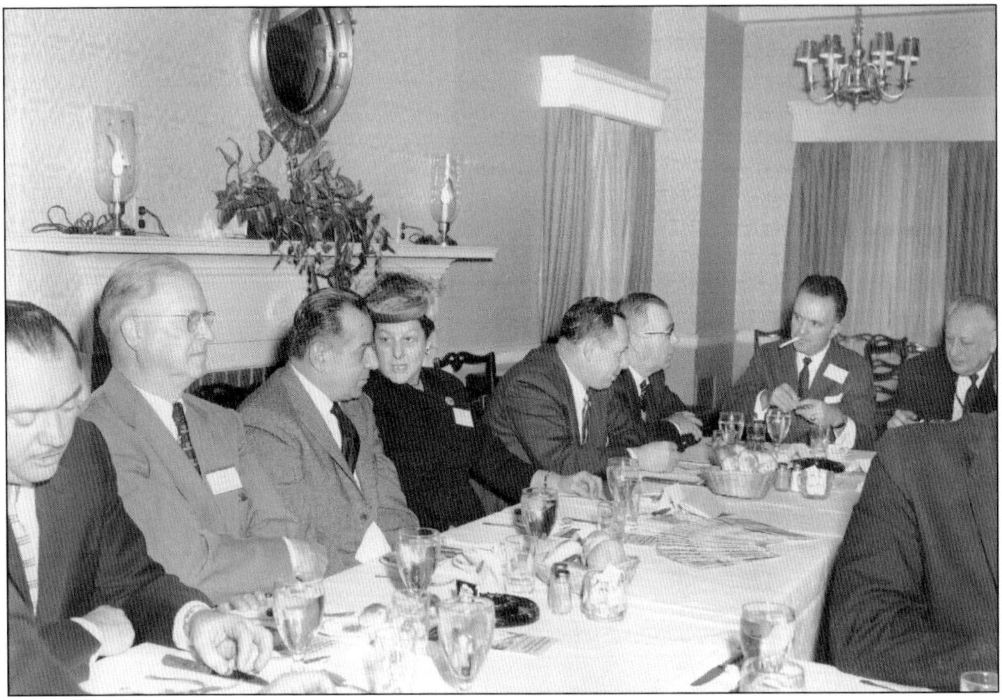

Construction moved so quickly on the Garden State Parkway that it seemed as though new sections were opening constantly. In another opening ceremony in 1955, this time at the Clifton terminus in Passaic County, Commissioner Katharine E. White is visible in the center. To the right is executive director D. Louis Tonti.

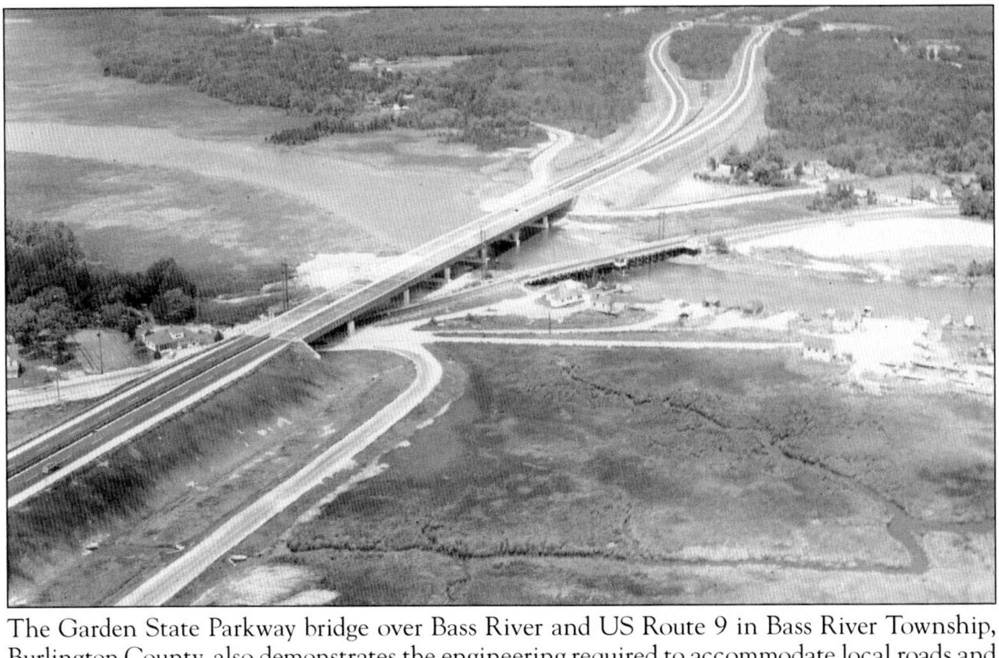

The Garden State Parkway bridge over Bass River and US Route 9 in Bass River Township, Burlington County, also demonstrates the engineering required to accommodate local roads and traffic. The Parkway crosses several major waterways, including the Passaic, Raritan, and Mullica Rivers as well as the Great Egg Harbor Bay.

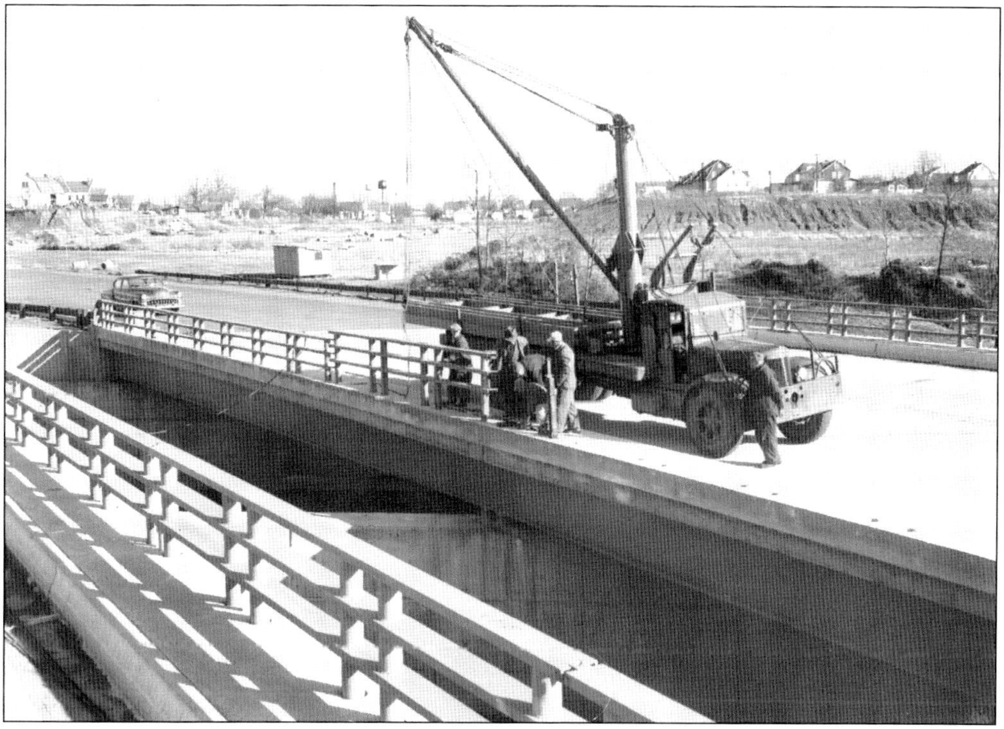

Workers install a section of the distinctive angled tri-rail railing that was a characteristic of the Garden State Parkway. This railing design added to the sleek, modern appearance of the roadway, providing a recognizable style for travelers on the Parkway and intersecting roads. The railing and other metal infrastructure were painted the distinctive Parkway green color, a sage green shade. This was one of the many treatments that helped to set the Parkway apart from more mundane and utilitarian roads. While uniform in appearance, the post spacing could vary by a foot, based on the length of the bridge on which it was being placed. Later, safety requirements would include chain link fencing on the overpasses. Eventually, the requirements of more modern safety standards for crash protection from larger vehicles would lead to the removal of these rails throughout much of the Parkway.

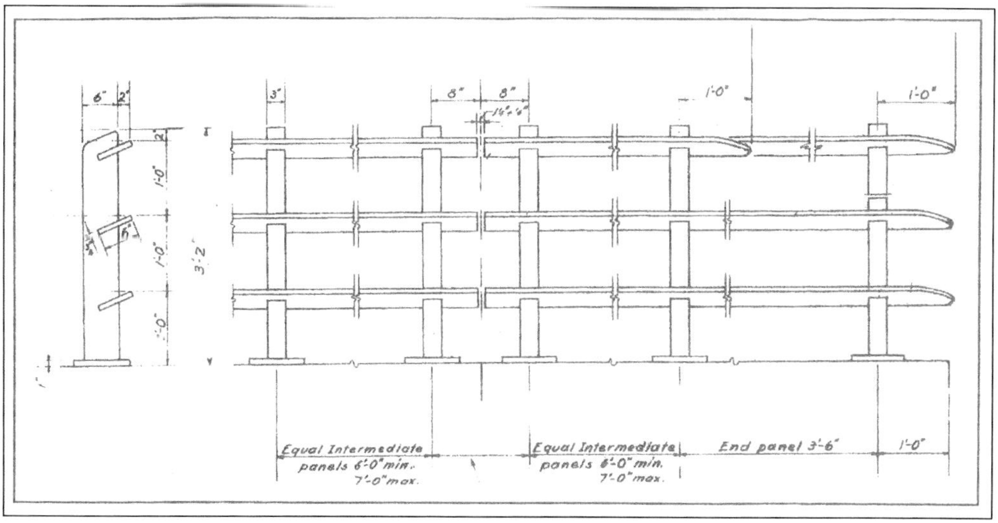

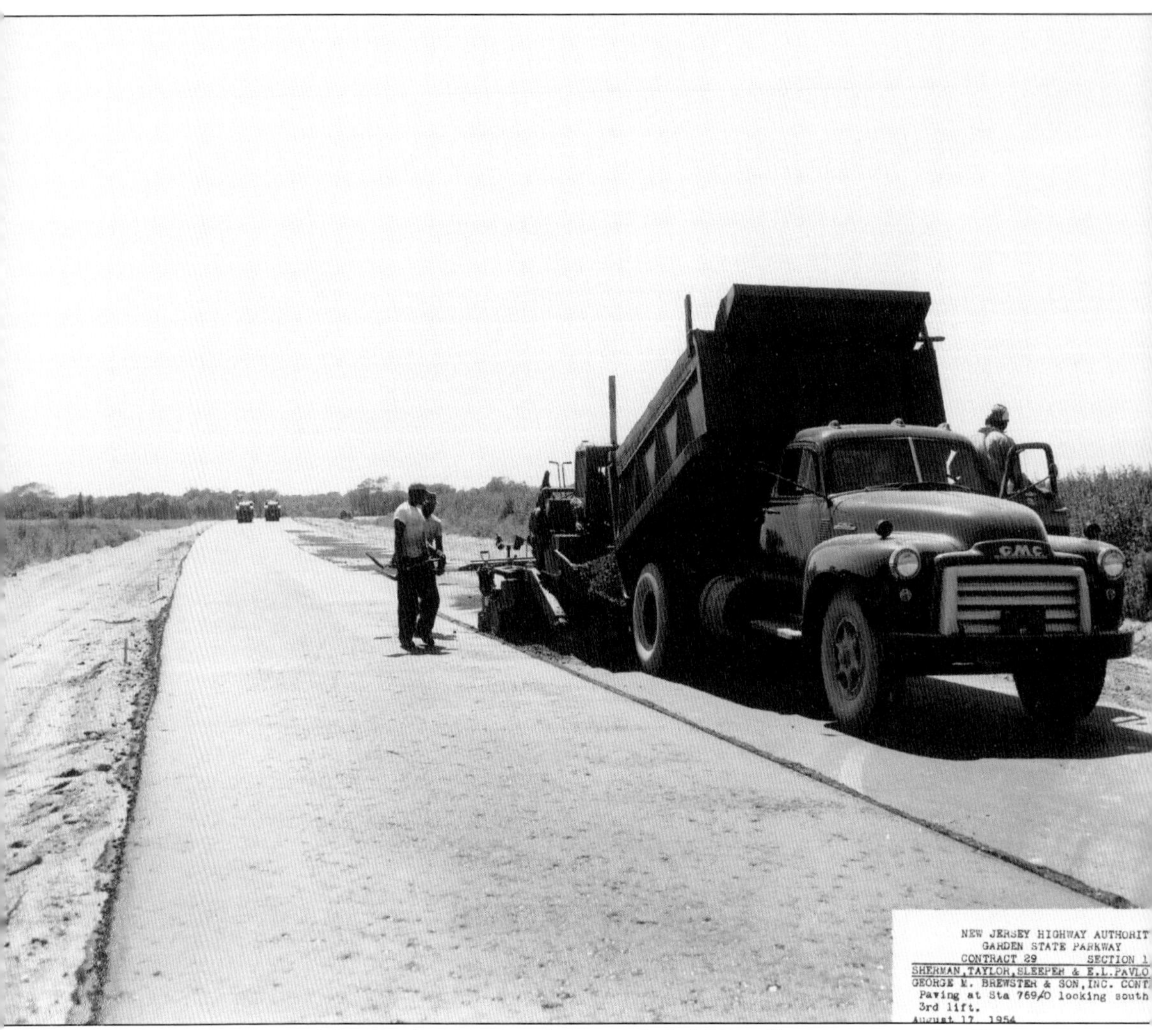

The construction of the Garden State Parkway included 7.7 million square yards of bituminous concrete (asphalt) and required the efforts of thousands of people. Governor Driscoll understood the benefits of employing large labor forces in the construction of highways and had the backing of the American Road Builders Association, a broad-based lobbying group. This effort followed on the large-scale public works projects that were undertaken during the Depression under the Franklin D. Roosevelt administration. Much work was curtailed during World War II because of the resources required to supply the needs of the war effort. With the economic boom that took place following the war, infrastructure needed to keep pace. Road building supplanted railroads as the focal point of the ground transportation network. The development of suburbs and population growth outside of cities coincided with the flourishing of the automobile age that could carry people to and from work and recreation.

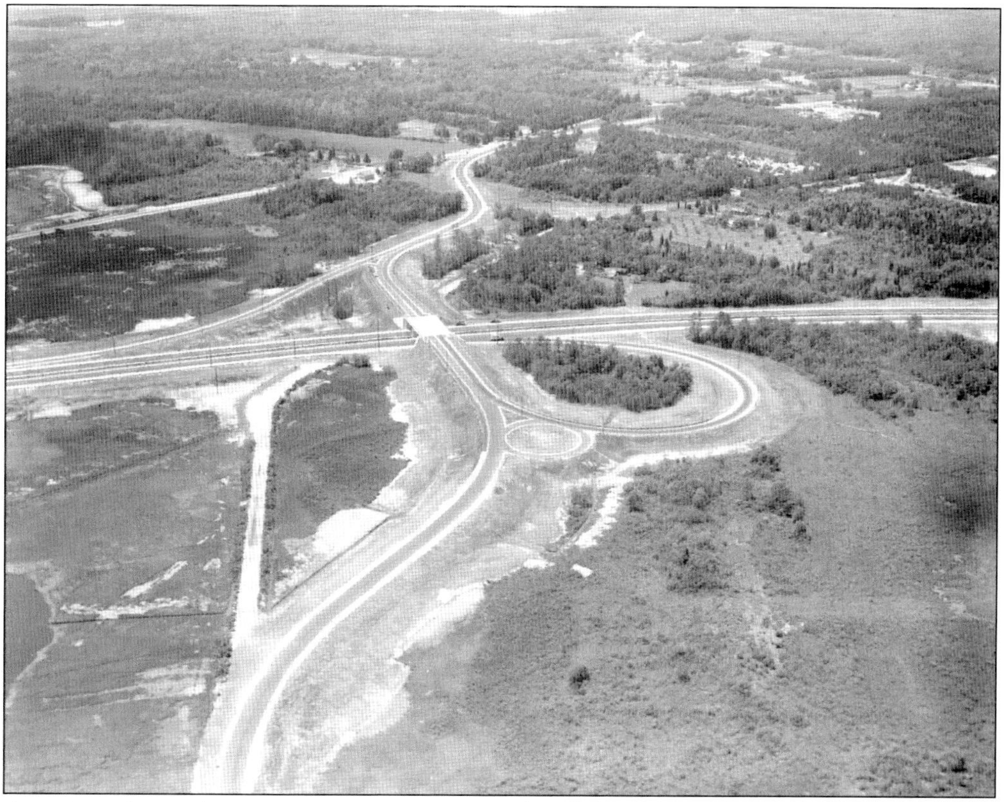

A variety of interchange arrangements were employed throughout the Garden State Parkway. This partial configuration is Interchange 50 at Amasa Landing Road (New Jersey Route 9) in Bass River Township, Burlington County. The Parkway median has been eliminated to reduce the roadway and structures size for the crossings of the Mullica and Bass River, where single bridges are used to carry the Parkway over these waterways.

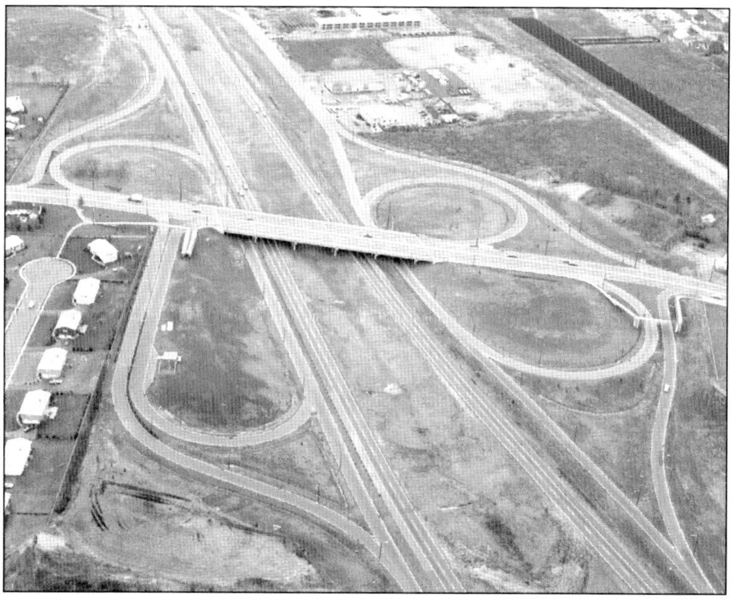

The Paramus ramp (Interchange 165) at East Ridgewood Avenue in Paramus, Bergen County, illustrates another interchange configuration. The designs were dictated by the amount of land available and the volume of traffic that the interchanges would need to handle. Connections to the local road network were crucial for the success of the Garden State Parkway as a commuter route.

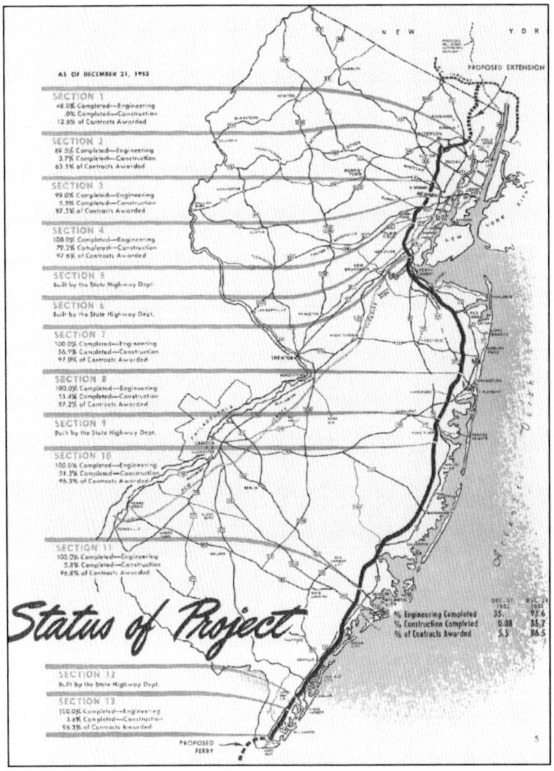

During the construction of the Garden State Parkway, effort was made to keep the public informed about the progress of the project. Following the initial contract that was awarded in 1953, the pace of design and construction quickened. It was understood that the Parkway would have a tremendous impact on shore tourism, so emphasis was placed on opening as much of the roadway as possible in time for the 1954 summer season.

The construction of the Garden State Parkway over North Wildwood Boulevard in Middle Township, Cape May County, utilized some of the 623,000 cubic yards of structural concrete needed to complete the roadway. In addition to the labor required for the construction, many more people were involved in the material manufacture and supply chain necessary for such a massive undertaking.

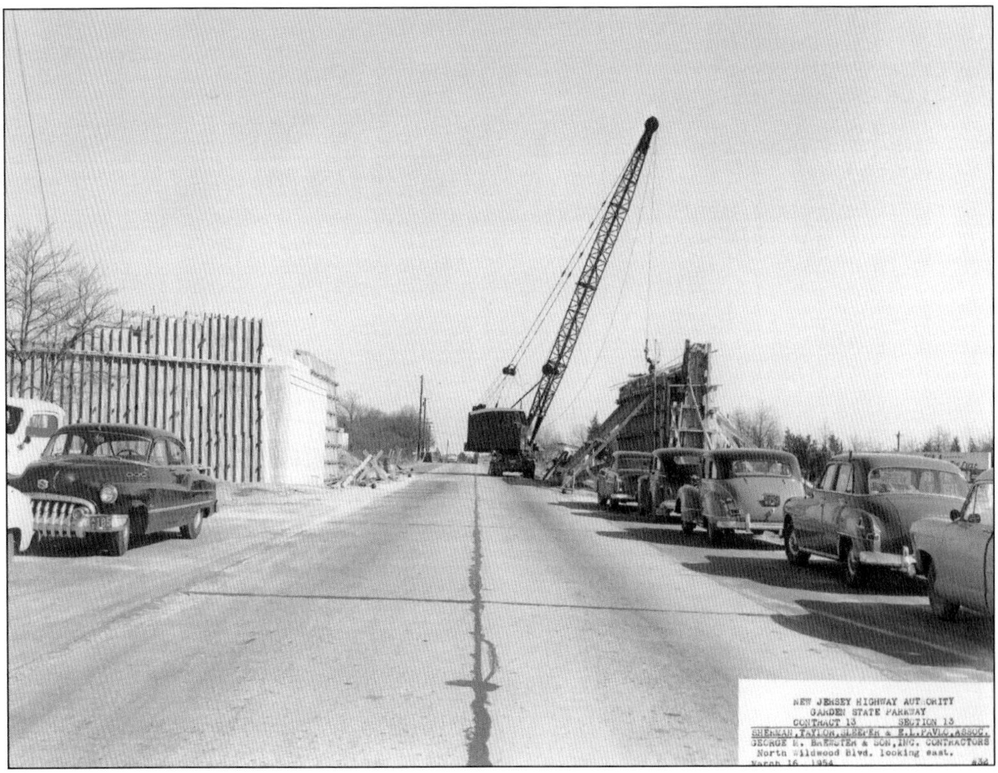

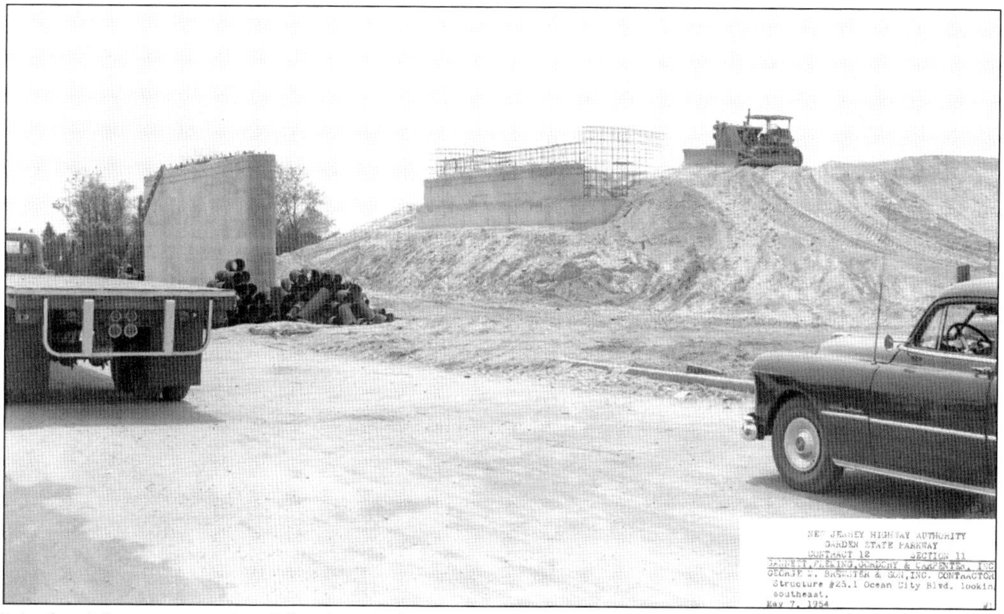

Much of the excavated soil for the roadway was used for embankments to allow the Garden State Parkway to cross over local roads. Here in Atlantic County, the reinforcing steel framework for the abutment is readied for additional concrete prior to placing the girders that will carry the Parkway to the support pier. For four-lane roads and larger, it was often necessary to use multiple bridge spans for the Parkway overpasses. Once again, the rounded bridge supports with two band reveals along the top are demonstrated in this photograph.

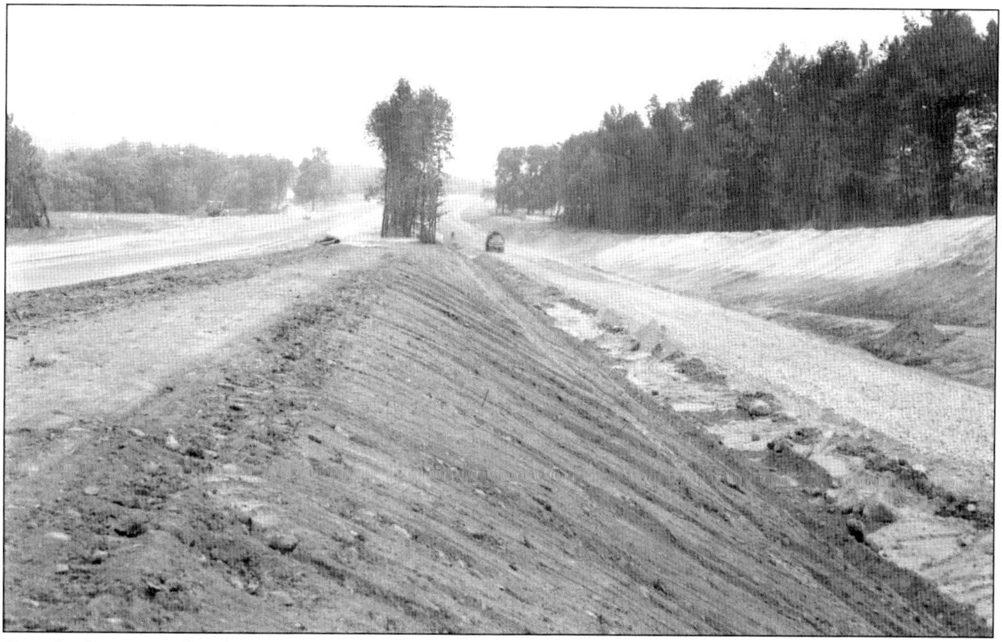

Gently sloping embankments provided runoff areas for motorists. The separation between opposing lanes of traffic minimized the potential for head-on crashes and added to the open feel of the Garden State Parkway. It also necessitated extensive land modification in many portions of the Parkway, requiring considerable landscape design to keep natural elements.

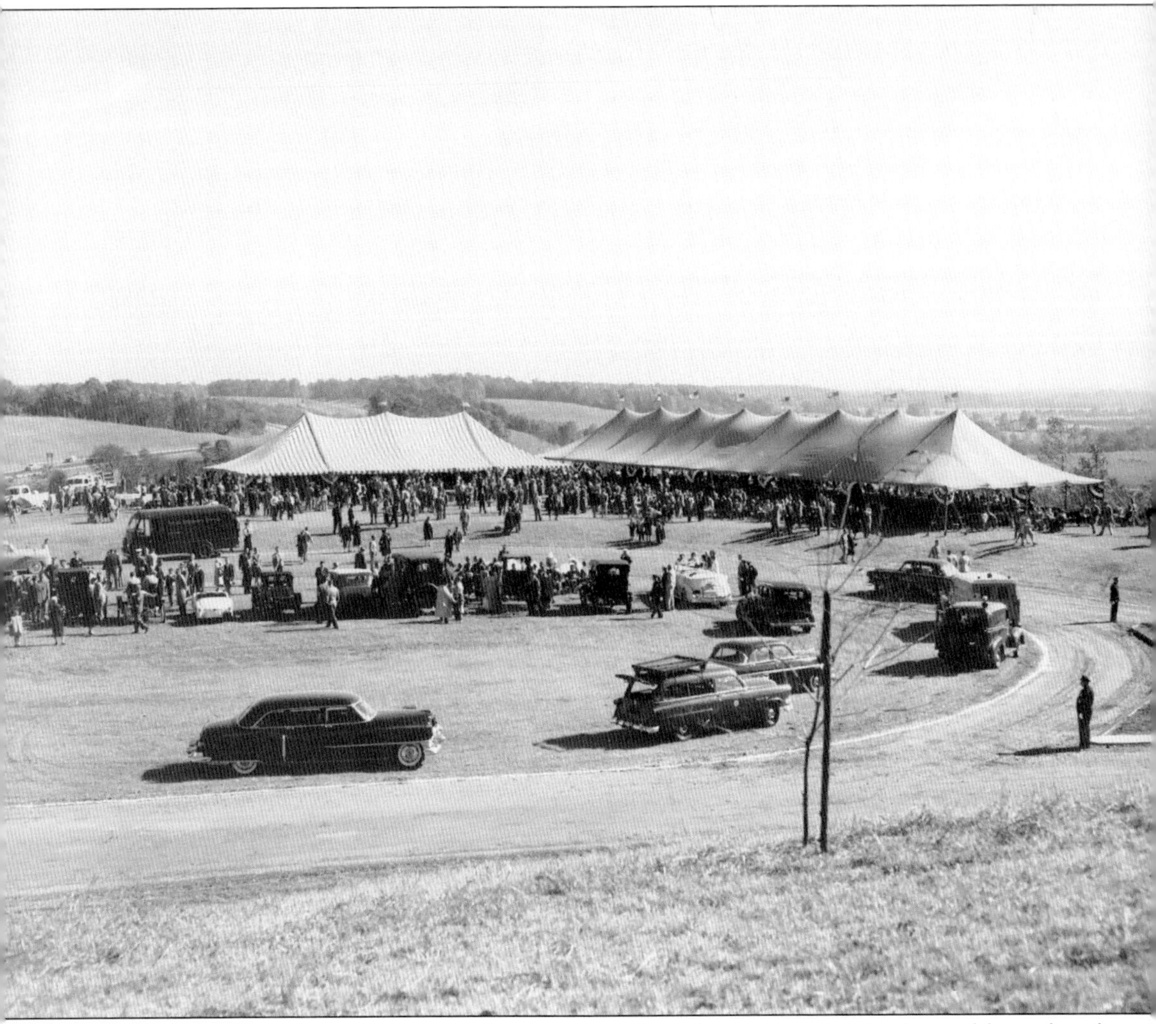

On August 4, 1954, eighty miles of uninterrupted roadway opened to both northbound and southbound drivers. Before the end of the month, more roadway was opened, which resulted in 113 miles of uninterrupted travel. On September 18, 1954, the southern end of the Garden State Parkway opened in Cape May. Pictured is the grand opening ceremony for the Parkway held at Telegraph Hill in Holmdel on October 23, 1954, where Governor Meyner and his predecessor, Governor Driscoll, presided over the state's accomplishment. More than 3,000 guests attended the ceremony and enjoyed a box lunch. Commissioner Katharine E. White, who was also the mayor of Red Bank, noted the sacrifices of many property owners along the route. However, news reporting of the event preferred to look forward, noting that the Parkway would represent the history of the area and would outlast any controversies or losses felt by property owners. By the time of this event, 143 miles of roadway had been completed of the ambitious road that would become a regional icon.

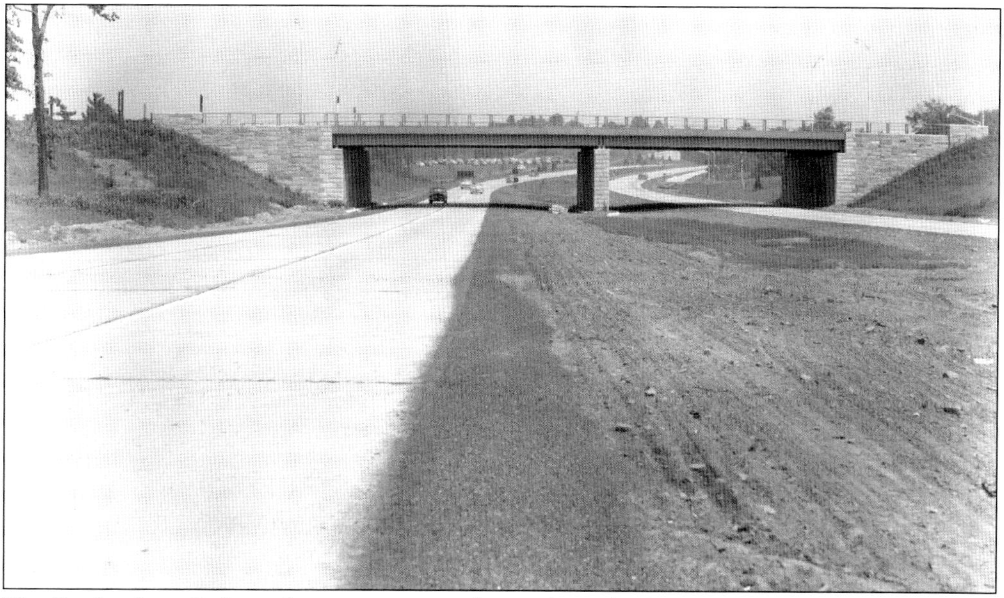

The Garden State Parkway design incorporated several standards and two basic surface treatments. The Galloping Hill Road Bridge in Kenilworth, Union County, pictured here, is an example of rolled-steel girder bridges on the Parkway, the most common form. The distinctive tri-rail, which tops the structure, was a basis for similar rail used in the sections constructed by the New Jersey Highway Authority. In the Union County portion originally built by the State Highway Department, stone facing was utilized with different stone on the quoins at the corners.

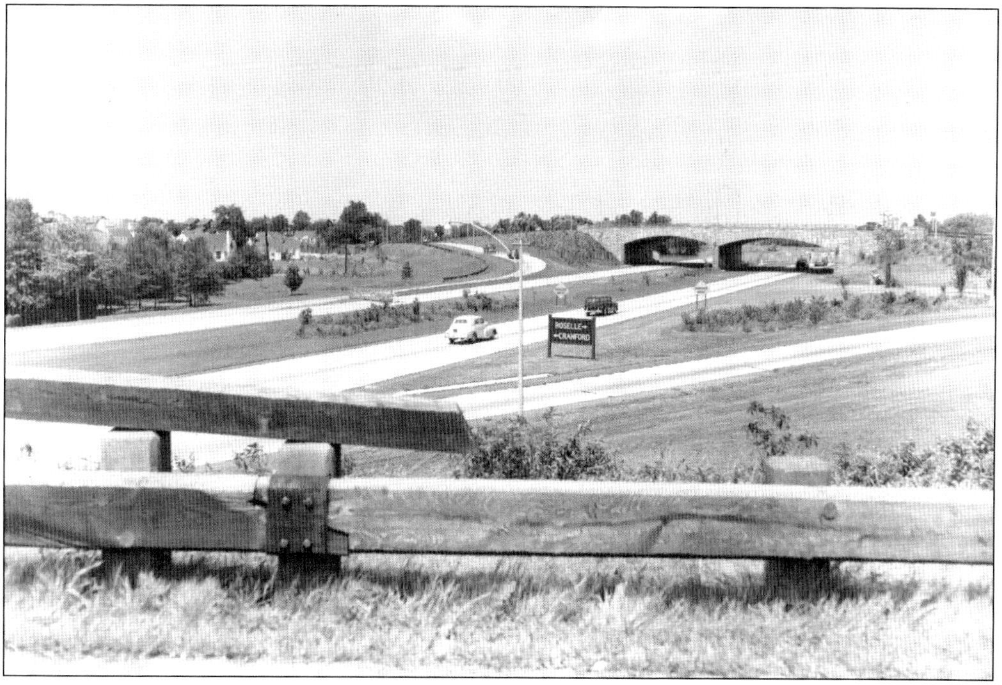

The stone-faced structures in the northern portions built by the State Highway Department include this graceful two-span bridge at Interchange 136 in Cranford Township, Union County. Rigid arch-frame bridges are common in the portions built by the state.

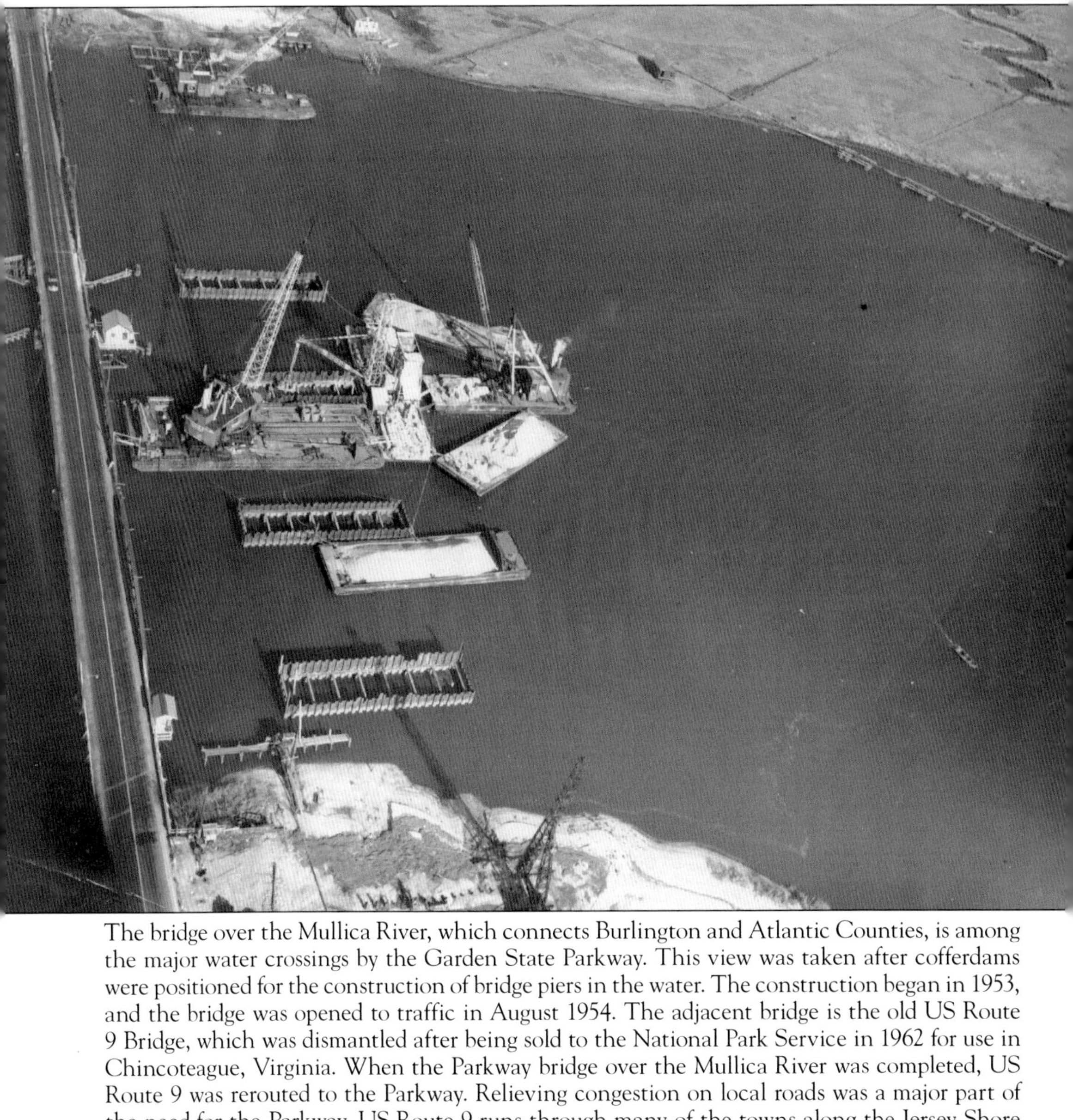

The bridge over the Mullica River, which connects Burlington and Atlantic Counties, is among the major water crossings by the Garden State Parkway. This view was taken after cofferdams were positioned for the construction of bridge piers in the water. The construction began in 1953, and the bridge was opened to traffic in August 1954. The adjacent bridge is the old US Route 9 Bridge, which was dismantled after being sold to the National Park Service in 1962 for use in Chincoteague, Virginia. When the Parkway bridge over the Mullica River was completed, US Route 9 was rerouted to the Parkway. Relieving congestion on local roads was a major part of the need for the Parkway. US Route 9 runs through many of the towns along the Jersey Shore and widening would have resulted in many more business and residential displacements. The Parkway successfully allowed greater access to small shore communities without impacting them directly with the roadway.

In sections where the median was narrow, such as over the Passaic River, which separates Bergen and Passaic Counties, engineers designed only a single bridge to carry all lanes. In addition, the northern portion of the state was already more heavily developed, limiting the amount of land used for the Garden State Parkway. It was still isolated as much as possible from the surrounding landscape.

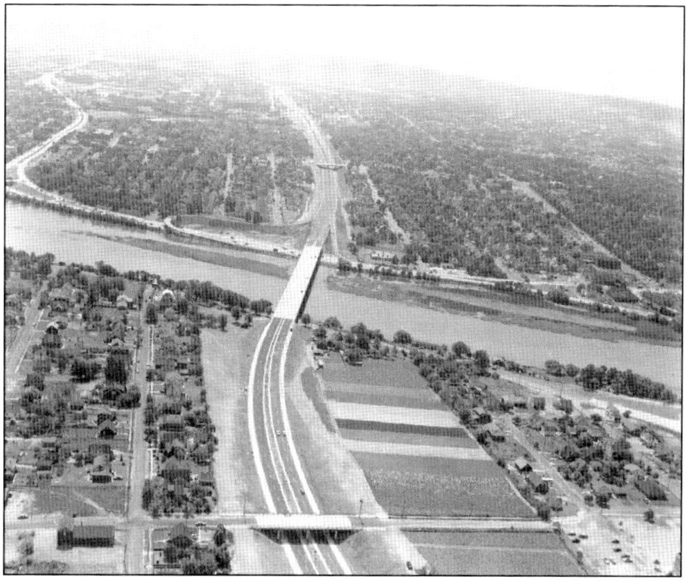

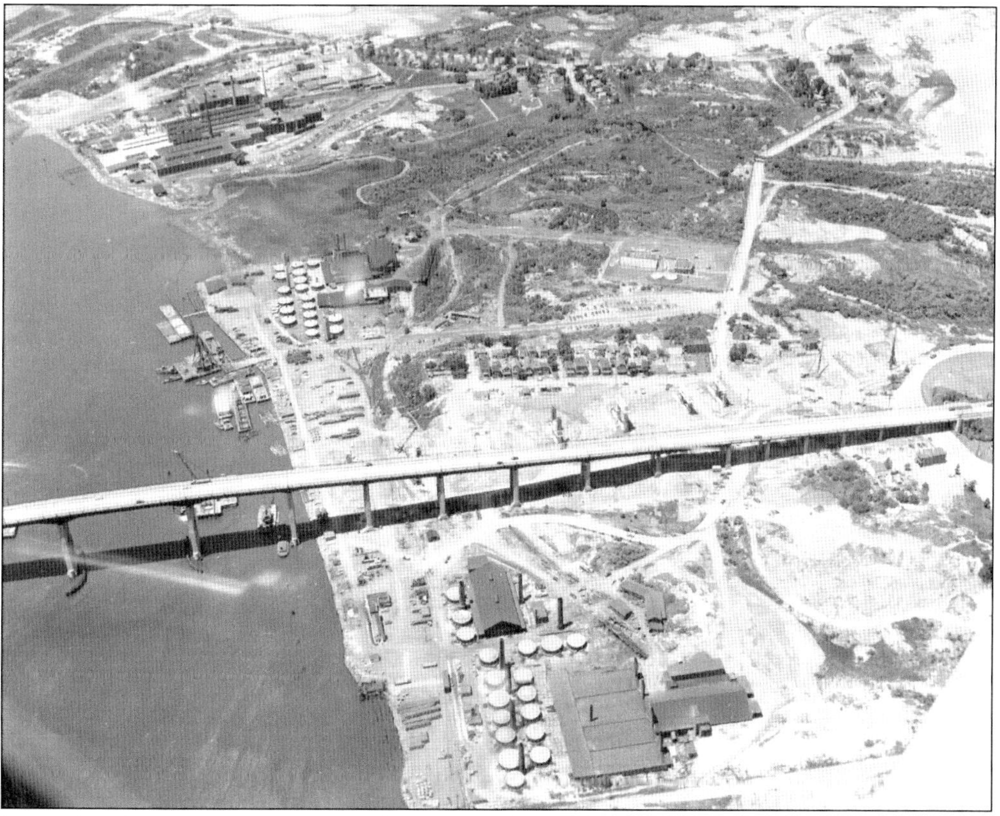

Soon after the start of construction, the piers on the north side of the Raritan River in Middlesex County are taking shape for the Garden State Parkway crossing, behind the existing Route 9 Bridge. The Raritan River was used for commercial shipping, and the industries along its banks are visible. This required a large span that allowed for shipping clearance and would be able to accommodate a high traffic volume.

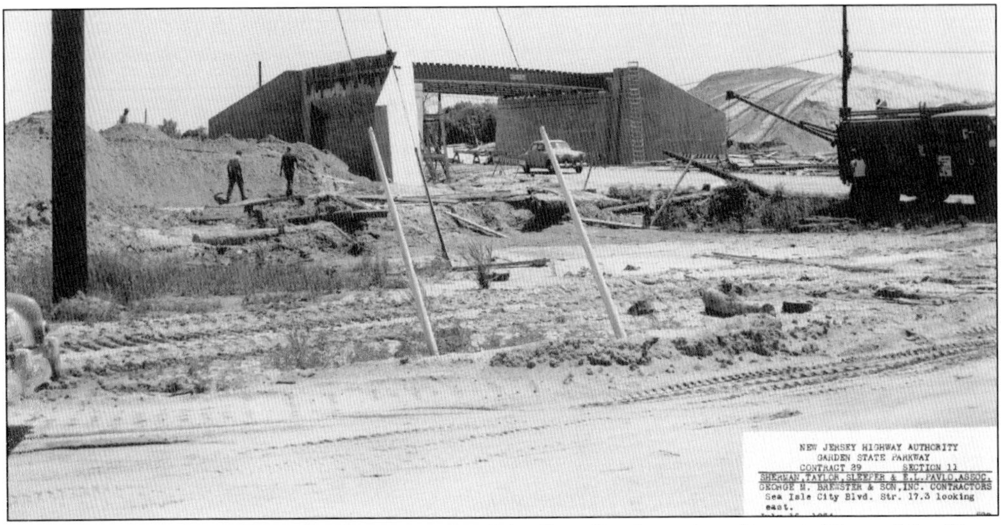

The Garden State Parkway bridges over Sea Isle City Boulevard in Dennis Township, Cape May County, show the use of rolled steel girders on concrete abutments that maintain the consistent look of the Parkway. The two reveals are along the wall just below the girders, in typical Parkway fashion.

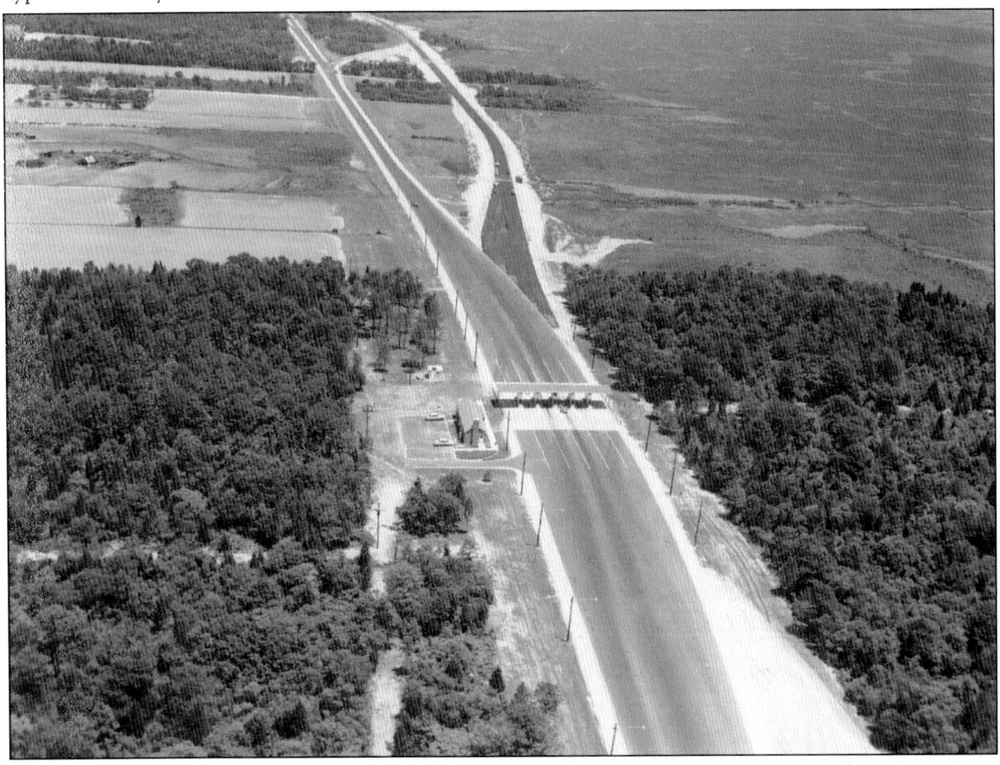

The southbound roadway approaching the Cape May Toll Plaza in Upper Township, Cape May County, carries traffic in both directions prior to the completion of the northbound roadway, as shown in this view in 1955. The incomplete northbound roadway is the darker section in the upper right. This partial construction allowed the Garden State Parkway to open for traffic while still under construction. The delays were minimal, with the entire roadway opened in very short order.

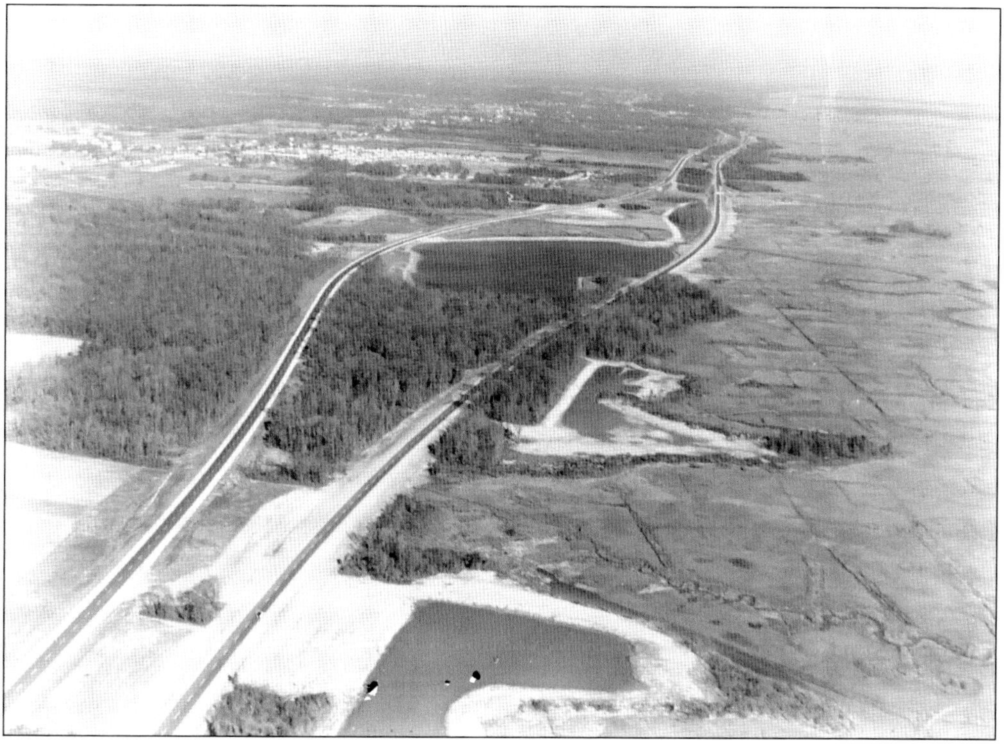

In Cape May County, the Garden State Parkway is at the edge of the marshes and a forest of pines near Wildwood. This is the Parkway concept, where the natural landscape—sometimes enhanced by the designers—was made visible for the travelers. The Parkway has allowed millions of travelers to experience and enjoy a New Jersey that is natural and scenic.

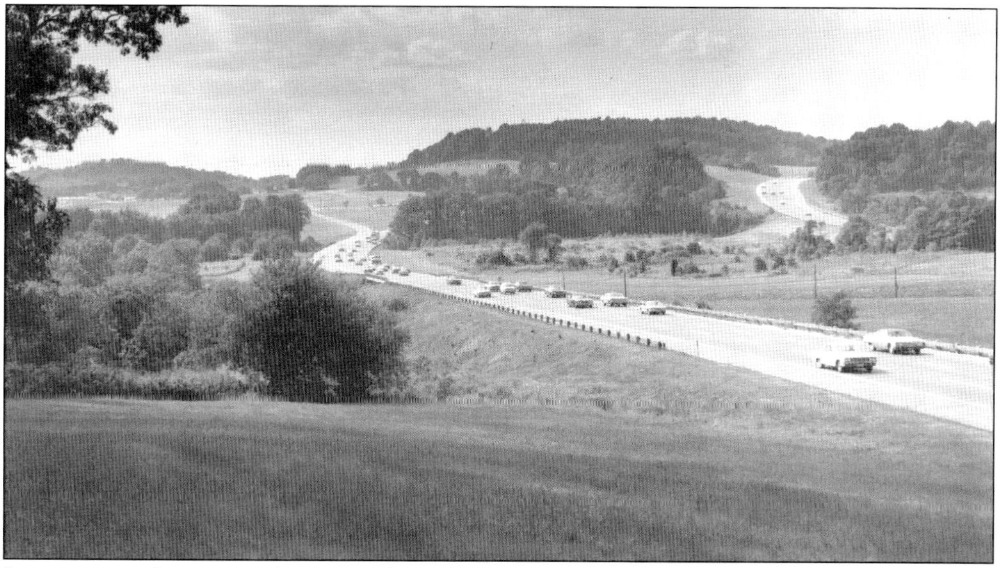

In contrast to the portion that passes through the New Jersey Pinelands, this stretch in Monmouth County with Telegraph Hill in the background passes through more open, rolling topography. The Garden State Parkway design allowed for areas of scenic driving separated from views of development, including billboards. The landscape was used in concert with the road design.

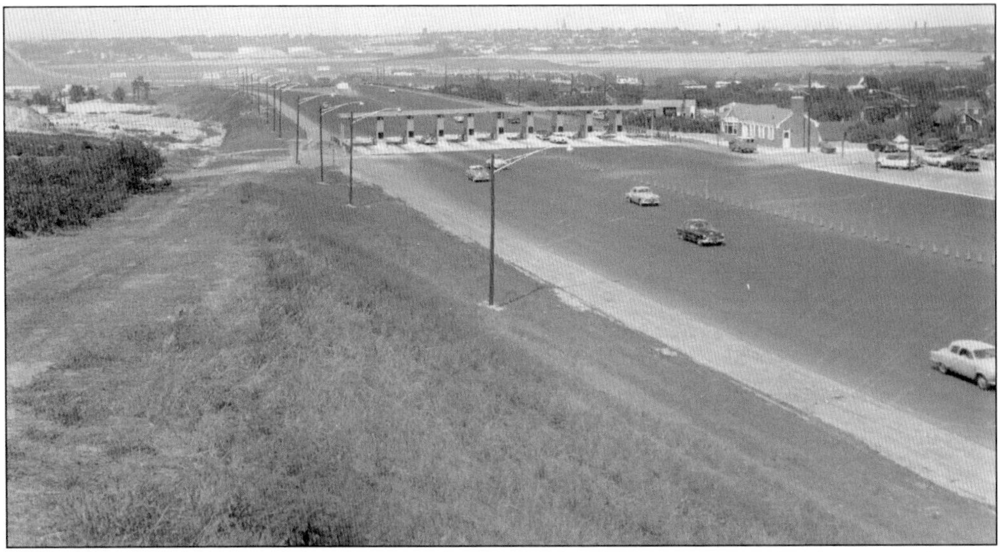

The newly completed Raritan Toll Plaza in Sayreville, Middlesex County, demonstrates a barrier toll, which forced motorists to slow down and served to meter traffic. Such plazas were intended to pay off the bonds as well as fund operation and maintenance of roadways. The administration buildings were designed in the Colonial Revival style, adding to the ambiance.

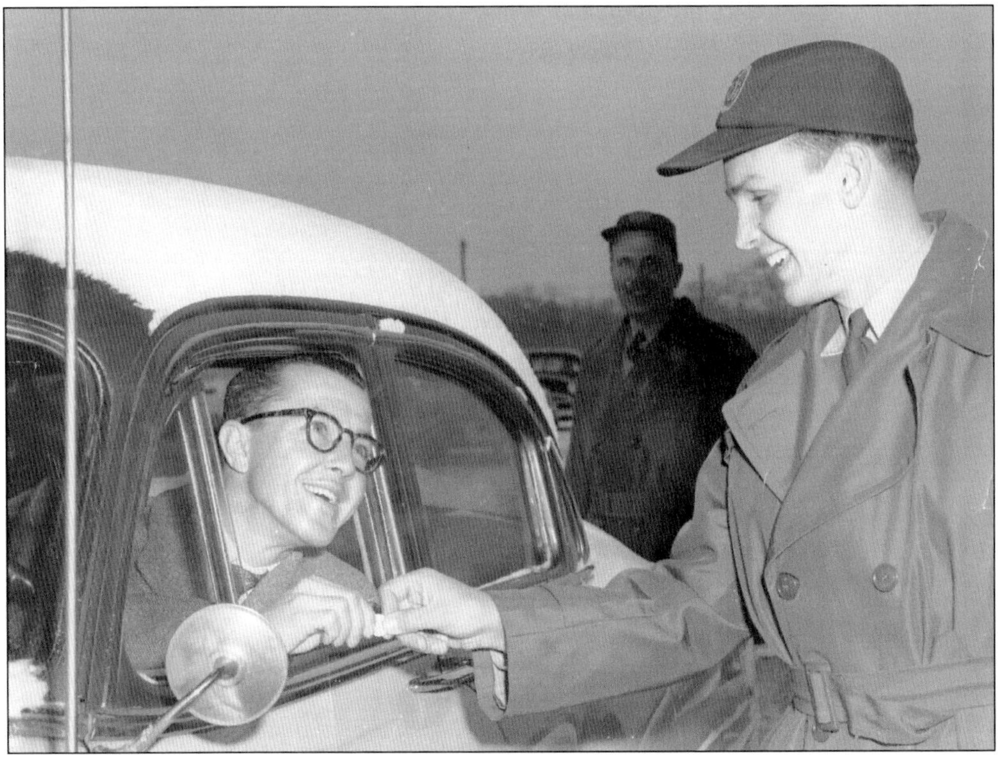

On January 15, 1954, a mere two years after Governor Driscoll signed the New Jersey Highway Act, the first section of the Garden State Parkway constructed by the New Jersey Highway Authority opened for business. This photograph commemorates the toll paid by George Vraken of Linden to Edward Cichowski at the Union Toll Plaza in Hillside Township, Union County, three days later.

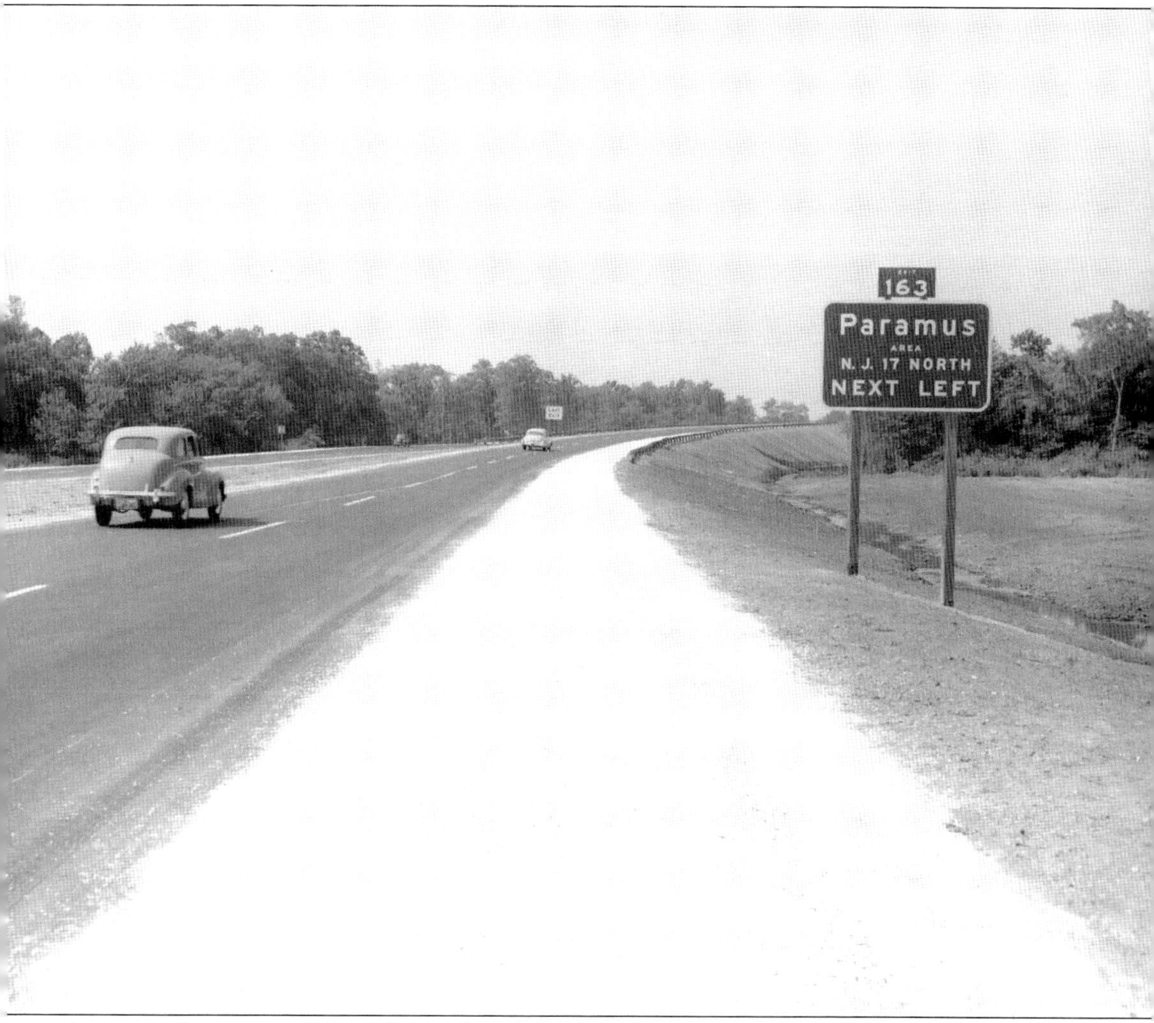

Above, travelers are approaching the north end of the Garden State Parkway as originally completed. It now stretched all the way from Cape May and provided a continuous route for commuters and vacationers from within and outside of New Jersey. A connection to the state line had been in the works, and it would soon be completed, extending the Parkway the length of New Jersey.

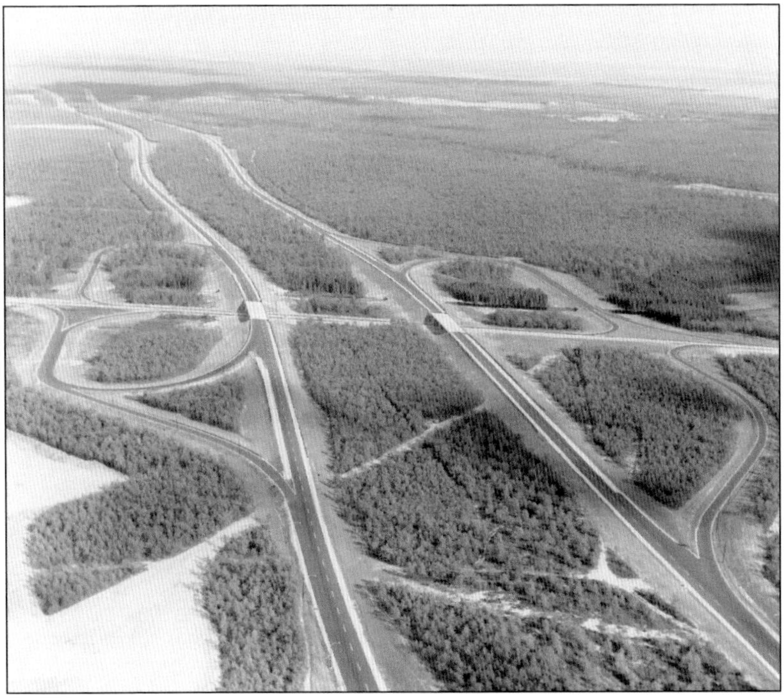

Interchange 63 (State Route 72) in Stafford Township, Ocean County, shows the blending of modern, high-speed road design and the preservation of large expanses of forest. While state and county roads were intersected with interchanges or bridges, many sand roads that were used by local residents for recreation were cut off by the new road.

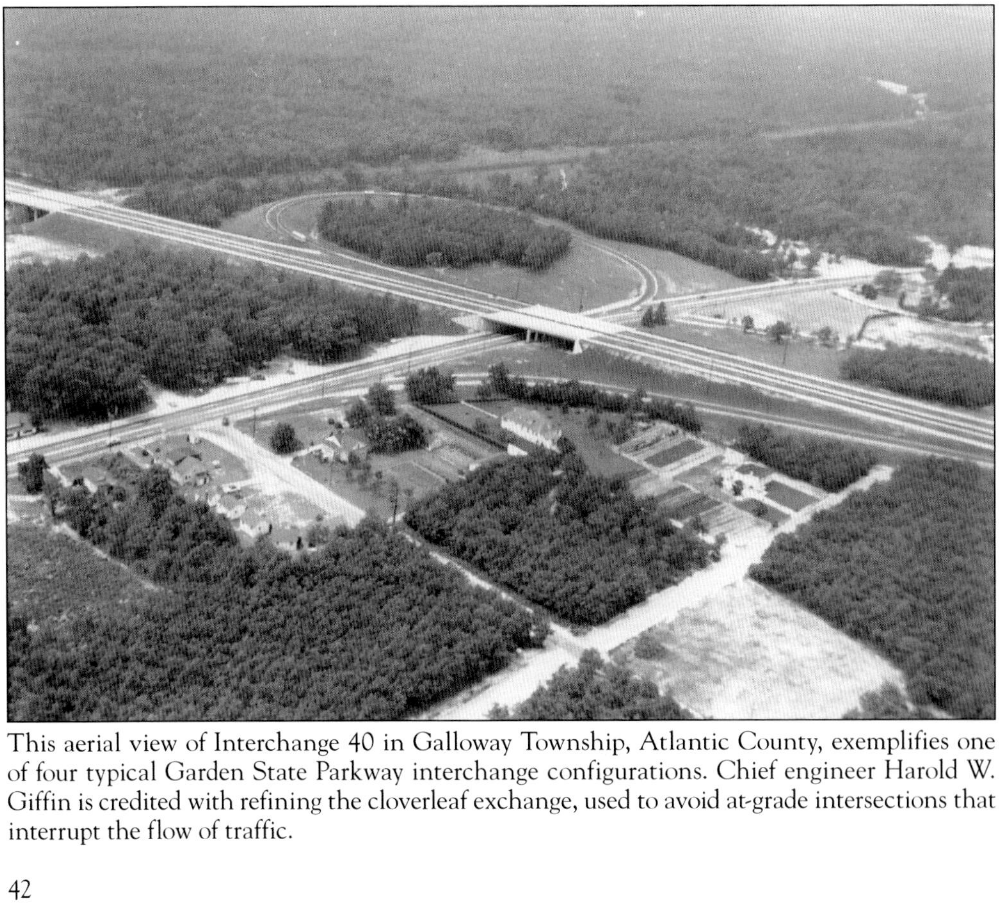

This aerial view of Interchange 40 in Galloway Township, Atlantic County, exemplifies one of four typical Garden State Parkway interchange configurations. Chief engineer Harold W. Giffin is credited with refining the cloverleaf exchange, used to avoid at-grade intersections that interrupt the flow of traffic.

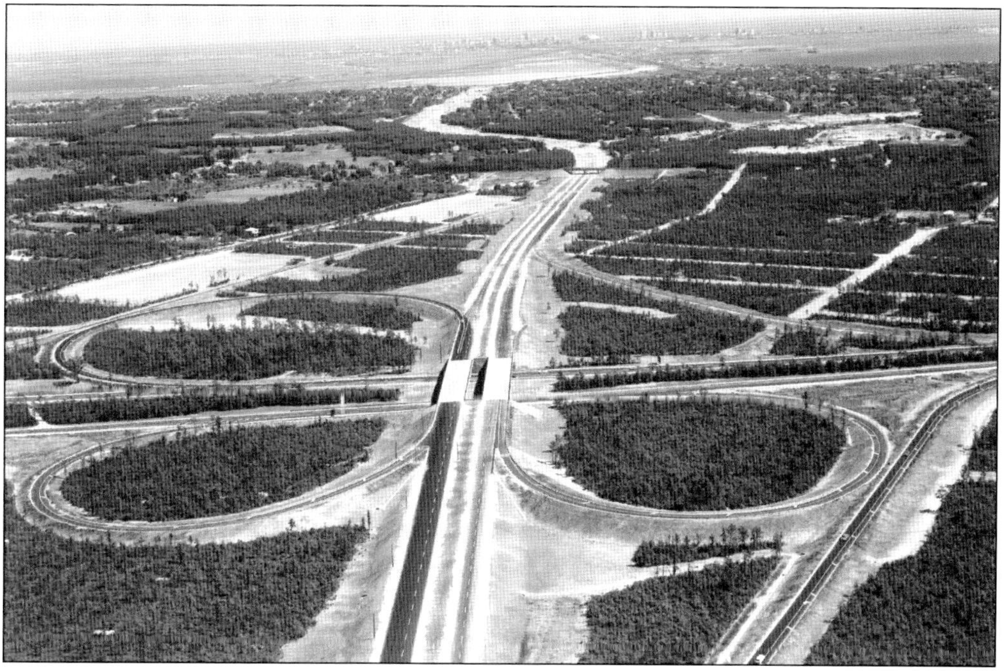

A more complete cloverleaf interchange configuration was used at the Garden State Parkway and Atlantic City Expressway at Interchange 38 in Egg Harbor Township, Atlantic County. Note the retention of the natural landscape to enhance a picturesque drive. The idea was not only to get people where they were going, but to make it safe and pleasurable as well.

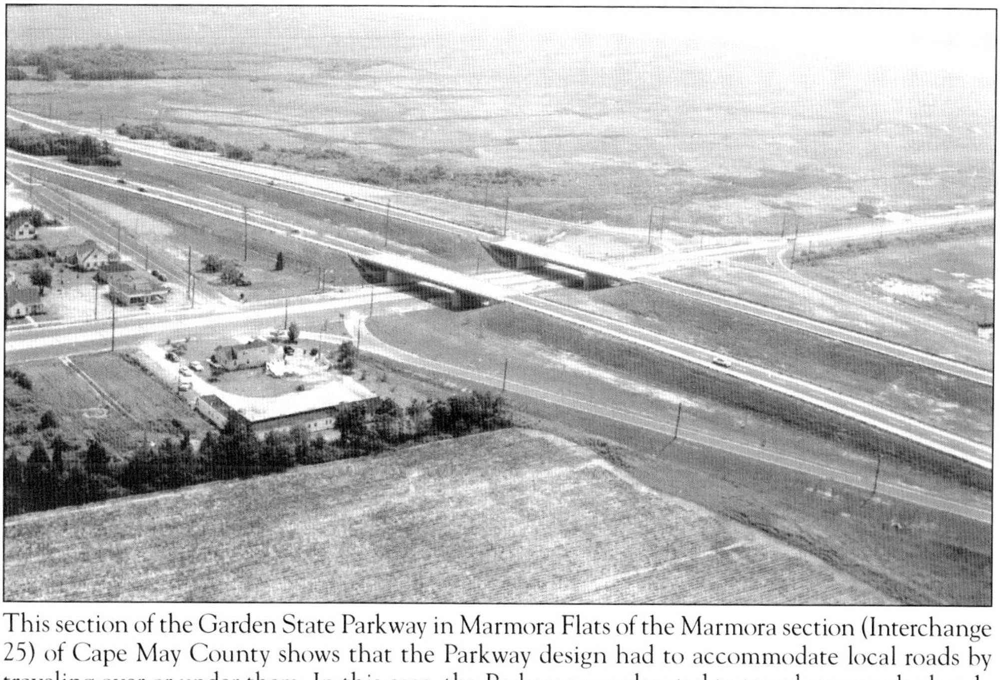

This section of the Garden State Parkway in Marmora Flats of the Marmora section (Interchange 25) of Cape May County shows that the Parkway design had to accommodate local roads by traveling over or under them. In this case, the Parkway was elevated to travel over roads already present. The exit and entrance ramps are in a simple diamond pattern that allowed traffic access in all directions.

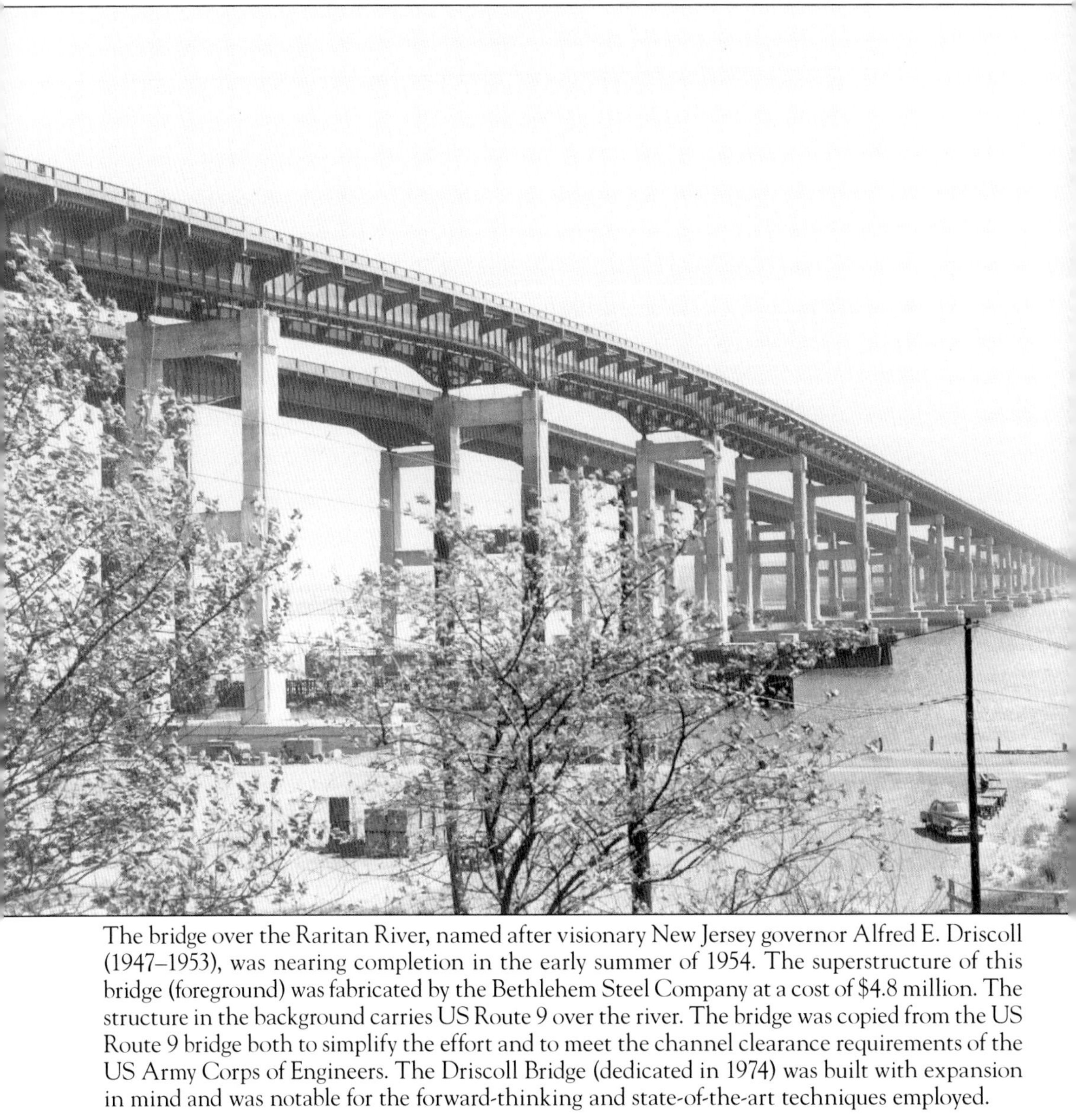

The bridge over the Raritan River, named after visionary New Jersey governor Alfred E. Driscoll (1947–1953), was nearing completion in the early summer of 1954. The superstructure of this bridge (foreground) was fabricated by the Bethlehem Steel Company at a cost of $4.8 million. The structure in the background carries US Route 9 over the river. The bridge was copied from the US Route 9 bridge both to simplify the effort and to meet the channel clearance requirements of the US Army Corps of Engineers. The Driscoll Bridge (dedicated in 1974) was built with expansion in mind and was notable for the forward-thinking and state-of-the-art techniques employed.

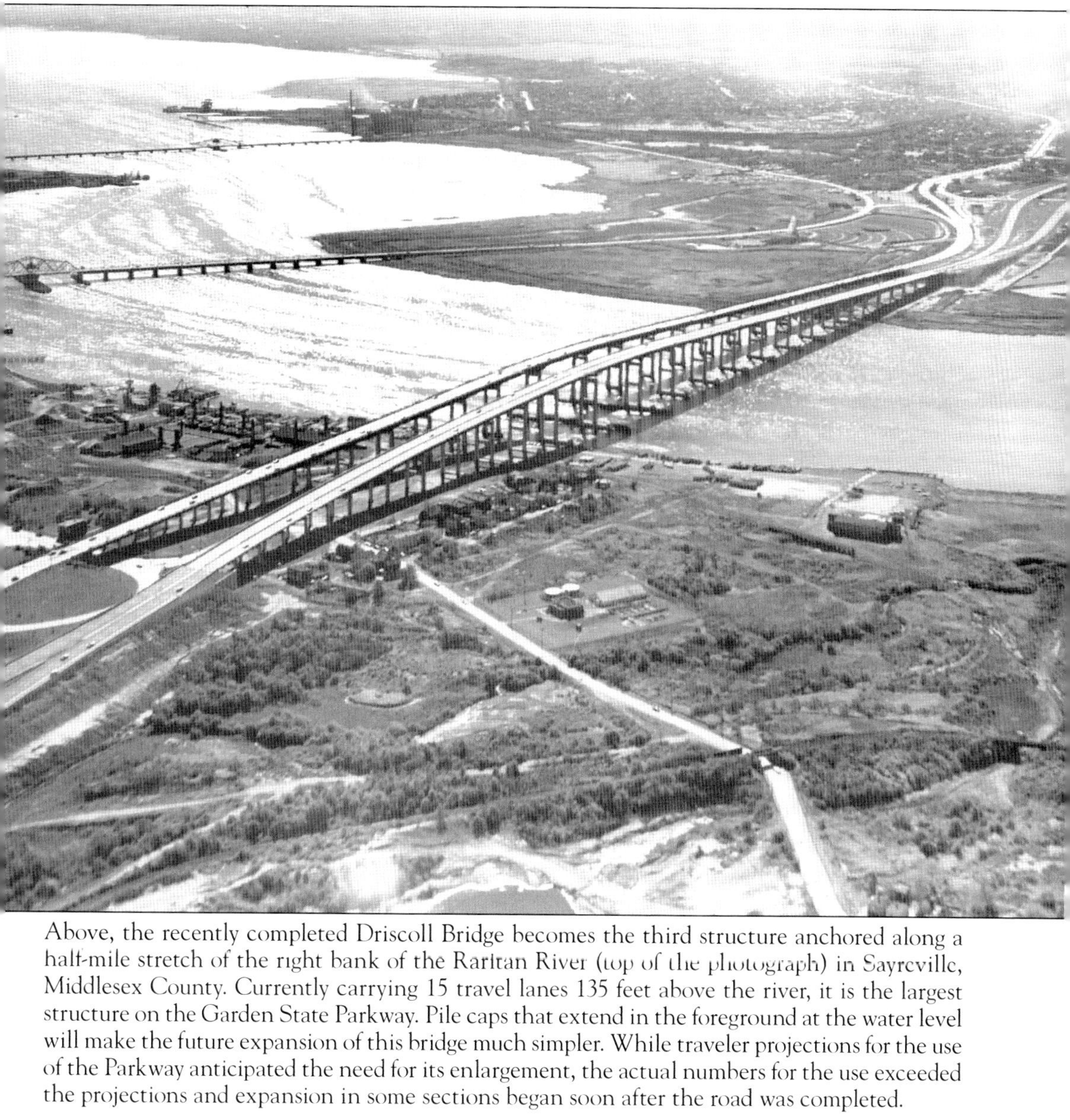

Above, the recently completed Driscoll Bridge becomes the third structure anchored along a half-mile stretch of the right bank of the Raritan River (top of the photograph) in Sayreville, Middlesex County. Currently carrying 15 travel lanes 135 feet above the river, it is the largest structure on the Garden State Parkway. Pile caps that extend in the foreground at the water level will make the future expansion of this bridge much simpler. While traveler projections for the use of the Parkway anticipated the need for its enlargement, the actual numbers for the use exceeded the projections and expansion in some sections began soon after the road was completed.

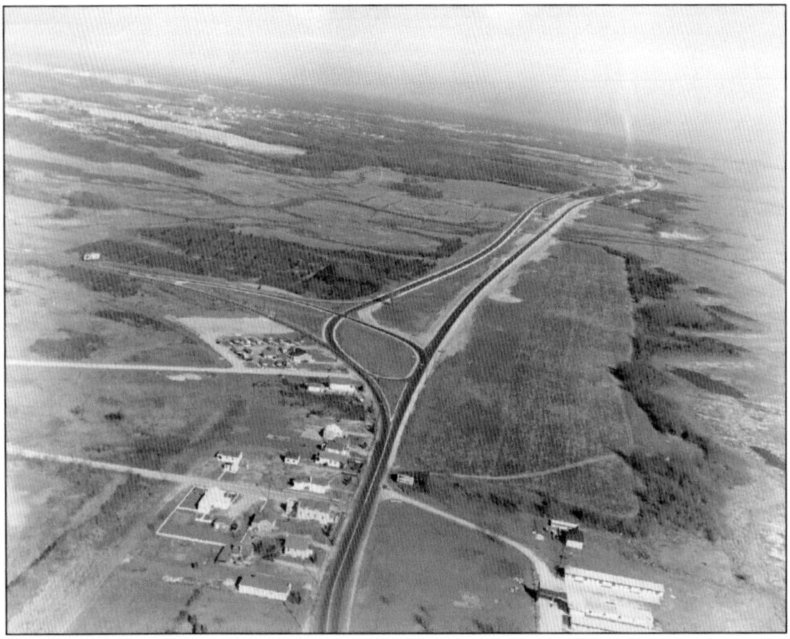

The southern terminus of the Garden State Parkway in Lower Township, Cape May County, is Milepost 0. Following completion, travelers would be able to ride the Parkway for 173 miles to the New York Thruway, or stop at places of interest in 10 counties along the route.

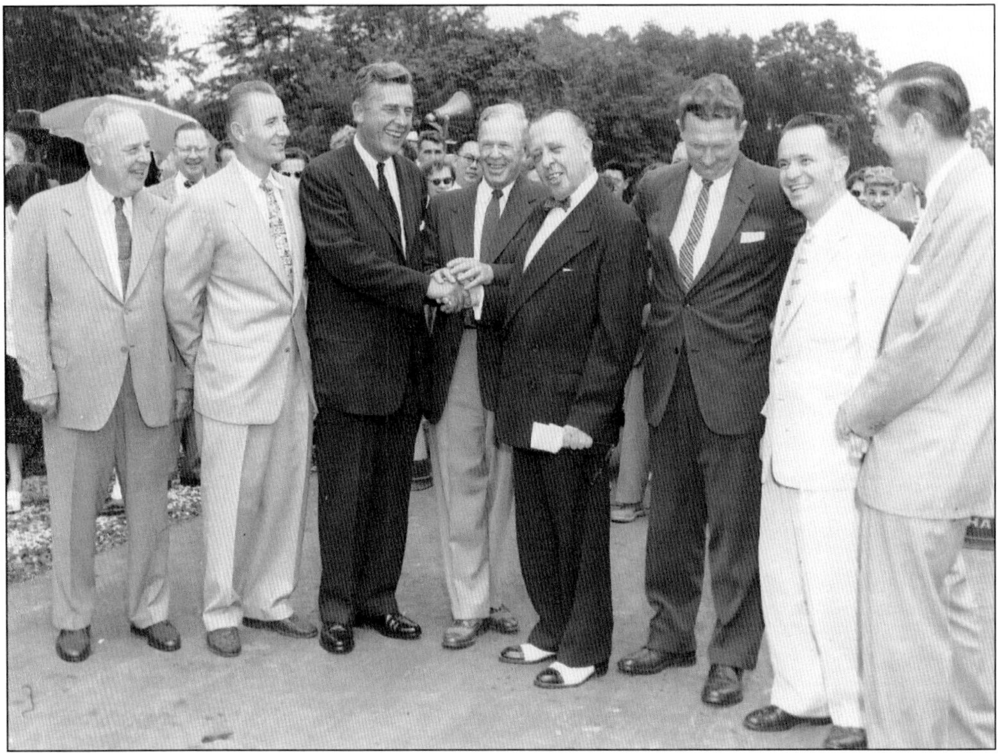

This celebration is for the formal opening of the northern portion and full operation of the Garden State Parkway on July 1, 1955. Shaking hands in the middle are Gov. Robert B. Meyner, chief engineer Harold W. Giffin, New Jersey Highway Authority chairman Orrie de Nooyer. Executive director D. Louis Tonti is to the right in the light suit. There was now only one remaining gap in the route to Cape May.

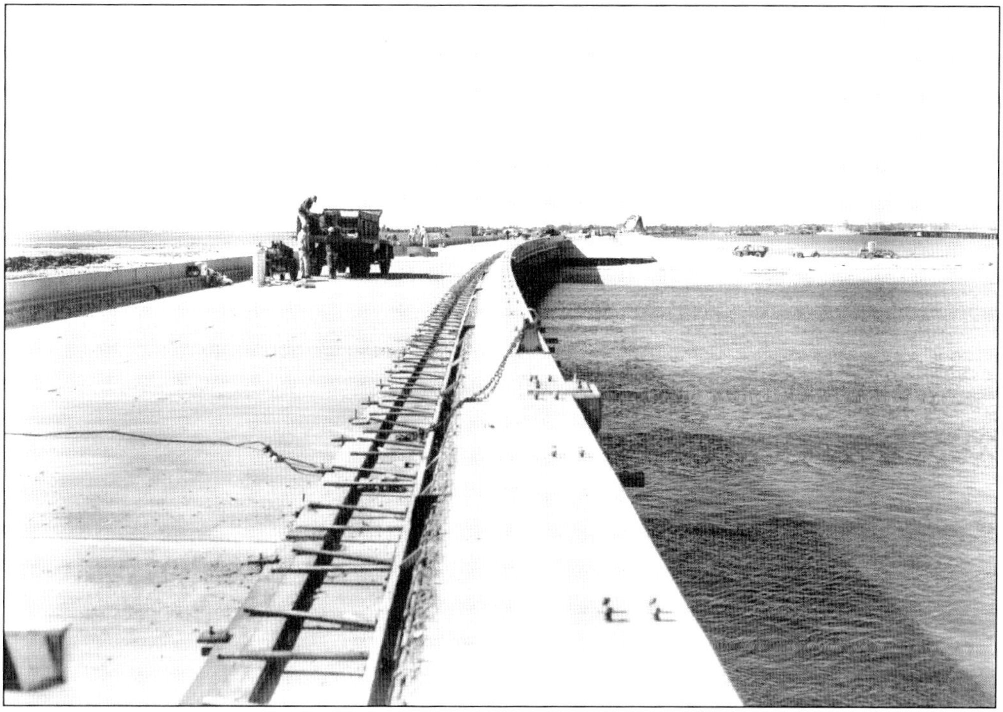

The Garden State Parkway bridge connecting Atlantic and Cape May Counties over the Great Egg Harbor Bay was the last piece of the main stem to be completed. Opened for traffic in May 1956, the bridge fulfilled the New Jersey Highway Authority's obligations to the bondholders. It is the longest structure on the Parkway, spanning one and a half miles. Originally, one lane in each direction was carried across this waterway. This allowed traffic to use the Parkway until additional lanes could be opened, allowing for two lanes in each direction. The Beesley's Point Bridge is in the background below.

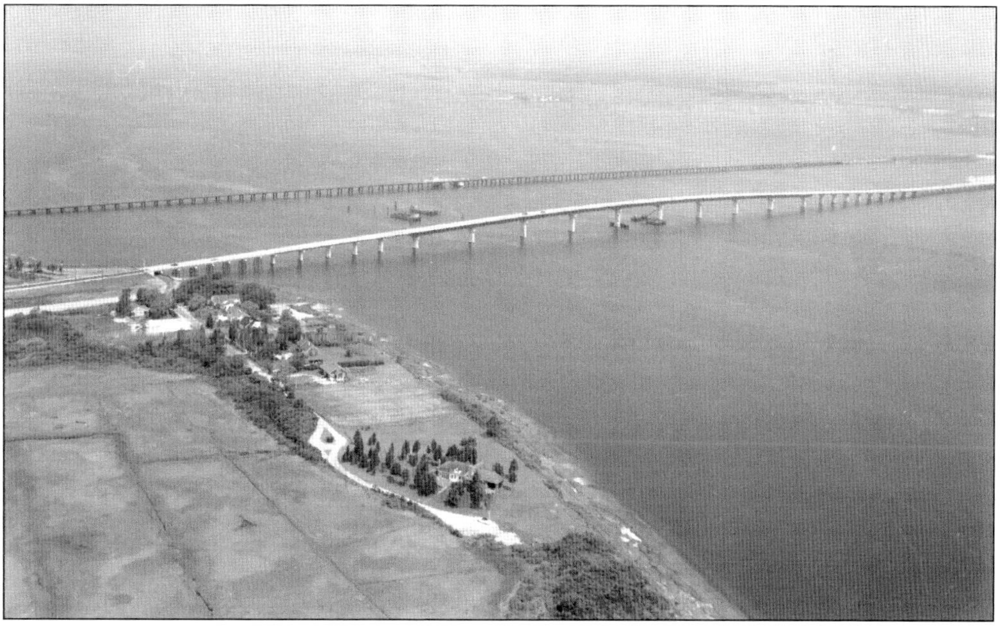

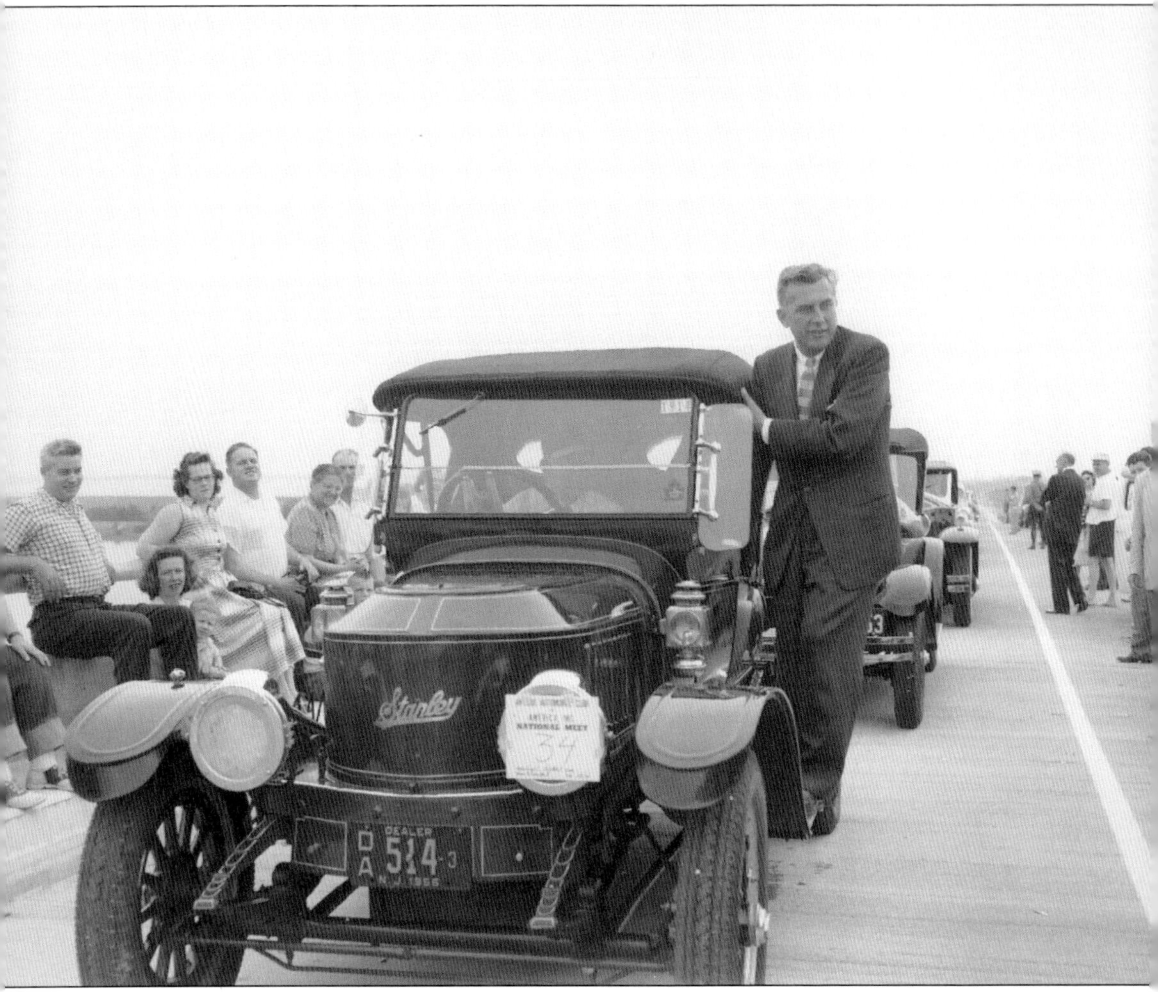

Gov. Robert B. Meyner gets his first trip across the newly opened Garden State Parkway bridge over the Great Egg Harbor on June 16, 1956, riding the running board of a Stanley Steamer that was part of the antique automobile parade. Governor Meyner continued with the work Governor Driscoll had started and oversaw the completion of the second major road-building project for New Jersey. The New Jersey Turnpike and the Parkway helped transform the state and travel within it. Both roads have been memorialized in song. However it was the Parkway that inspired a fan club at Stonewall Jackson High School in Manassas, Virginia.

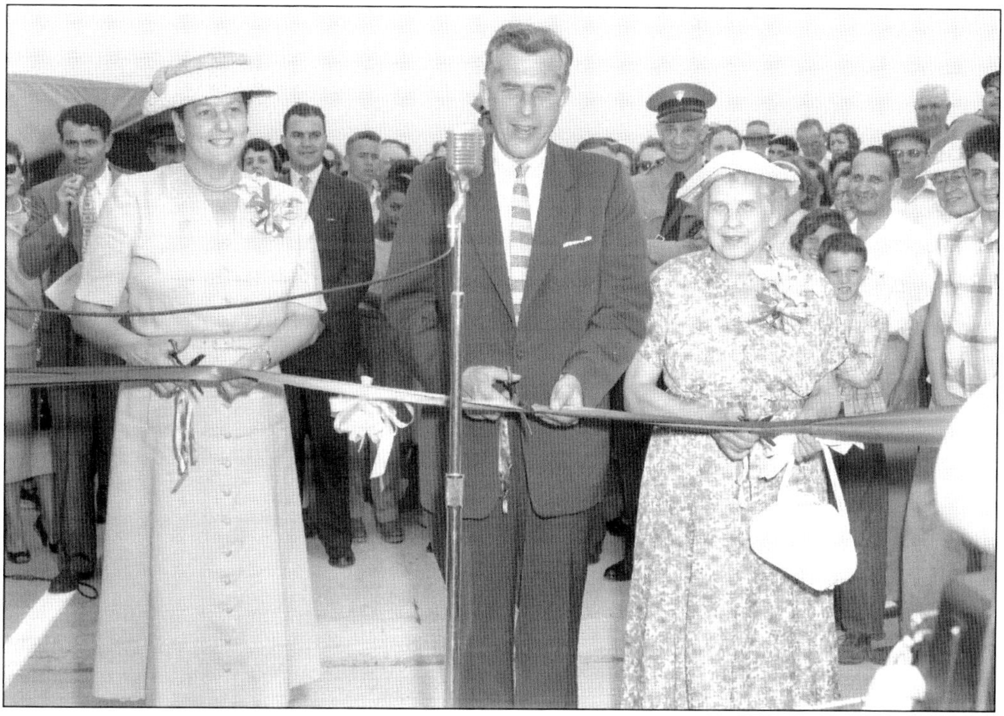

Governor Meyner and his mother, Sophia Meyner (right), joined chairman Katharine E. White at the opening ceremony of the Great Egg Harbor Bridge on June 16, 1956. While this event signified a milestone for the new road, it would not mark the full completion of the original route, which work crews were rushing to complete.

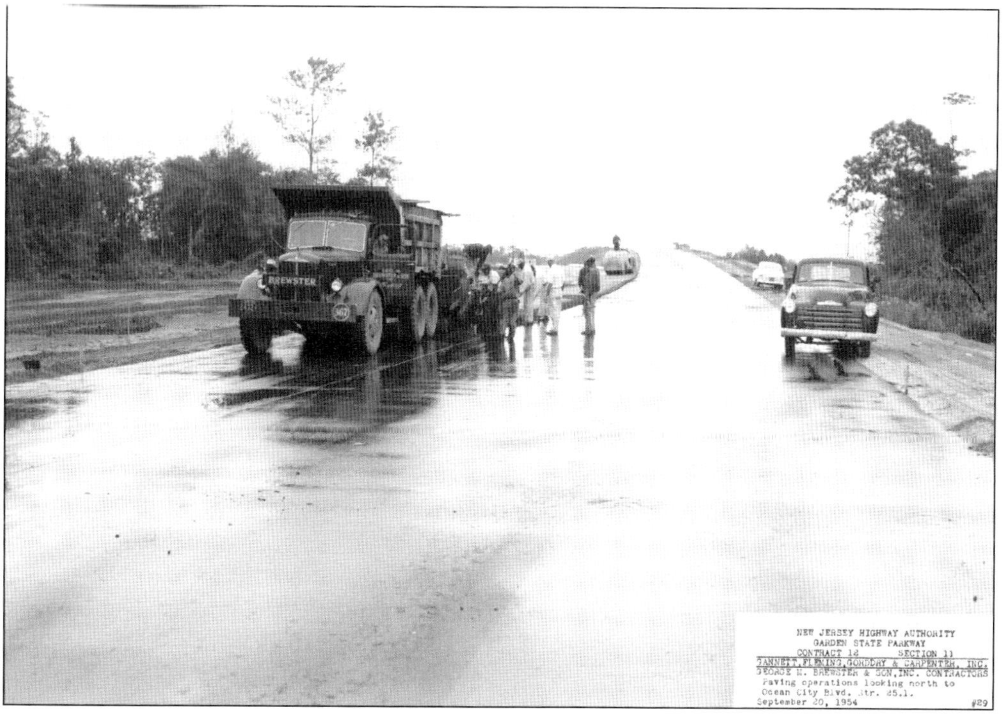

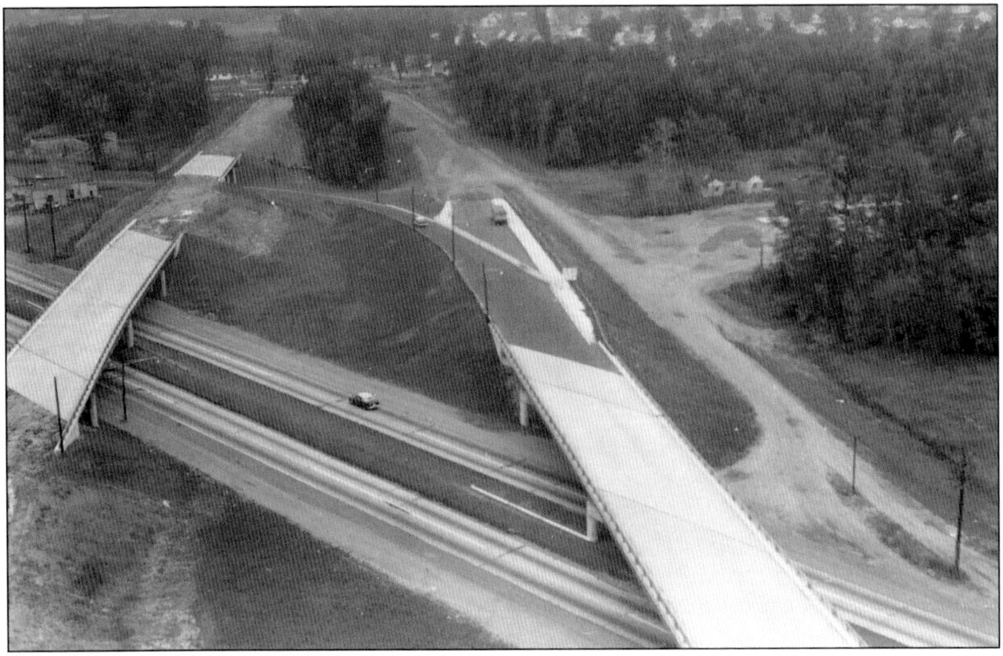

In 1956, the northern end of the Garden State Parkway connected to Route 17 in Paramus, Bergen County. However, by the time the original 164-mile stretch had been opened with the completion of the Great Egg Harbor Bay Bridge, ground had already been broken for a nine-mile connector with the New York Thruway, which would be completed the next year and finish the original 173-mile roadway.

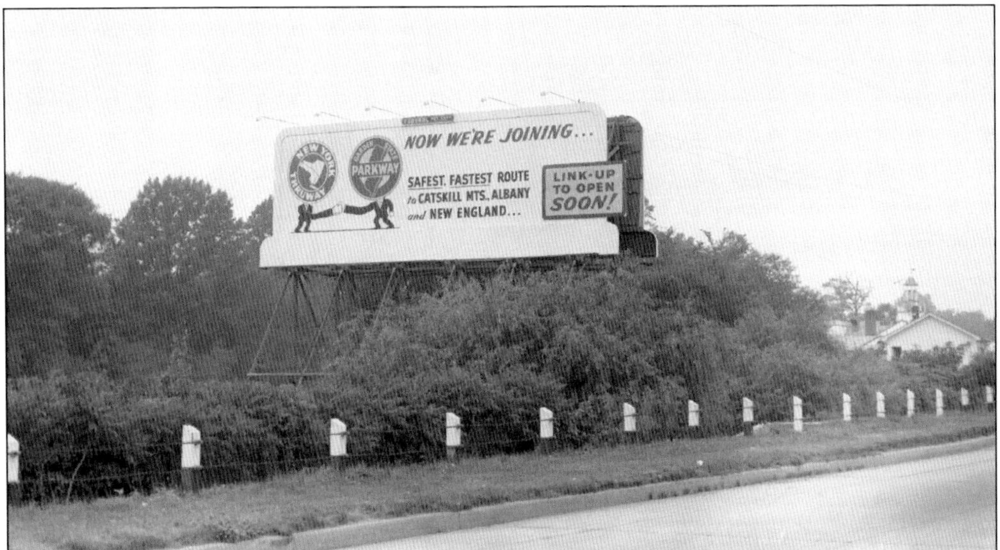

The completion of the Garden State Parkway required the cooperation of many state and local officials. In order to make it the success envisioned, cooperation would need to extend beyond state borders. Connection with the New York Thruway offered a greater benefit to the commuters and vacationers of the region.

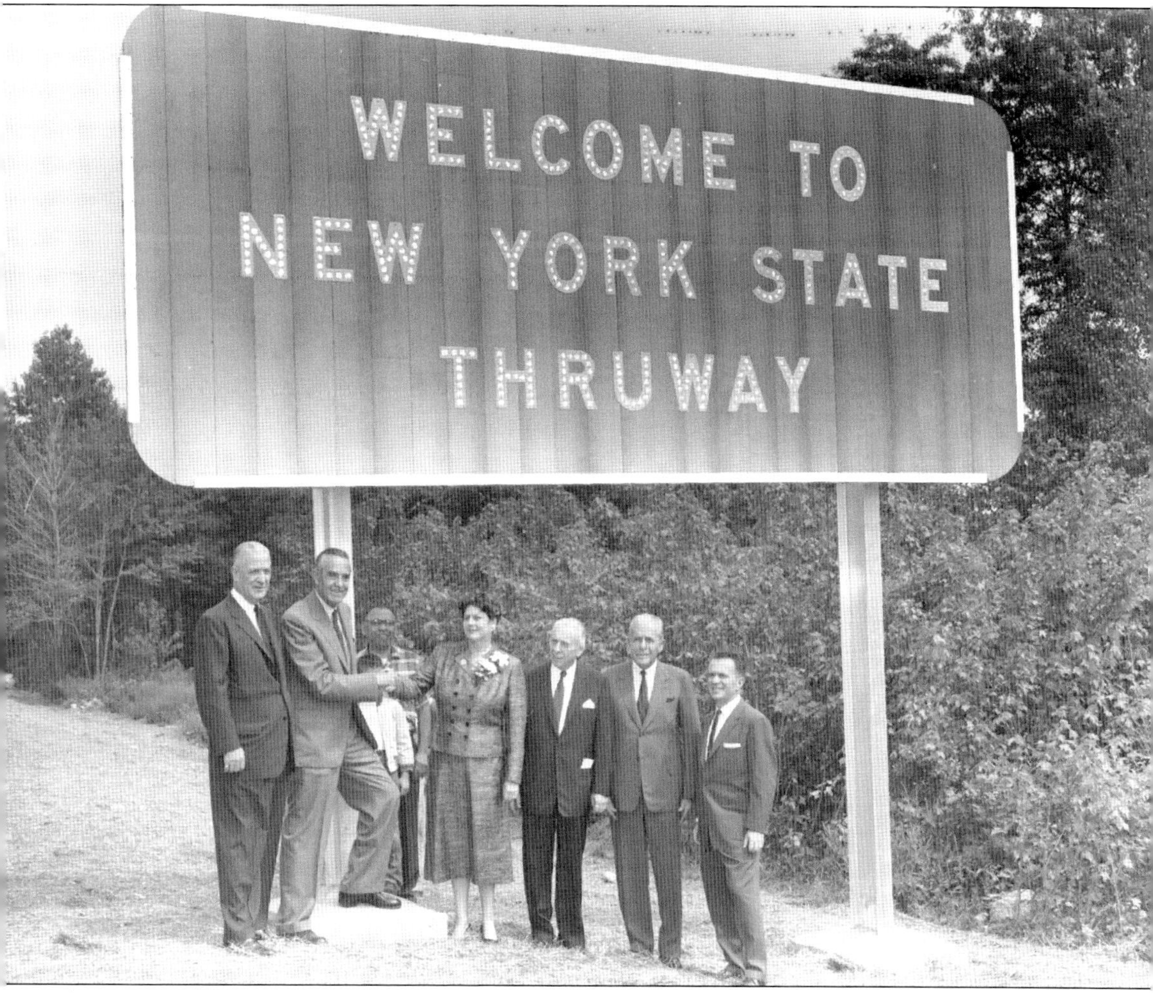

The opening ceremony of the New York Thruway connection was held on August 30, 1957. Pictured are, from left to right, New York Thruway member D. Martin, New York governor Averill Harriman, New Jersey Highway Authority chairman Katharine E. White, New Jersey Turnpike member J. Morecraft, New Jersey Department of Transportation representative R. Palmer, and New Jersey Highway Authority executive director D. Louis Tonti. The New York Thruway connection opened the last portion of the original 173-mile parkway after being under construction for a little over a year.

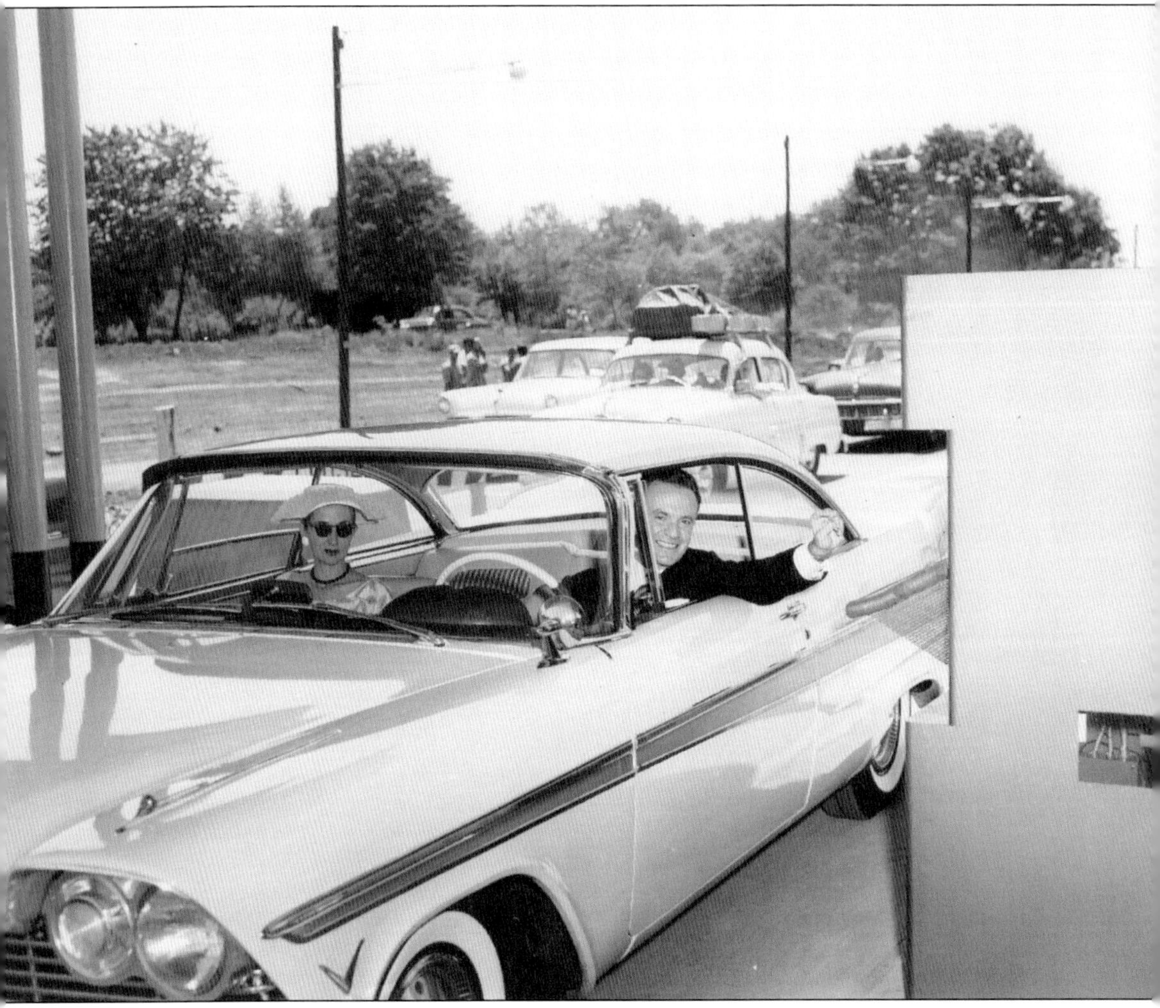

Highway authority executive director D. Louis Tonti and his wife pass through an automated tollbooth as they entered the New York Thruway in 1957. The Garden State Parkway was complete from Cape May to the New York state line. The extension would now open up the state's tourist destinations for easy travel from the north and expand the commuting potential. The immense success of the Parkway also meant an immediate expansion of the roadway to handle the traffic.

Three

The Unique Highway Authority and Its Parkway

The Garden State Parkway provided not only an easier commute for travelers in the northern portions of the state, but also granted tourists easier access to the shore. During World War II, shore industries declined as men were shipped overseas and women left at home to enter the professional world. Vacations became too expensive for many families, and the shore suffered their loss. After the construction of the Parkway, though, the shore was reborn better than ever expected as housing developments and shopping centers popped up around interchanges.

Because families no longer spent significant periods of time simply driving to and from the shore, more people could vacation there without having to take time off from work. This meant that the shore opened up to middle and working class families instead of remaining a playground for only wealthier families. The Boardwalk in Atlantic City and Wildwood saw growth in motels and cottages. Businesses grew to accommodate more visitors. Upper middle class tourists began to flock to Stone Harbor, Bay Head, and Beach Haven.

The first year the Parkway was in service, the 10 counties it traversed earned an extra $300 million in tax ratables thanks to new construction, tourism spending, and resident dollars. By 1958, these 10 counties earned tax ratables four times higher than other counties in the state thanks to permanent population growth as well as increased tourist dollars. The Parkway successfully ignited New Jersey's economy and improved the lives of state residents and tourists.

When the state legislature granted the New Jersey Highway Authority the power to design and construct the Parkway, it also gave the New Jersey Highway Authority the ability to build recreational facilities. Thus was born the Garden State Arts Center, now known as the PNC Arts Center, in Holmdel, Monmouth County. Architect Edward Durell Stone, who partnered in such famous venues as Radio City Music Hall and the original Museum of Modern Art in New York City and who was primarily responsible for the design of the Kennedy Center in Washington, DC, created the Garden State Arts Center. It opened in 1968 as an open, circular amphitheater that could seat 5,302 under the roof and another 5,500 on the lawn.

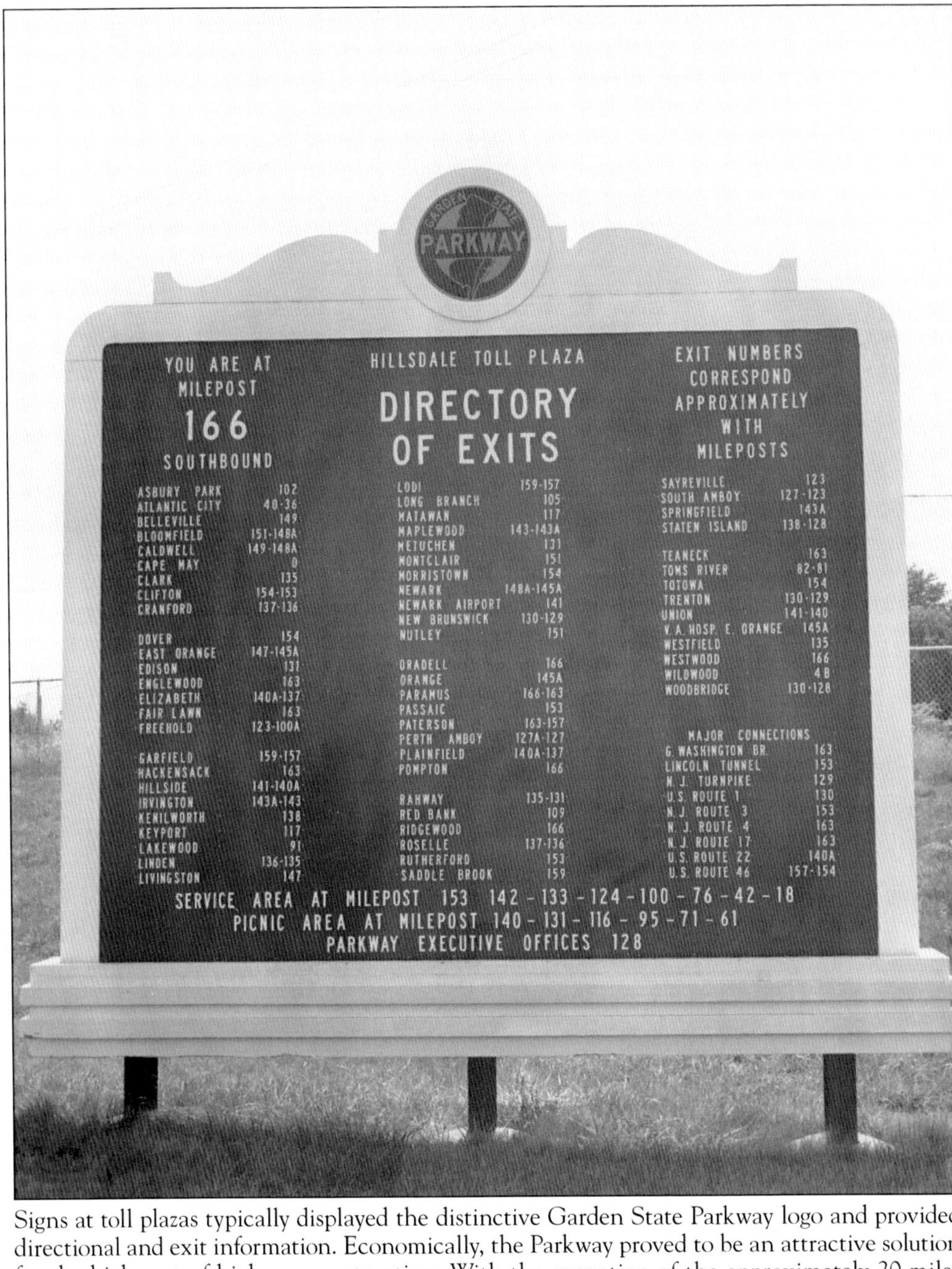

Signs at toll plazas typically displayed the distinctive Garden State Parkway logo and provided directional and exit information. Economically, the Parkway proved to be an attractive solution for the high cost of highway construction. With the exception of the approximately 20 miles of the Parkway, then known as Route 4, constructed by the State Highway Department, the Parkway was built without using taxpayer dollars. It continues to be a self-sustaining roadway today, unlike most other roads in the nation. This made the project virtually free for state and local governments and did not drain taxpayer wallets. In fact, the road has boosted the economy of New Jersey and added revenue at the local and state levels. It was a source of jobs when built and continues to employ engineers and contractors to keep the road safe and meet the needs of ever increasing traffic.

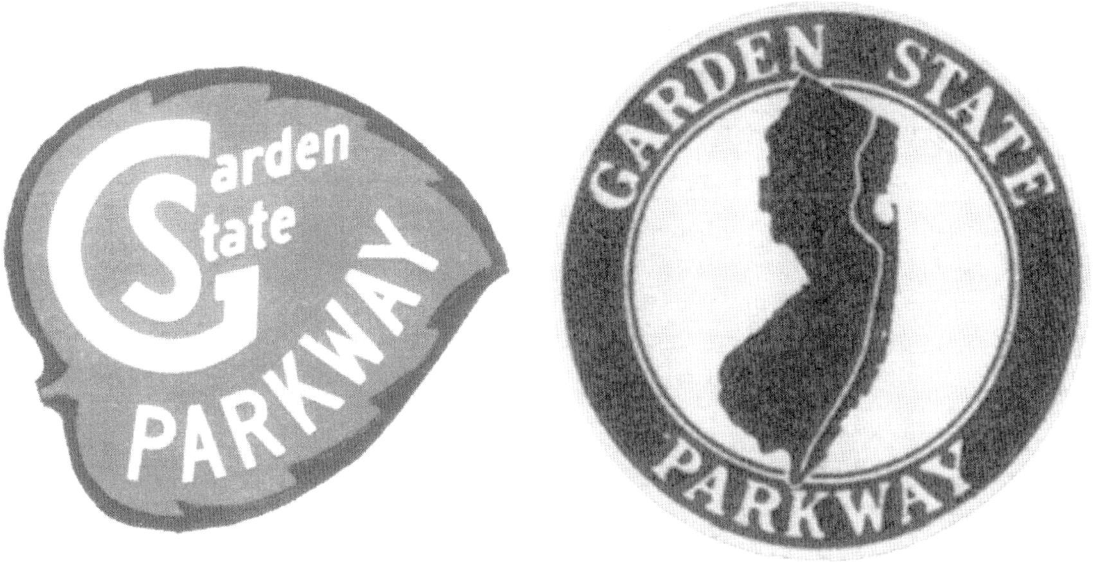

These are two of the original logos used for the Garden State Parkway in its early years. From the outset, the Parkway was established as a different kind of road, and the logo went through an evolution in the 1950s. The circular logo employed the road layout within the state, reflecting the area covered and amount of territory serviced. Up until the construction of the Parkway, roads were not designed to be both scenic and fast. Upon its completion, the New Jersey Highway Authority estimated that the trip from Paterson to Atlantic City along the Parkway was 2.6 hours and cost only $1.75 in tolls, while the same trip on local roads would have taken 3.7 hours. This was a savings in time and money spent on gas. Today, this trip costs $5.25 with tolls collected in one direction. Travelers can stop along the way at any of the service areas, which feature restaurants, phones, restrooms, gas stations, and picnic areas. Not only could motorists travel through New Jersey faster, they could also take breaks along the way without departing from the Parkway.

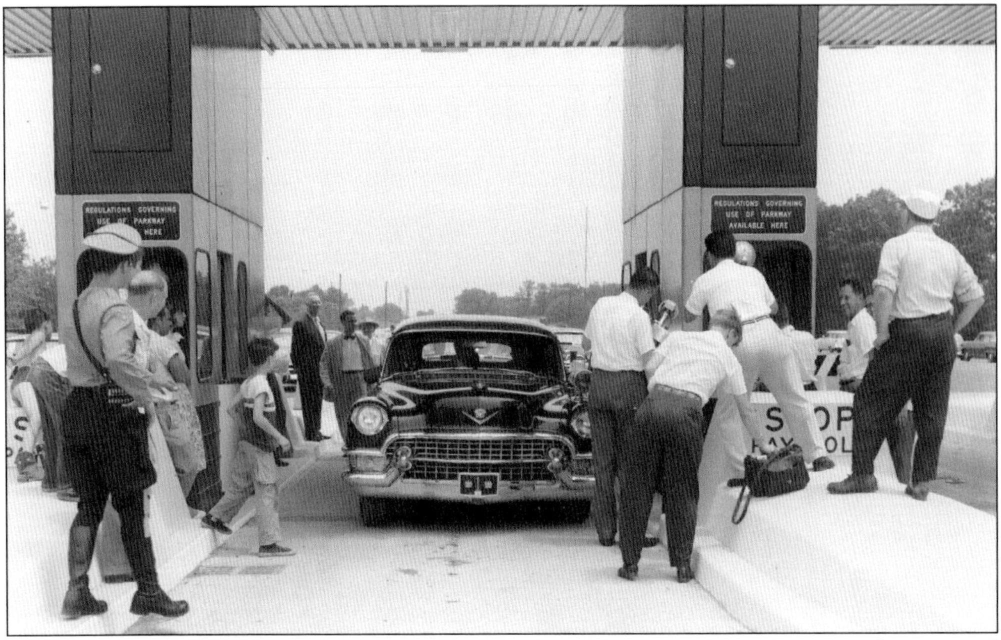

The Bergen Toll Plaza opening in Saddlebrook, Bergen County, in 1955 was a milestone and worthy of local and media attention. The public relations department made sure to keep everyone informed about the progress of the project and demonstration of its value.

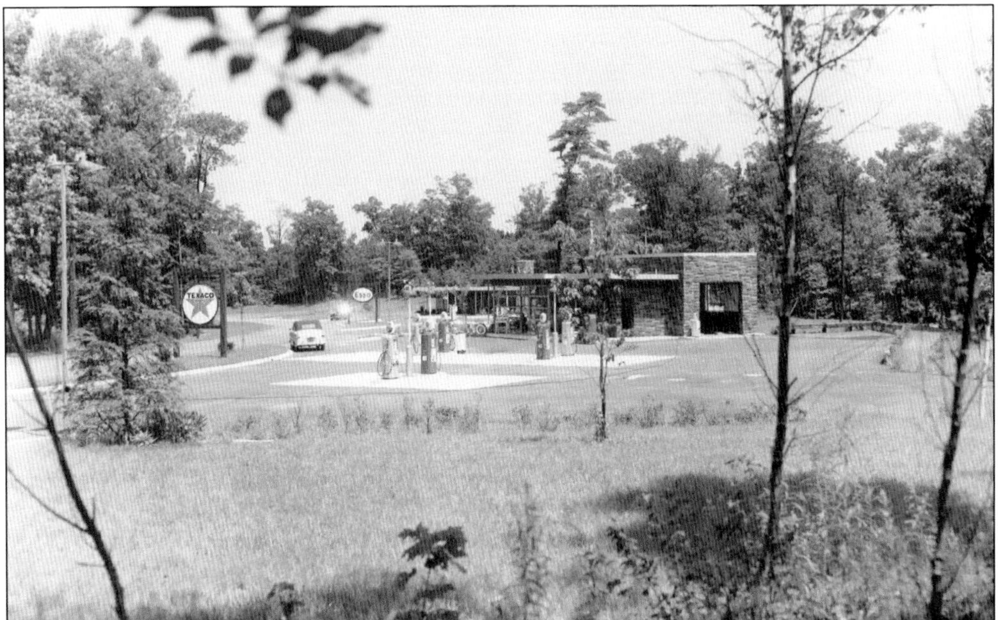

This gas-only stop constructed as part of the state section in Union County includes a Texaco gas station in the foreground with an Esso station sign in the distance. The other gas stations associated with the Garden State Parkway were operated by Cities Service and Atlantic. As is the case here, some of the facilities were limited in their services. The station includes stone facing similar to the Parkway structures of the area and is surrounded by open, naturalistic landscaping.

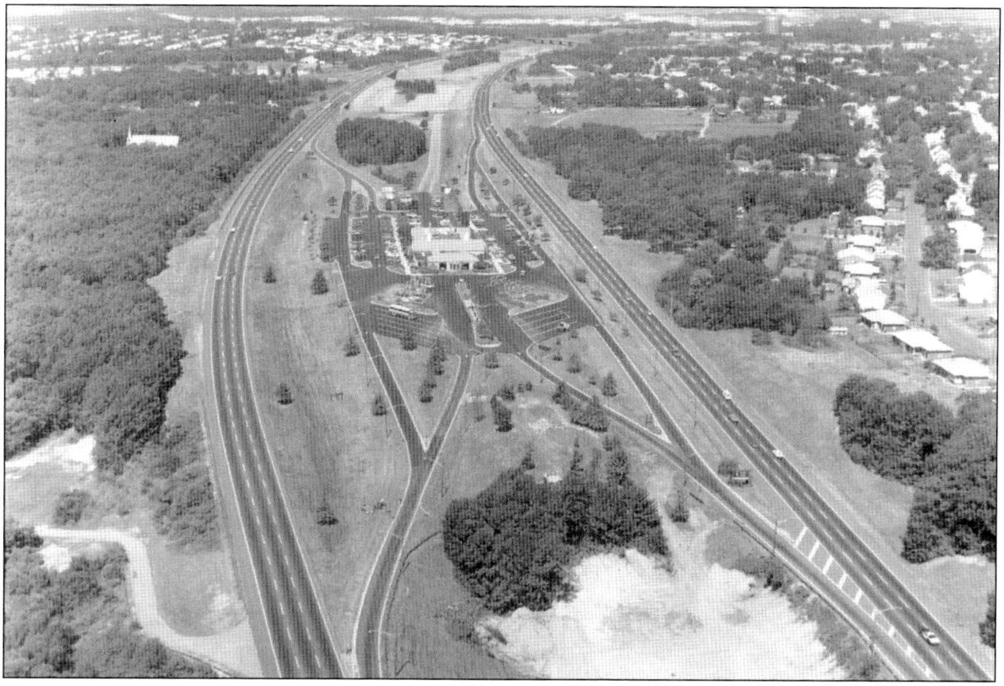

Innovatively designed service areas such as Cheesequake in Sayreville, Middlesex County, were located between opposing lanes of traffic within the median and were accessed from both sides of the Garden State Parkway when space would allow. Not only did this lessen the amount of land needed, it also reduced the number of individual facilities typically required for two directions of travel.

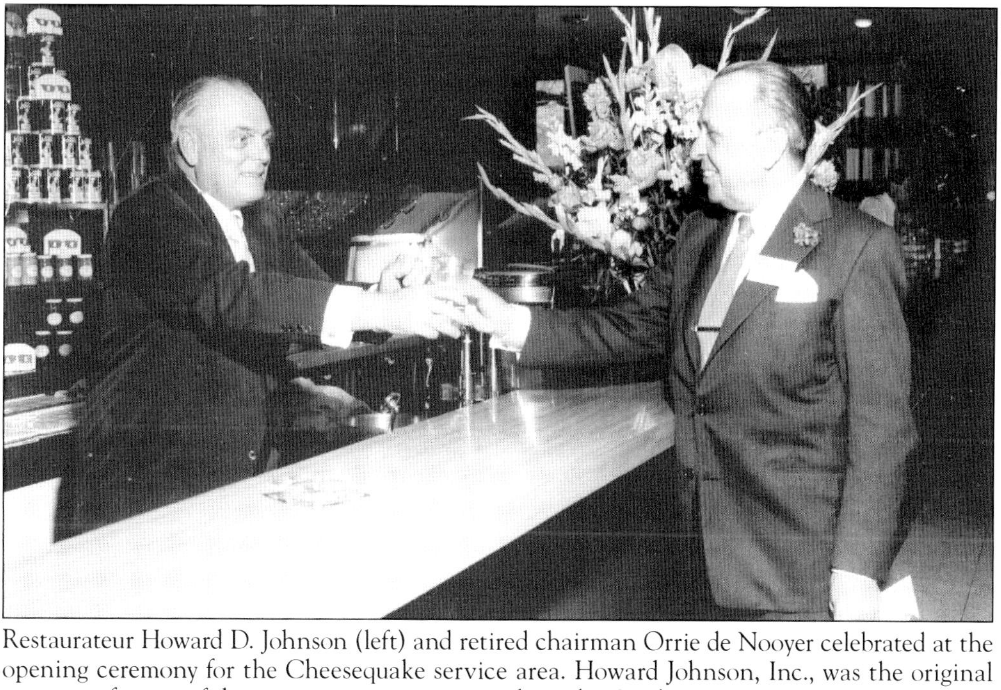

Restaurateur Howard D. Johnson (left) and retired chairman Orrie de Nooyer celebrated at the opening ceremony for the Cheesequake service area. Howard Johnson, Inc., was the original operator of seven of the service area restaurants along the Garden State Parkway.

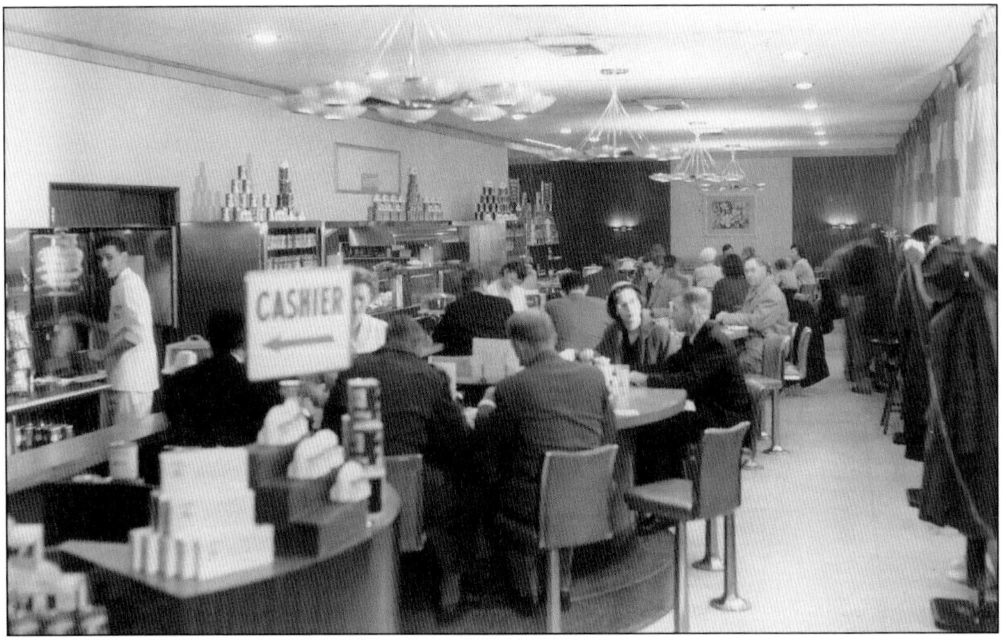

Service areas offered sit-down restaurants such as this. Howard Johnson, Inc., was the first vendor to occupy the service area restaurants, but the southernmost four were managed by Walter Reade, Inc., starting in 1956. In 1959, Holiday House took over management of the Walter Reade facilities. Lease income from the vendors helped to fund the Garden State Parkway and the New Jersey Highway Authority administration.

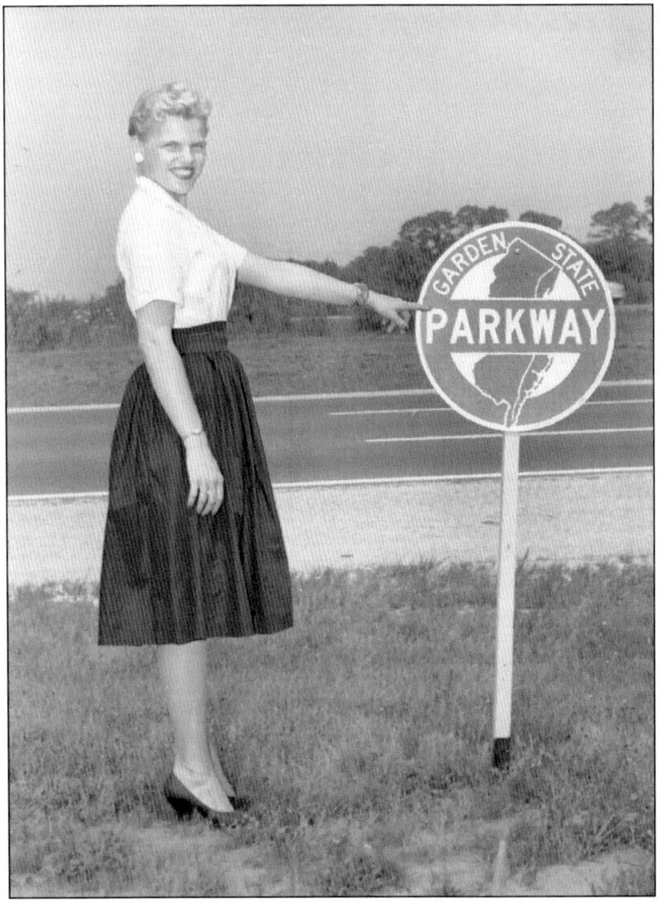

This promotional photograph exhibits the parkway signs posted periodically along the highway and to direct drivers to the road from the local network. This new parkway logo was unveiled in 1956. The signs were constructed of non-illuminated, reflective green and white metal with a distinctive parkway logo.

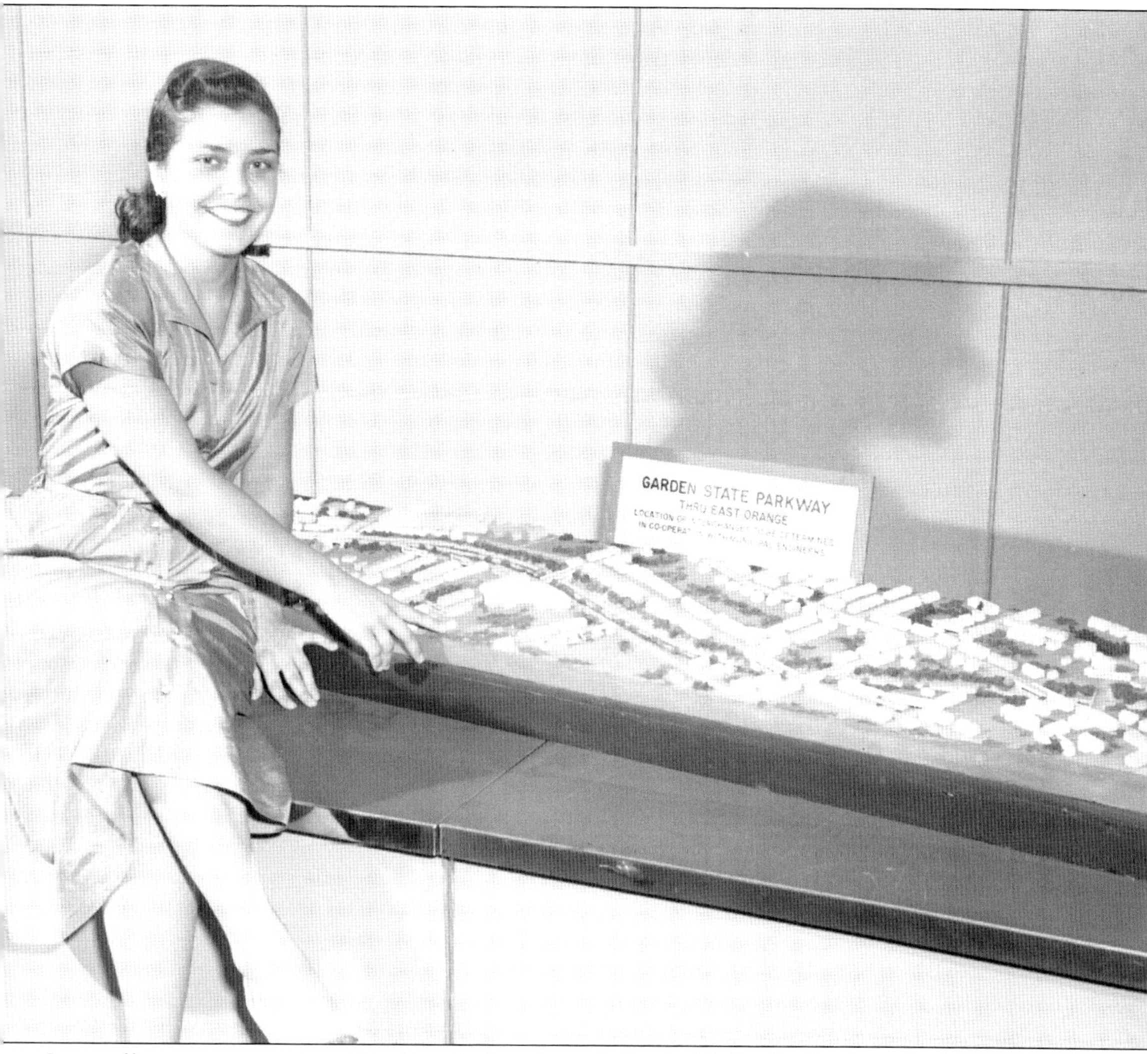

In an effort to prove to the public that the bonds needed to build the Garden State Parkway and that the additional tolls were a sound investment, the New Jersey Highway Authority operated a public relations department. The department promoted the Parkway not only to residents of New Jersey but also to the rest of the nation. The public relations department created exhibits at service areas, trade shows, and visitor centers across the state extolling the importance of the Parkway. This exhibit in 1953 showed a model of the Parkway through East Orange in Essex County. The public relations department of the New Jersey Highway Authority also documented many public events and New Jersey Highway Authority occasions and made sure that the benefits of the road were well known.

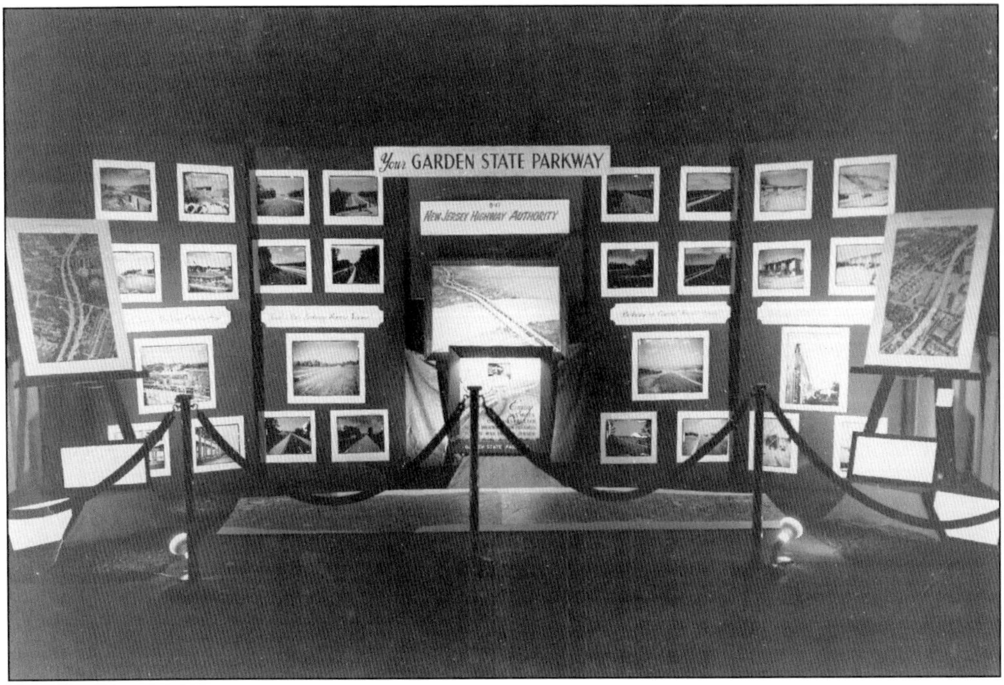

The promotional exhibit at the Public Works Congress in 1954 showed the typical display set up at various locations across the state. The exhibits helped assure the public that the Garden State Parkway was not only a worthwhile investment on their part, but necessary.

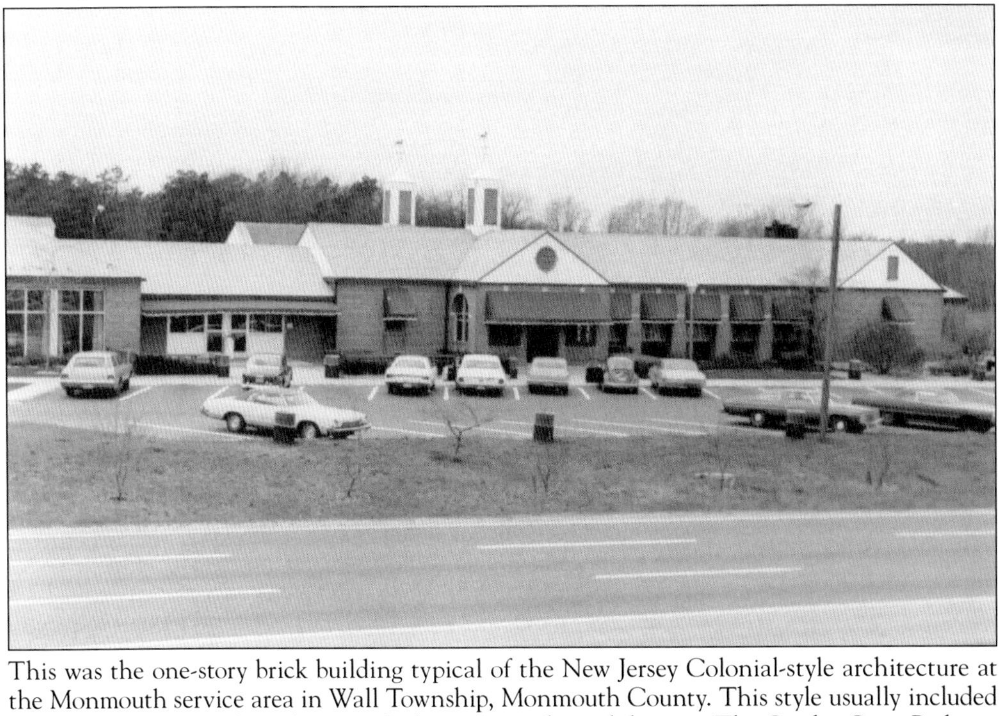

This was the one-story brick building typical of the New Jersey Colonial-style architecture at the Monmouth service area in Wall Township, Monmouth County. This style usually included gable roofs and a cupola with painted white trim and wood shutters. The Garden State Parkway designers carefully planned for a consistent look that was not utilitarian.

Chairman Katharine E. White and her grandson try out the small change room installed by Walter Reade at the restaurant in the Monmouth service area. This demonstrates some of the effort designers made to create a parkway that was convenient for motoring families. The New Jersey Highway Authority knew how important their role was in the tourism industry.

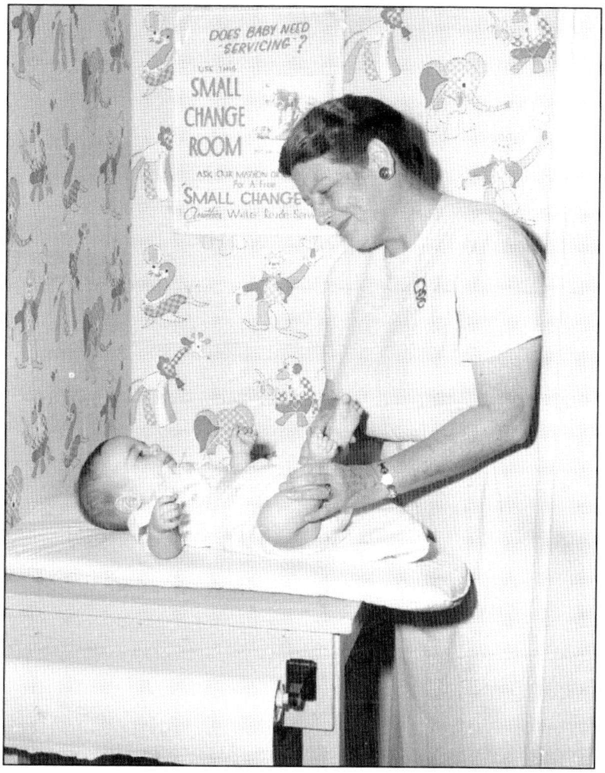

The Monmouth service area featured a full service gas station. Both cars and people could refuel along their way on the Garden State Parkway. Such facilities meant that parkway travelers did not have to exit the roadway while on their way.

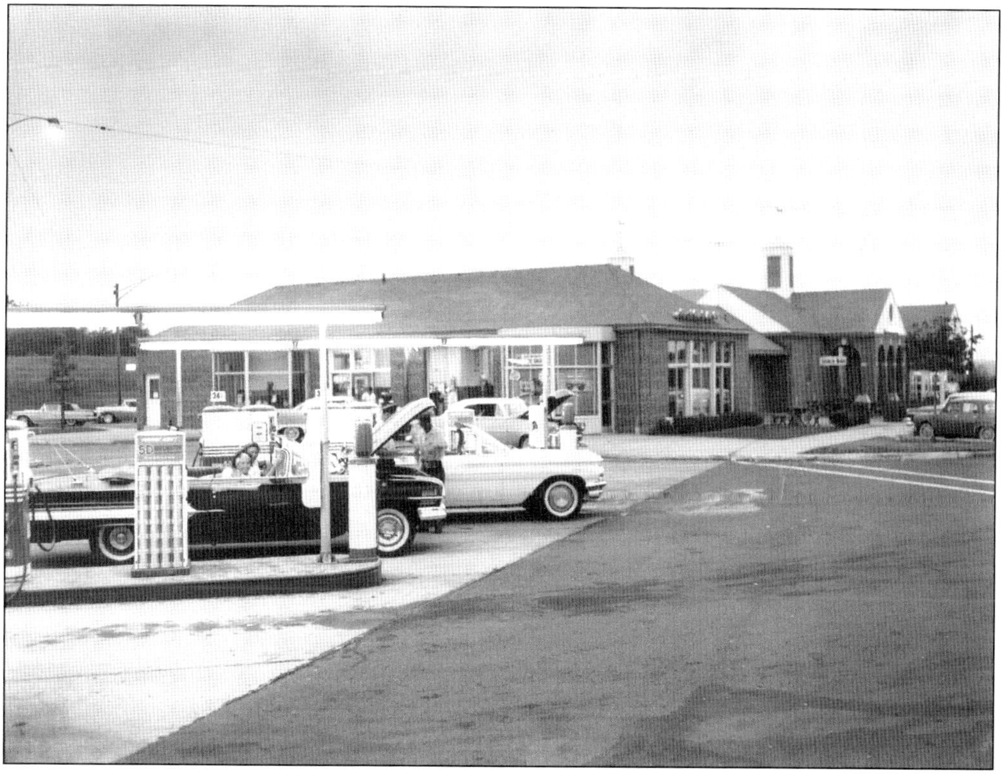

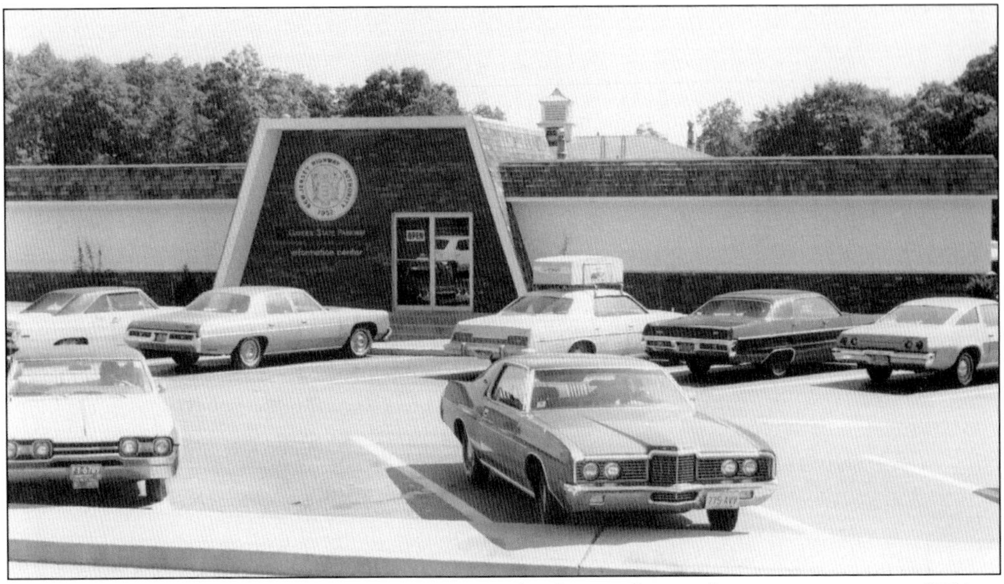

The Montvale service area in Bergen County also boasted an information center in 1974 as the Garden State Parkway continued its effort to make the highway a convenient route. As the northernmost facility on the Parkway, the Montvale service area plays a large role in the advertising of New Jersey to travelers coming from New York State and beyond.

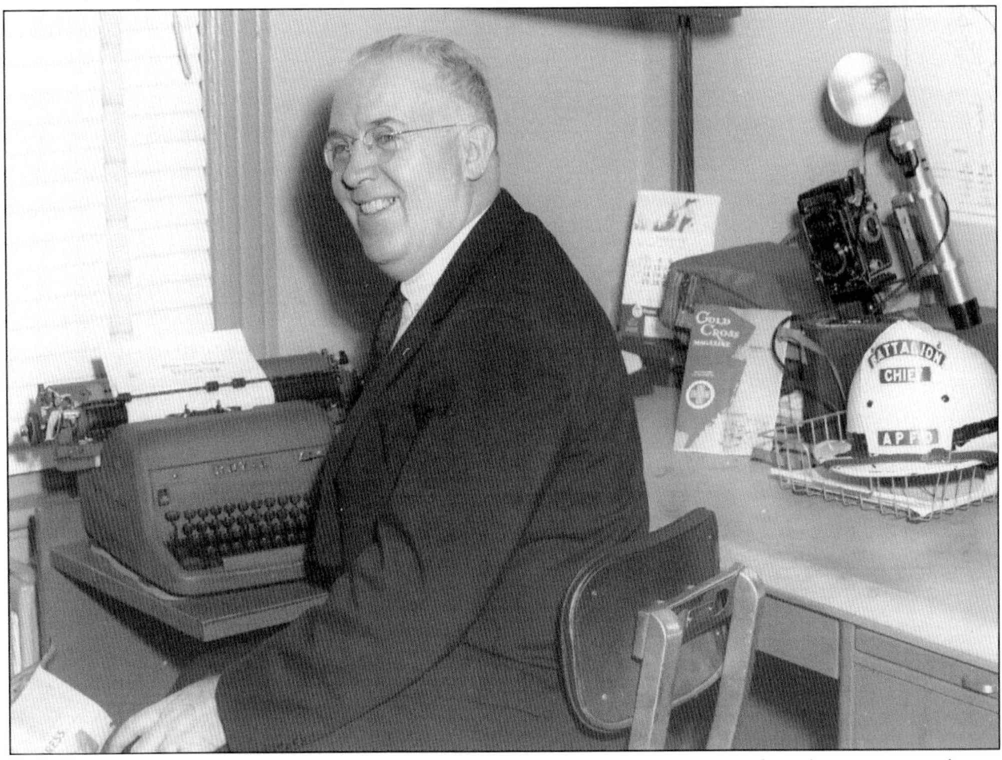

The public relations department of the New Jersey Highway Authority produced its own newsletter called the *Reporter*. It was an employee publication that provided news on employee activities and personal achievements. The *Reporter* was published monthly from 1955 until 2003.

Temper tantrums, splattered food on the floor, and frazzled parents were sometimes mandatory at the Bibbery. The children in this photograph, however, seemed to be doing well. This feature was one of several implemented at service areas to accommodate and encourage family travel.

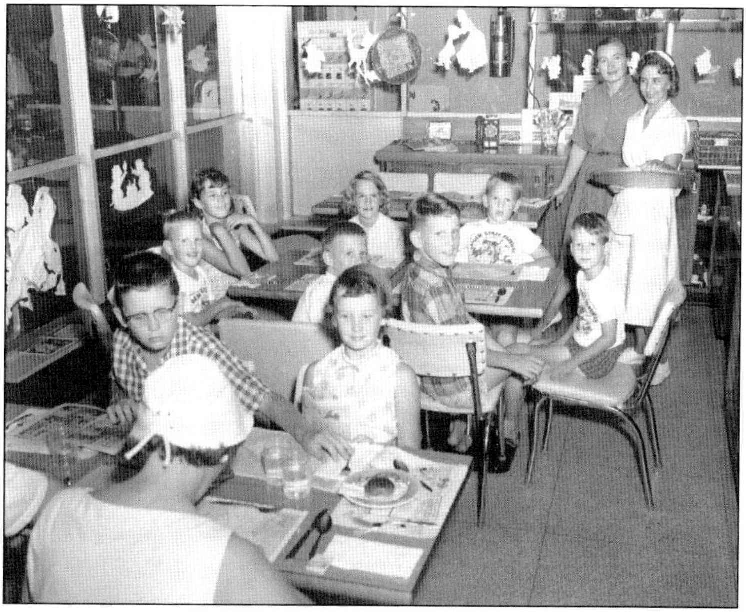

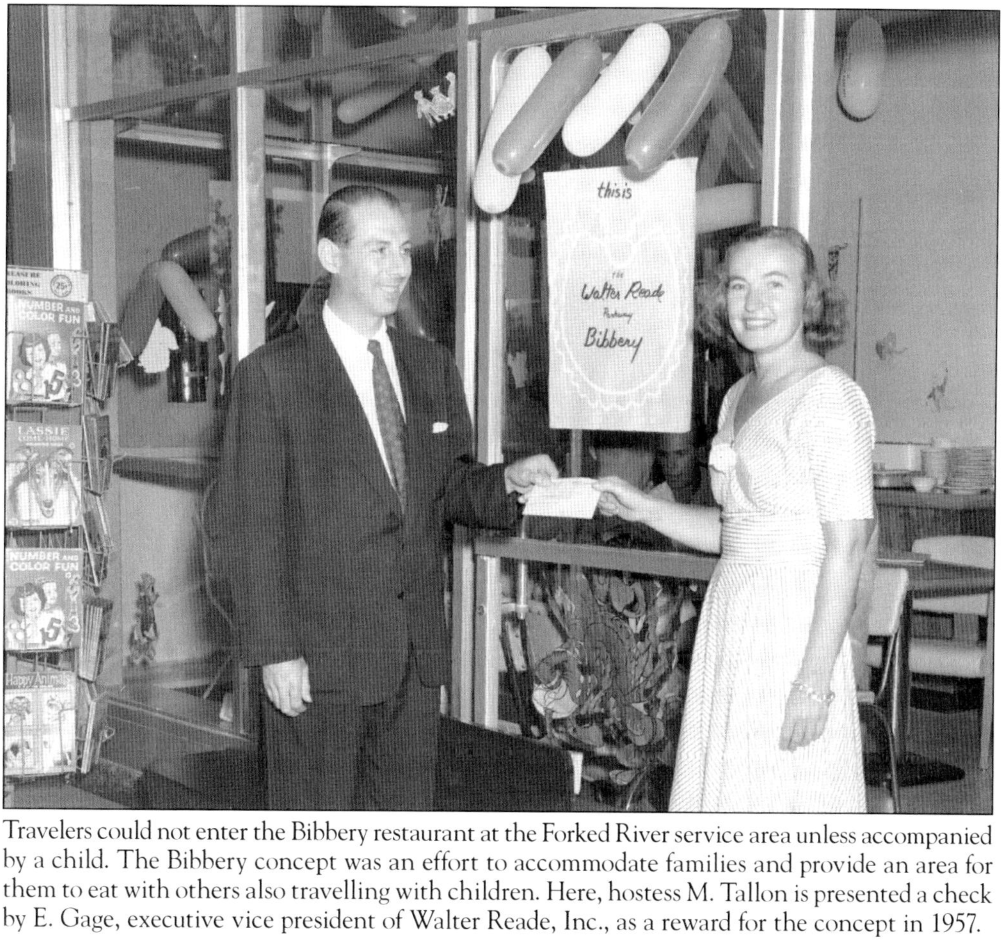

Travelers could not enter the Bibbery restaurant at the Forked River service area unless accompanied by a child. The Bibbery concept was an effort to accommodate families and provide an area for them to eat with others also travelling with children. Here, hostess M. Tallon is presented a check by E. Gage, executive vice president of Walter Reade, Inc., as a reward for the concept in 1957.

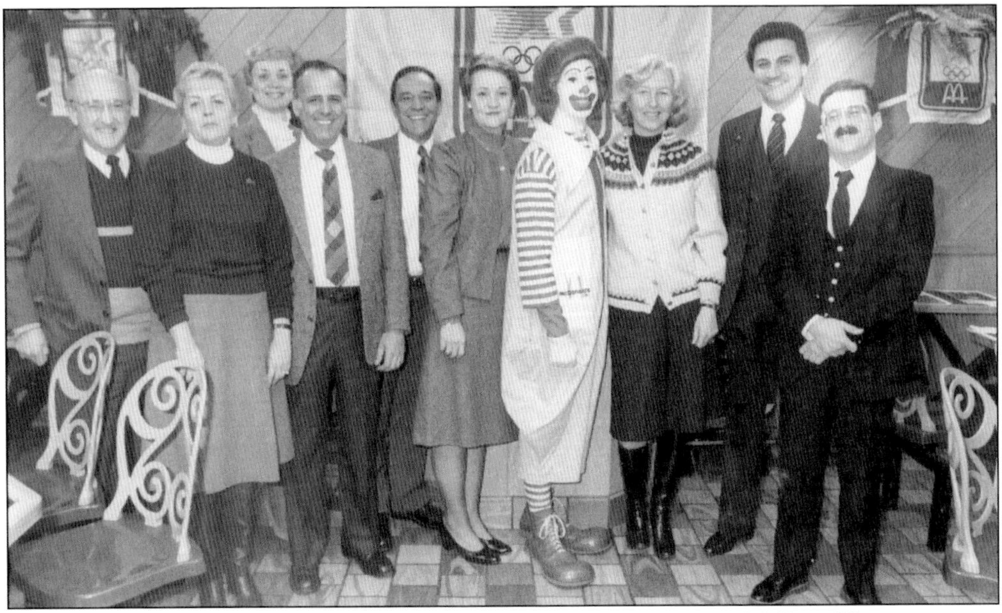

Celebrations were held at the Brookdale service area in Essex County at a McDonald's reopening in 1984. Pictured are, from left to right, personnel director Frederick Forrest, Pat Regan of personnel, E. Bell of personnel, building manager Angelo Paradiso, print shop manager Dick Gallo, arts center manager Patricia Horan, Ronald McDonald, director of public relations Ann McKee, F. Rubinetti, and assistant public relations director Dennis Ingoglia.

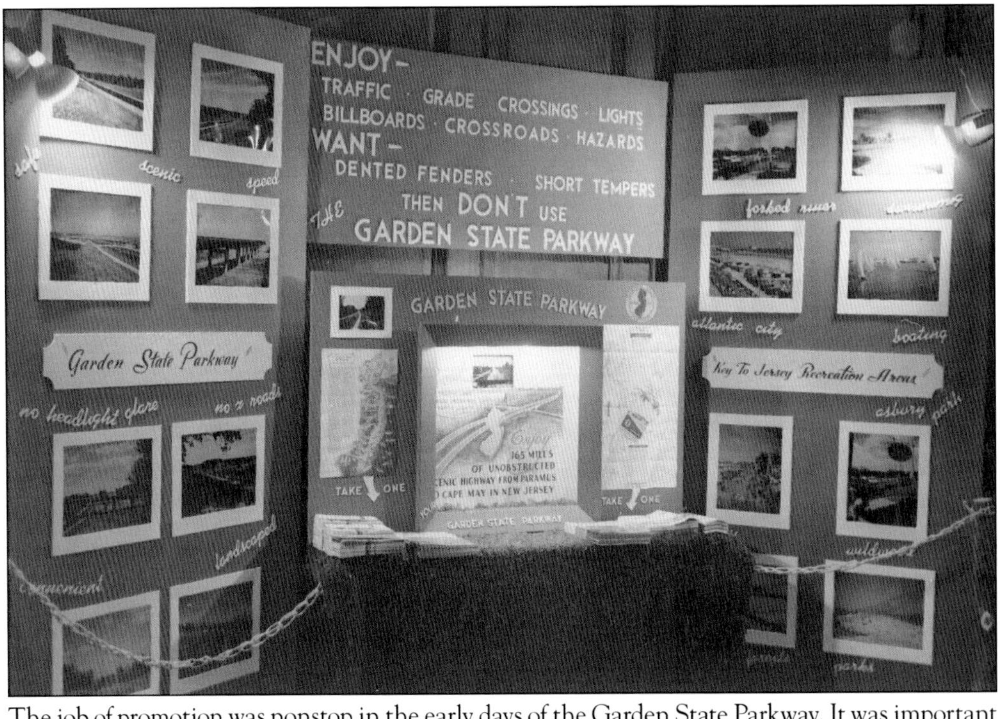

The job of promotion was nonstop in the early days of the Garden State Parkway. It was important to sell the road and ensure that the bonds were paid off. This 1955 display also illustrated a sense of humor as it promoted the value of the Parkway.

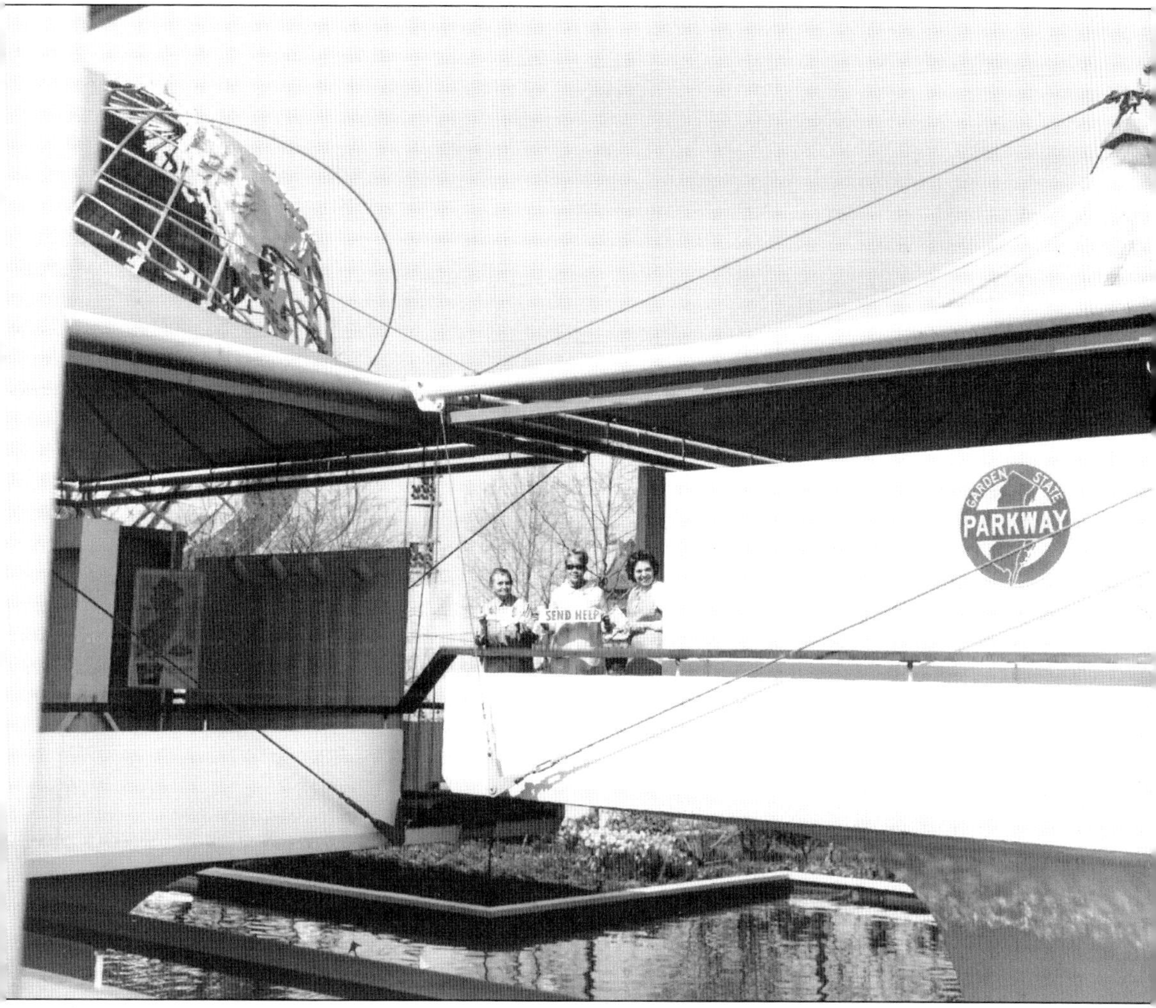

The promotion of the Garden State Parkway extended beyond New Jersey, including this exhibit at the 1964 New York World's Fair. The Parkway exhibit was featured in the New Jersey Pavilion at the fair. The representatives pictured here were enjoying themselves and taking time out from the events. Soon after completion, the Parkway gained a reputation as a significant achievement. Expansion and maintenance were always in the works, and so the roadway continued its promotion to the world. The impact it has had on New Jersey and the tourism industry has been a result of the emphasis on public relations and being a good partner for many interests.

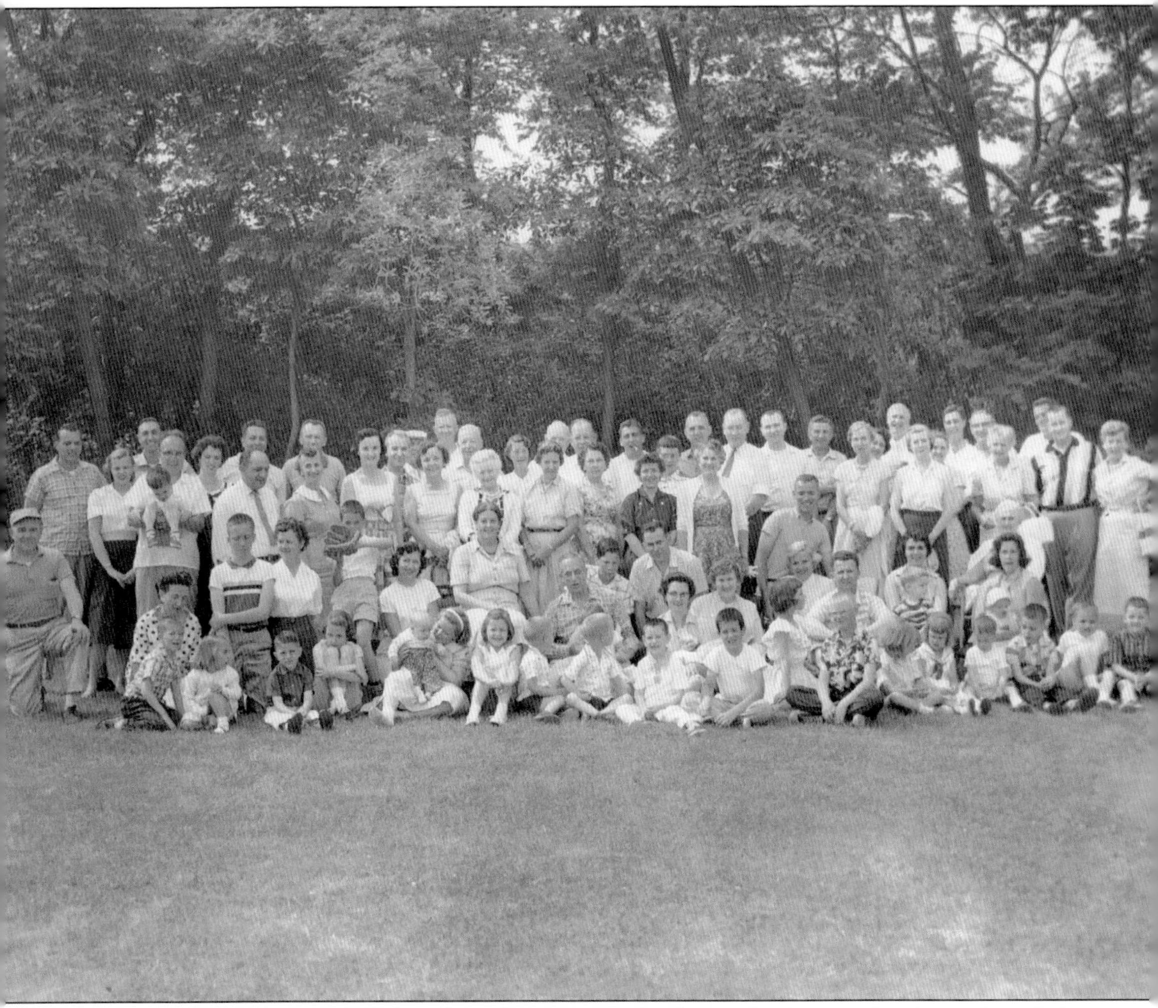

Chairman Katharine E. White hosted a picnic at her home for division heads, staff, and their families in June 1958. The event cost was shared by the employees who appreciated the opportunity to gather outside of work and socialize. The New Jersey Highway Authority created a workplace environment that nurtured a feeling of ownership and sense of pride for the Parkway. This camaraderie led to the establishment of activities such as bowling leagues. Chairman White is seated just left of center.

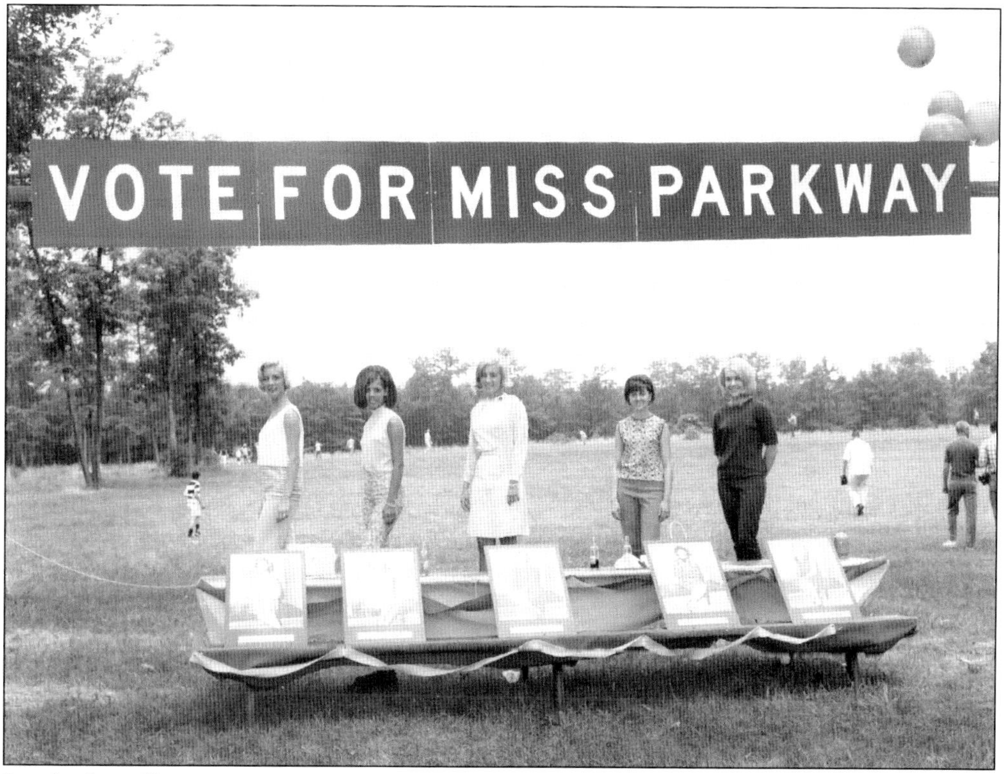

In a further effort to promote the Garden State Parkway, the public relations department sponsored competitions, such as the Miss Parkway Contest, which ran during the 1960s. Here, contestants for the 1966 title posed behind their publicity photographs at a picnic. The contest consisted of employees of the New Jersey Highway Authority who were voted on by their fellow employees.

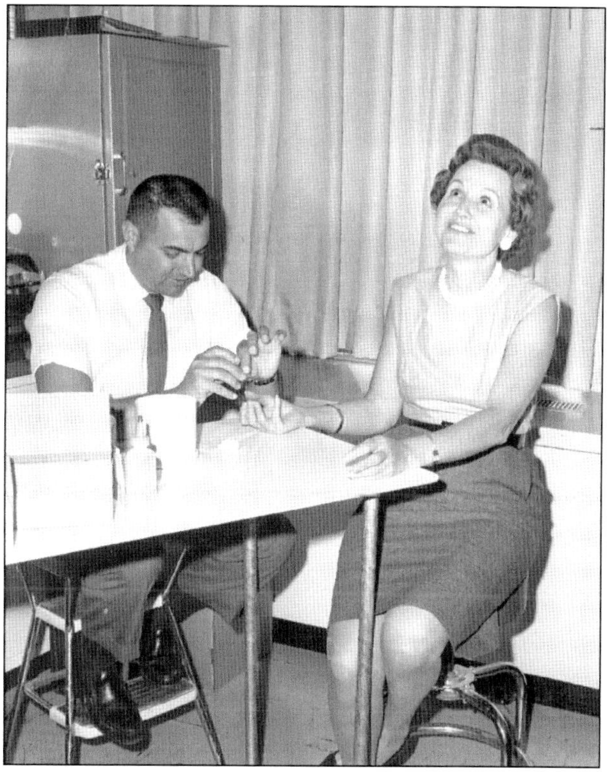

The New Jersey Highway Authority has long been involved in community activities such as blood bank drives. Here, Victor Calandriello of the operations section tests the blood of Bernice Panconi of the finance section in 1966.

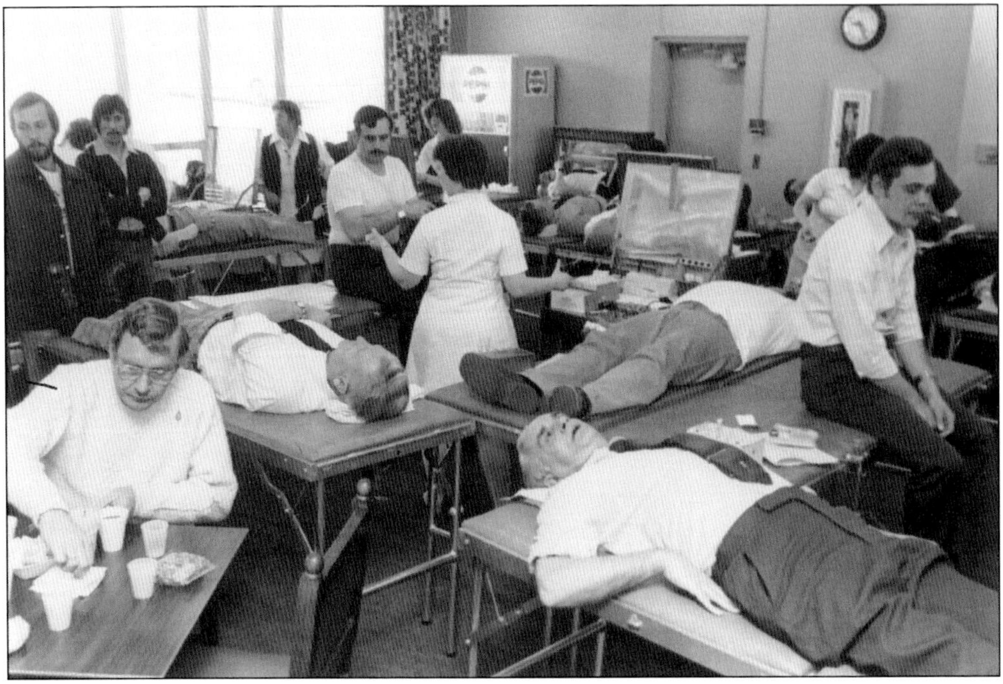

There was widespread involvement in the blood bank activities, as demonstrated here in 1978. Deputy executive director John Hughes (foreground) is donating blood while George Hrunka of building maintenance awaits his turn sitting on an adjacent table.

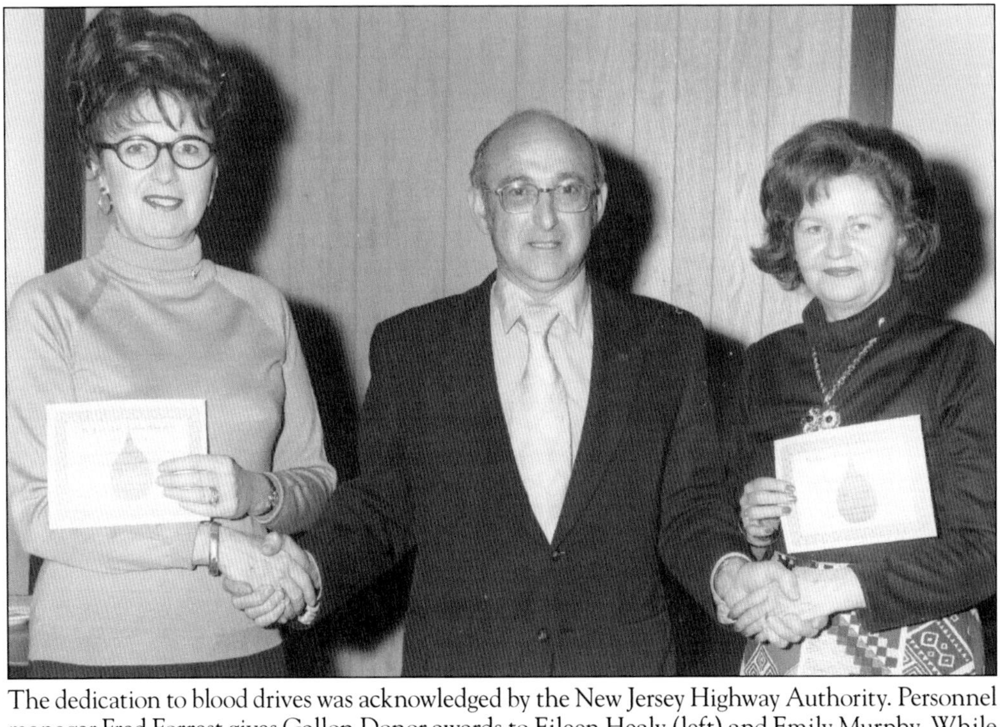

The dedication to blood drives was acknowledged by the New Jersey Highway Authority. Personnel manager Fred Forrest gives Gallon Donor awards to Eileen Healy (left) and Emily Murphy. While their dedication is unquestioned, there is no proof that the employees bled "Parkway Green."

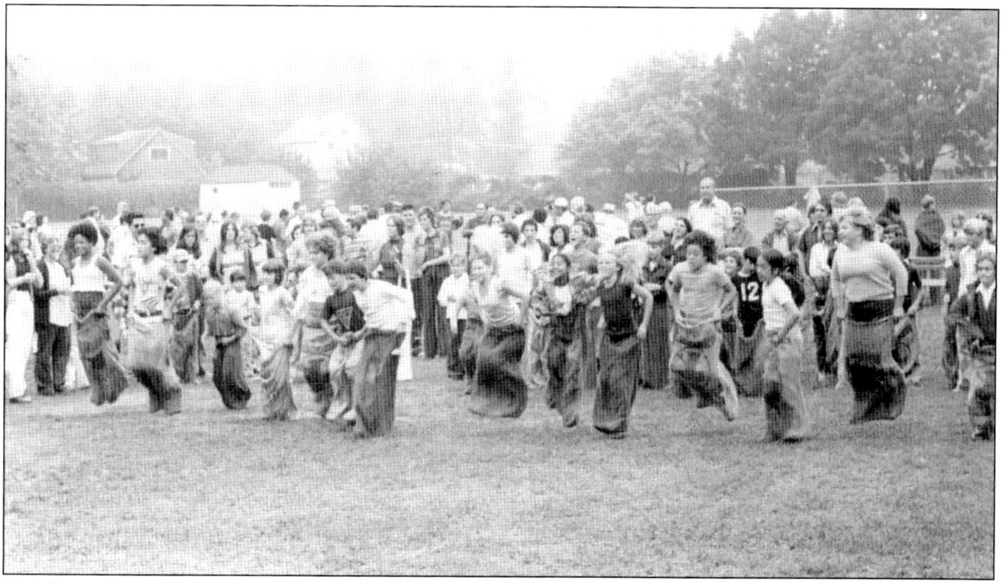

Employee children participate in a sack race at a New Jersey Highway Authority picnic in 1975. The event was held at the Old Cider Mill Grove in Union Township. Such activities allowed the employees to spend time together outside of work and their families to develop friendships.

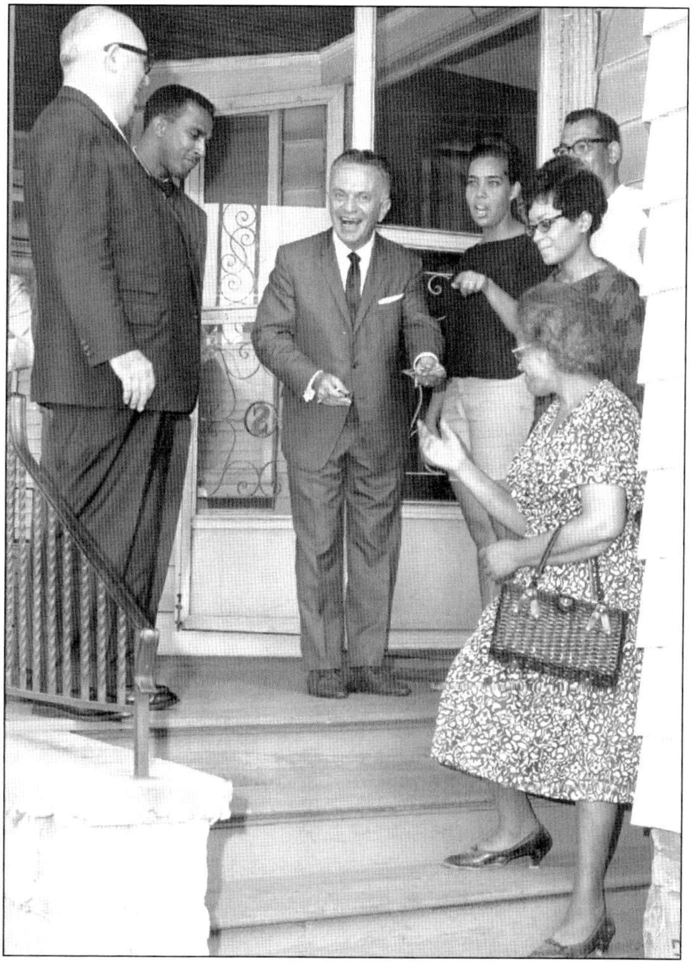

Executive director D. Louis Tonti loaned a house acquired by the New Jersey Highway Authority to the Johnson family after fire destroyed their home in 1965. The New Jersey Highway Authority home was made available until it was scheduled for demolition for Interchange 145 construction.

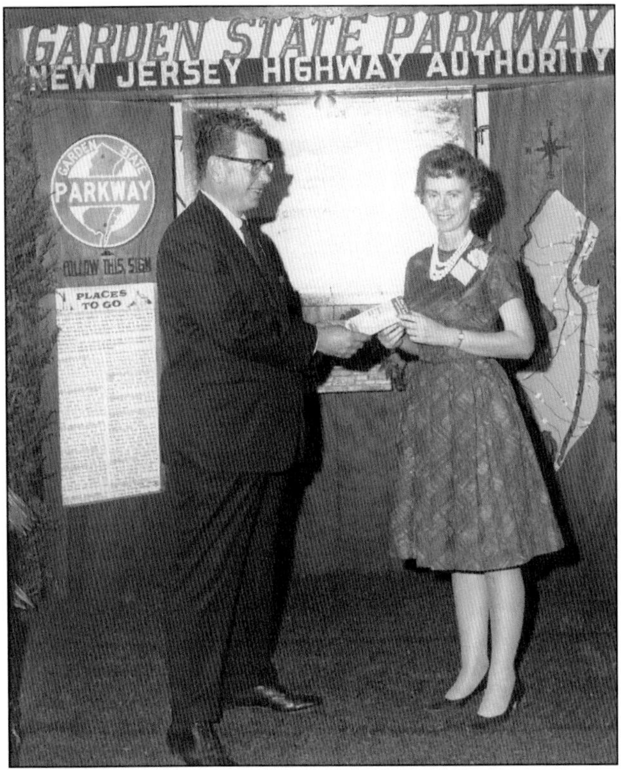

The New Jersey Highway Authority public relations department was still hard at work years after the final section of the Garden State Parkway was completed. Here, Gov. Richard J. Hughes participates with an unidentified woman in a traveling informational booth at a transportation show on September 19, 1963. The Parkway logo on the sign to the left of the governor was a well-known symbol by this time.

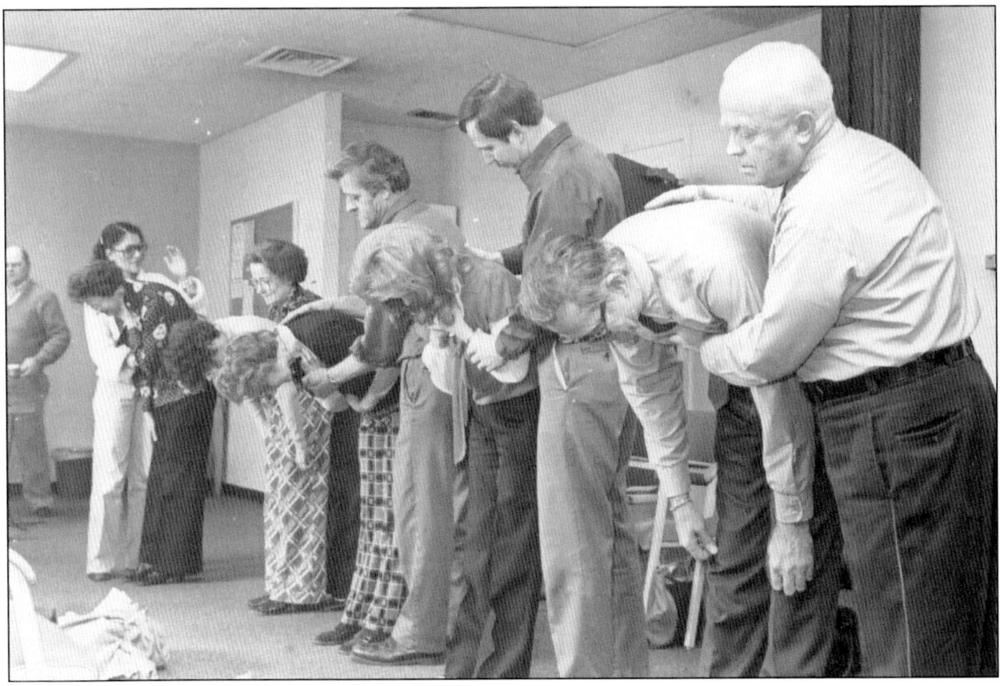

The New Jersey Highway Authority periodically provided first aid training for its employees. Here, a class in 1980 is instructed on assisting choking victims. Instructions were also given for CPR and minor medical emergencies.

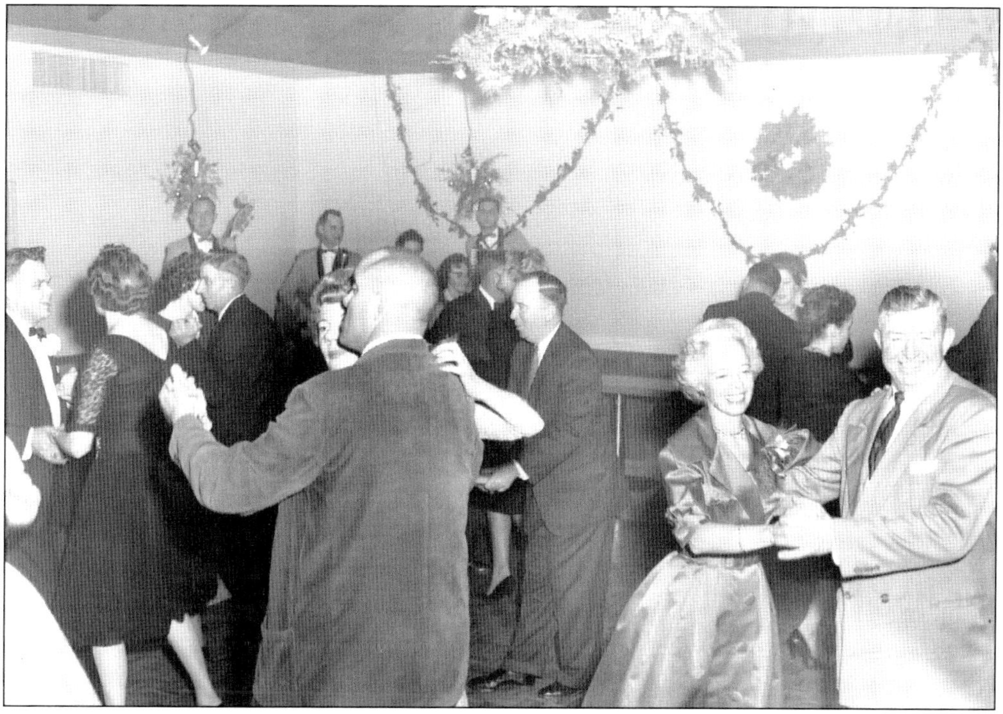

Highway authority employees and guests dance at the 1960 Christmas party. The event celebrated the season and provided an opportunity to see each other in a more formal, festive setting.

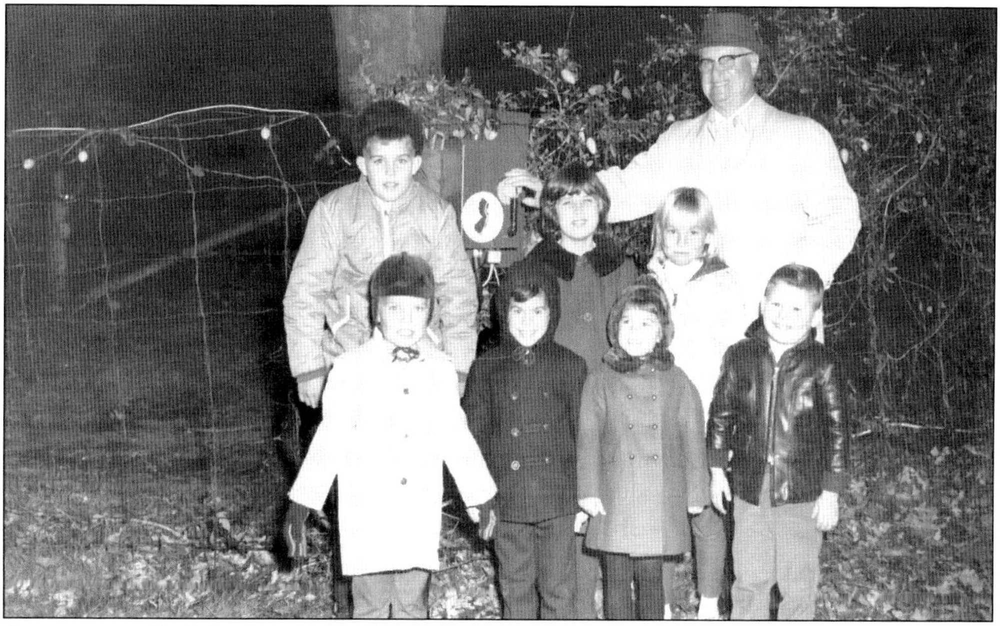

Commissioner Dr. John B. Townsend is ready to throw the switch for the lighting of the Shoemaker Holly at the eponymous picnic area in 1966. Such annual events provided a chance for children from the community to take part in celebrations. The Shoemaker Holly, estimated to be 300 years old, was preserved and protected from development by residents of Cape May County and named for the former owner of the property on which the tree grows.

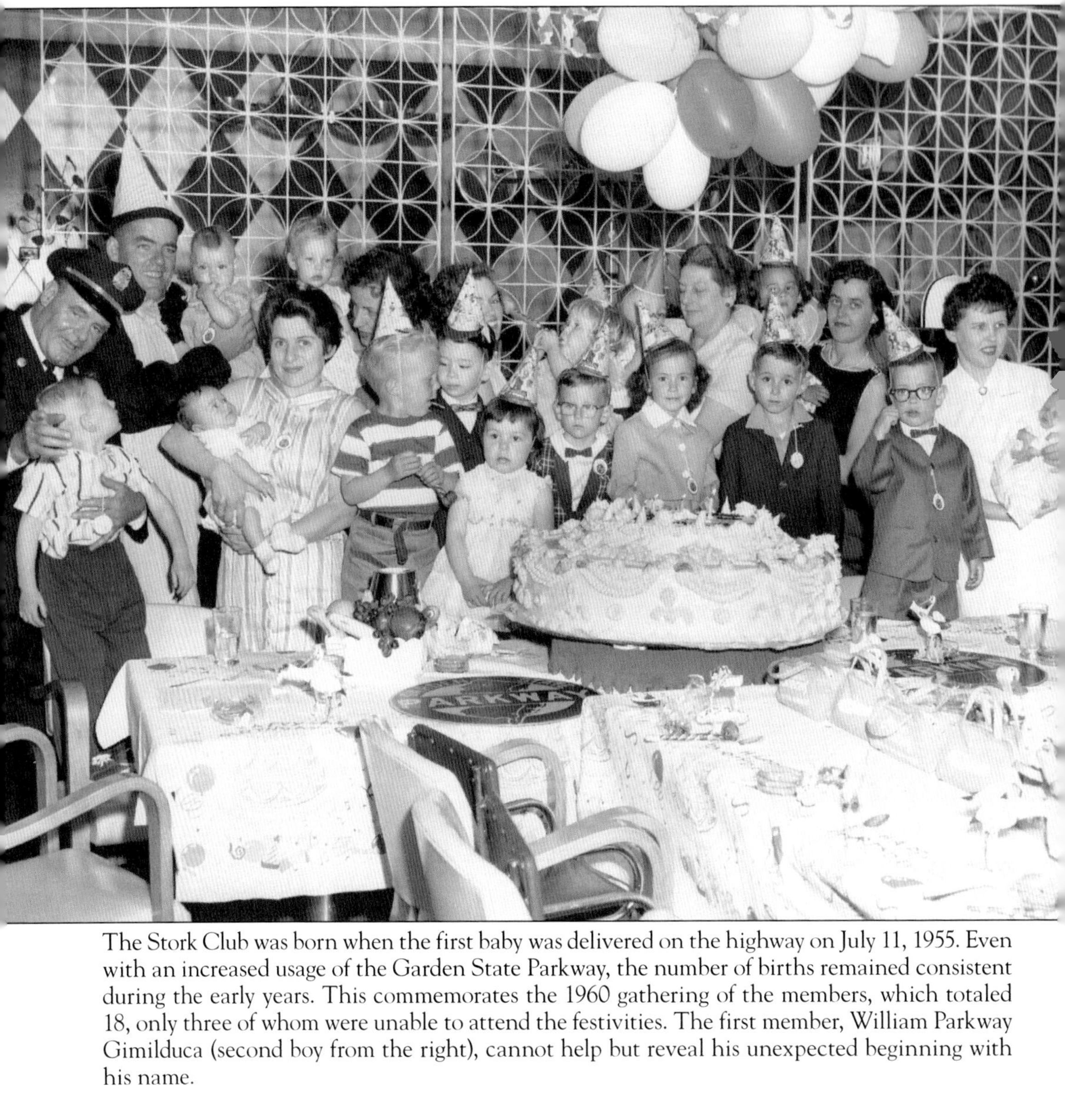

The Stork Club was born when the first baby was delivered on the highway on July 11, 1955. Even with an increased usage of the Garden State Parkway, the number of births remained consistent during the early years. This commemorates the 1960 gathering of the members, which totaled 18, only three of whom were unable to attend the festivities. The first member, William Parkway Gimilduca (second boy from the right), cannot help but reveal his unexpected beginning with his name.

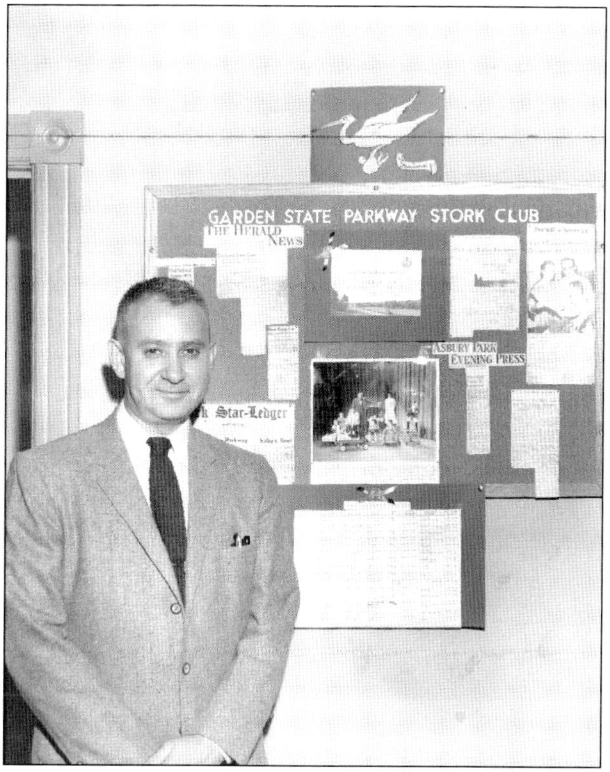

Milton Levy, the director of public relations for the New Jersey Highway Authority, poses with the Stork Club register of births in 1959, along with newspaper clippings that cover the births. The New Jersey Highway Authority held annual birthday parties for the Stork Club children, and by 1964, there were 23 members.

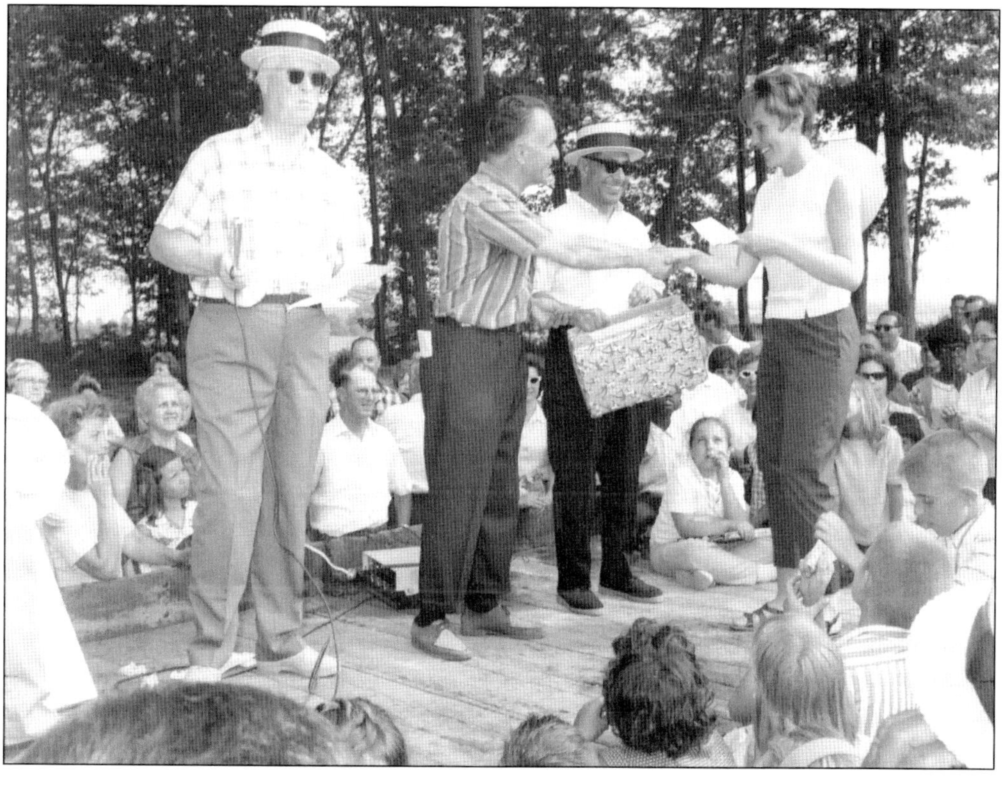

Executive director D. Louis Tonti hands out a prize at the 1966 employee picnic with the assistance of Commissioner Dr. John B. Townsend (left) and Vince Seminara of Finance. The picnic was held at Harvey's Grove in Shrewsbury, Monmouth County, in June. Employees contributed a few dollars per person to the Sunshine Club to help offset costs for functions during the year.

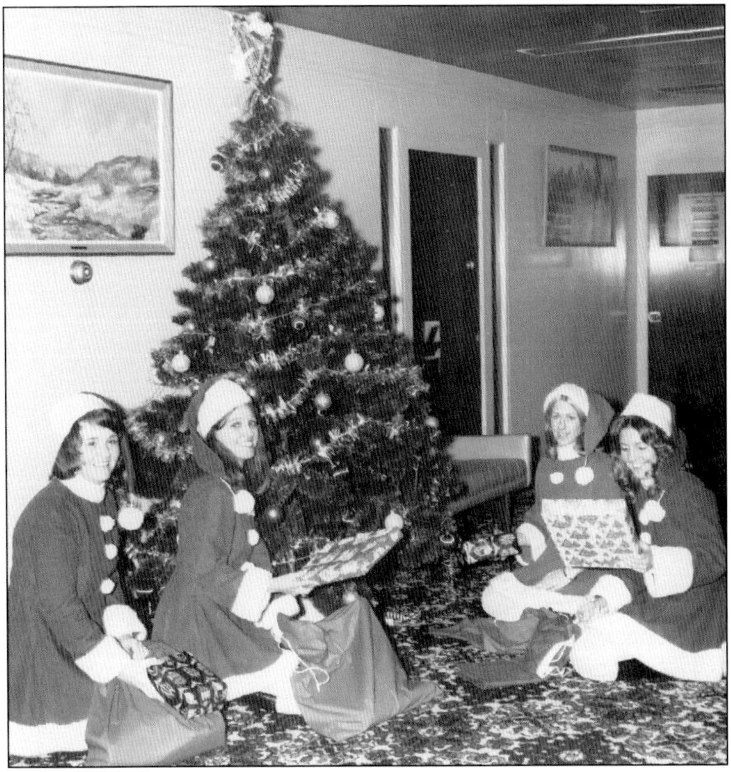

These Santa's Helpers place presents under the New Jersey Highway Authority administration building Christmas tree in 1974. From left to right, P. Horan, K. Ludwig, P. Bianchi, and D. Burley had also assisted in the lighting of the Christmas tree at the Garden State Arts Center. The New Jersey Highway Authority made the extended family of employees and the community part of the holiday season.

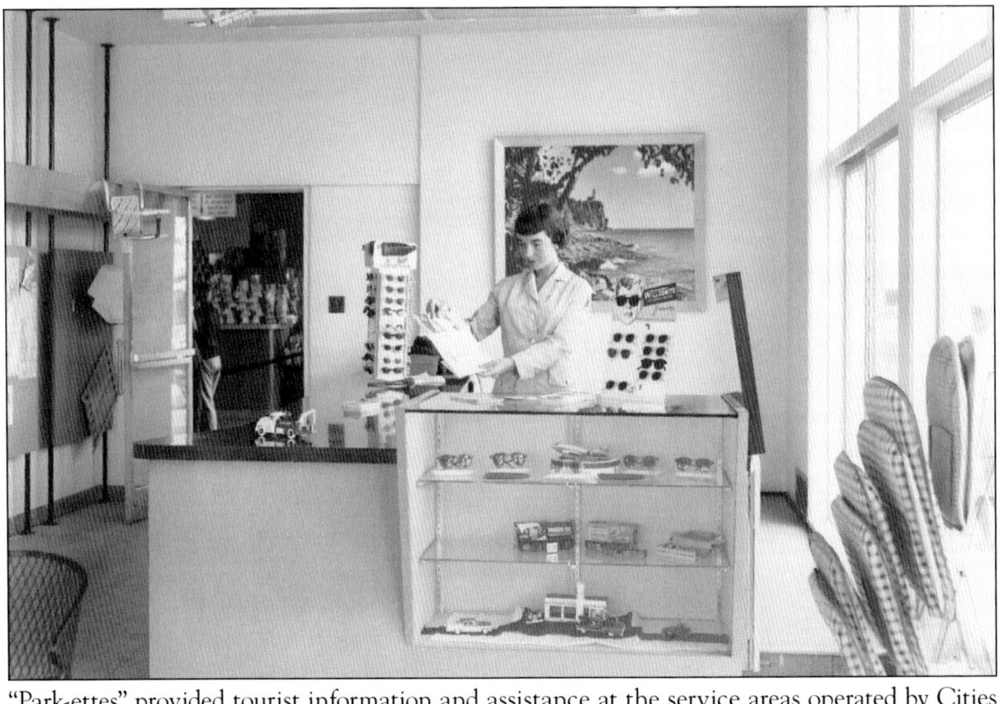

"Park-ettes" provided tourist information and assistance at the service areas operated by Cities Service along the Garden State Parkway. The emphasis on customer relations drove many of the Parkway facilities and designs.

Sources for information were not limited to the service plazas. The toll collectors provided assistance when necessary as well, such as here where senior citizen toll collector Samuel Mensch handed out a Garden State Parkway map in 1965. The additional attention by all the employees was part of the New Jersey Highway Authority's attitude towards providing courteous and friendly service to their patrons.

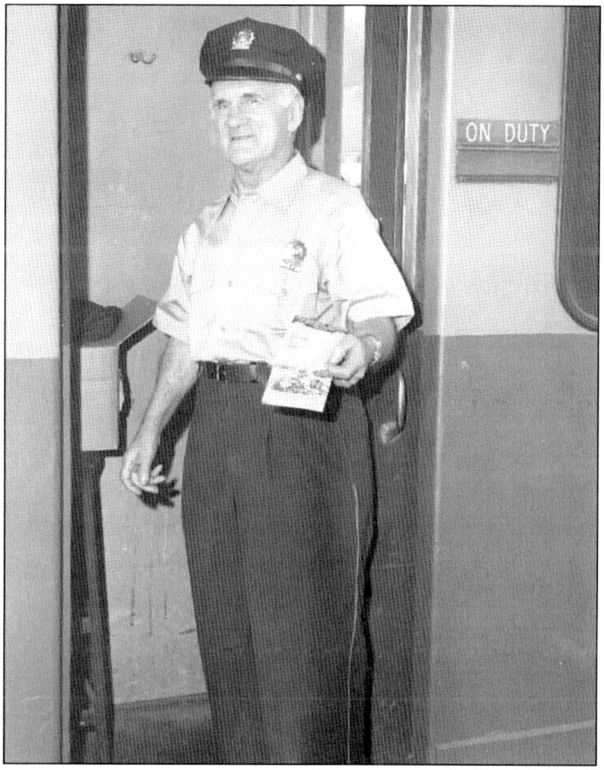

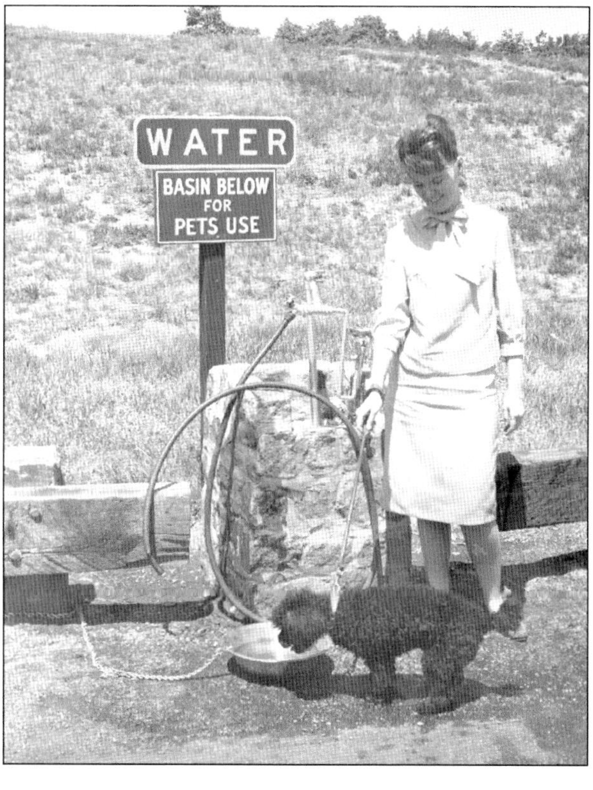

In 1964, a water basin for pets was provided at the Asbury Park Toll Plaza in Tinton Falls, Monmouth County. Such amenities were developed to encourage vacationers to travel with four-legged members of the family. Rest and service areas included places for all members of the family to stretch their legs and relax. The Garden State Parkway provided scenery during driving and stops with many areas that allowed travelers to see a nonurban New Jersey.

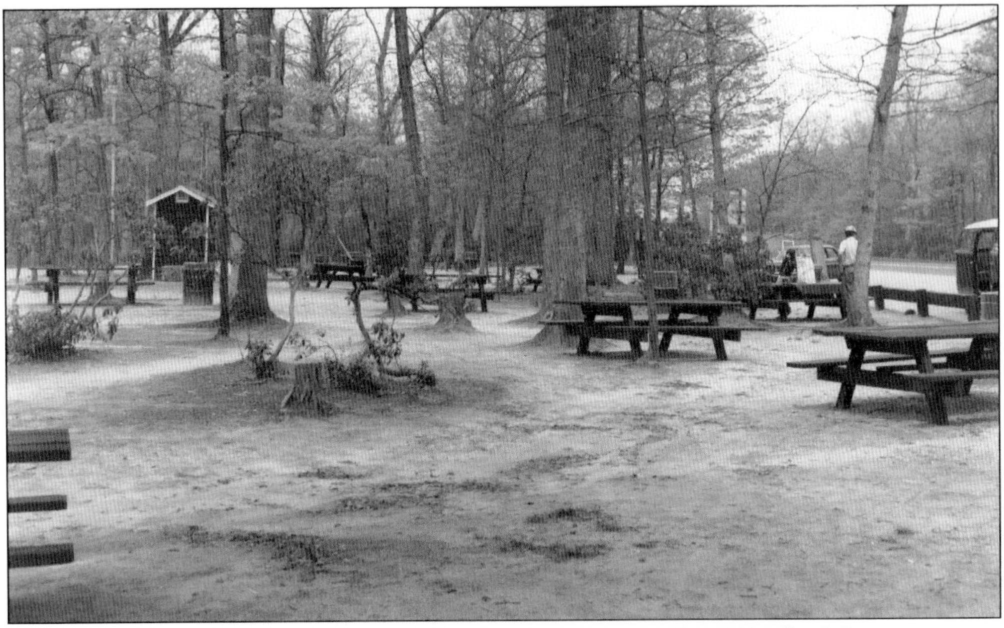

Patrons enjoy the Herbertsville picnic area in Ocean County. By 1969, all of the picnic areas included public phones, with this one being among the last to receive them. The areas were only open until mid-October, but patrons could access the phones year-round.

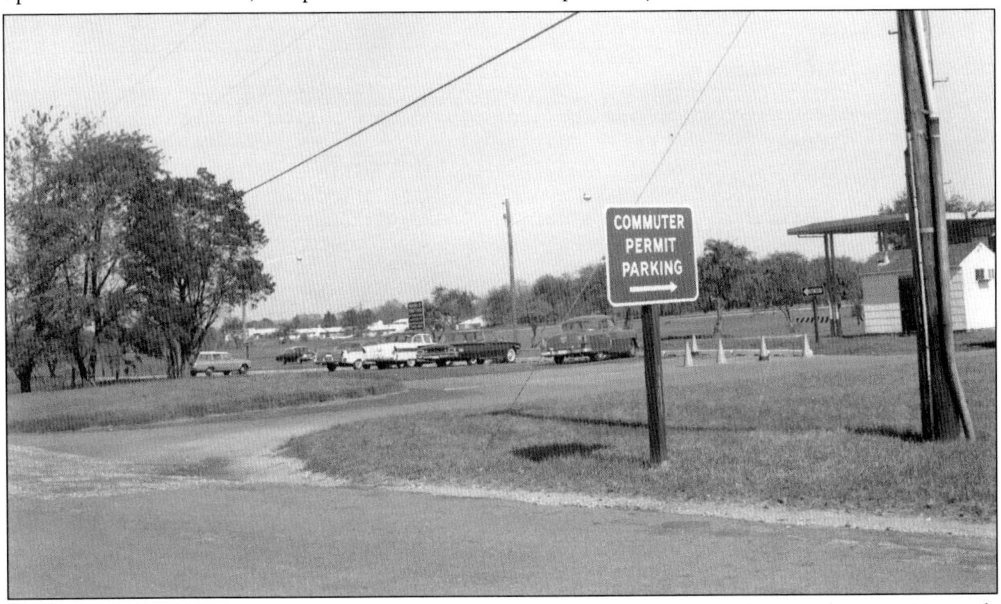

An experimental commuter parking lot was constructed at the Red Bank Interchange 109 south toll ramp in Middletown, Monmouth County, in 1962. The facility provided commuters with a location to meet for car pools in an effort to lessen the commuter traffic volumes on the Garden State Parkway. During 1970, the lot drew 1,820 daily users and 132 monthly patrons. At 25¢ per day, or $3 per month, the lot took in $819 for the year. By 1970, more than half of the construction cost had been recouped. Access and sales were handled by toll collectors at the interchange, keeping operating costs low. Seventeen free commuter parking lots now dot the length of the Parkway as an additional attraction to reduce the daily traffic on the road.

As exemplified in this photograph from the Raritan Toll Plaza in 1960, the position of the Garden State Parkway toll collector was only open to men at the beginning. Pictured are, from left to right, E. Christopherson, P. McDonough, and W. Whelan. Blackie, the mascot, sleeps after a rough day.

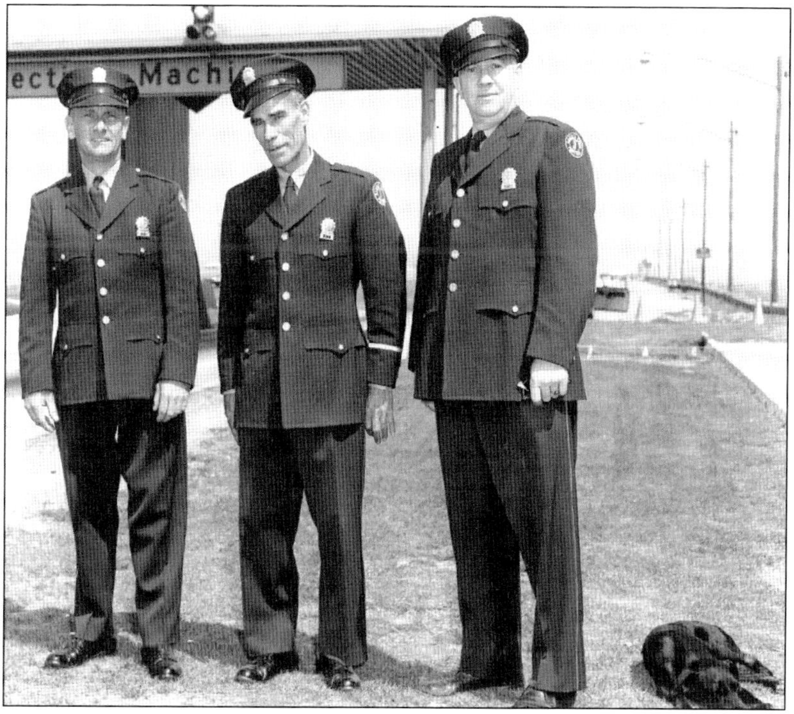

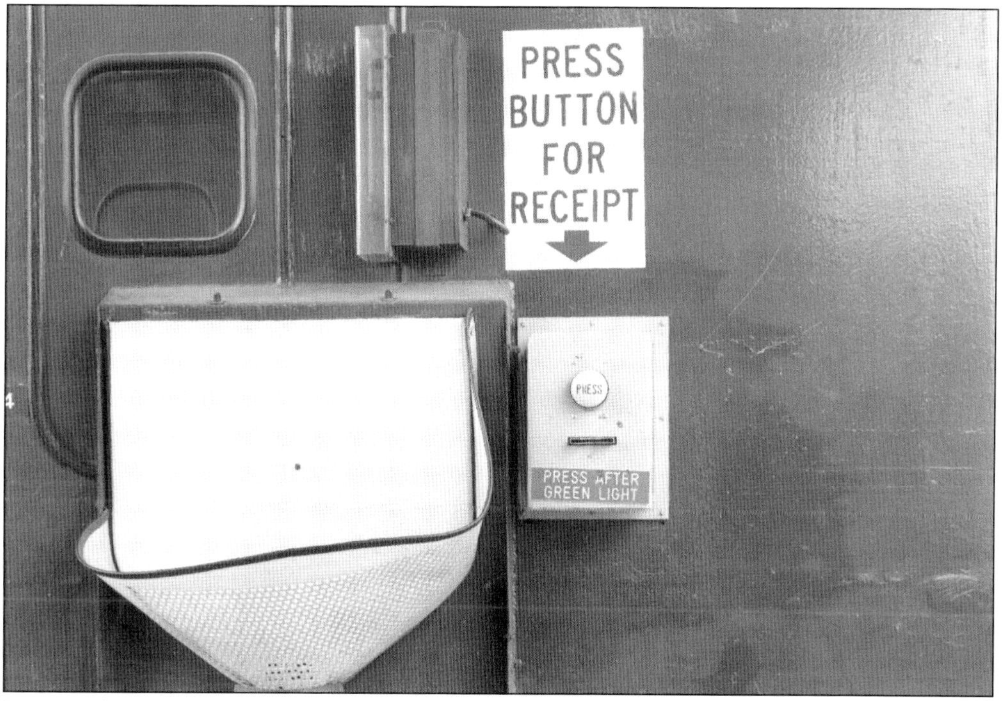

By 1973, this plaza offered drivers the option of using exact change and also getting a receipt. Such a system was needed for a road that was used by many business travelers. Today, many travelers use the E-ZPass system, which can track expenditures.

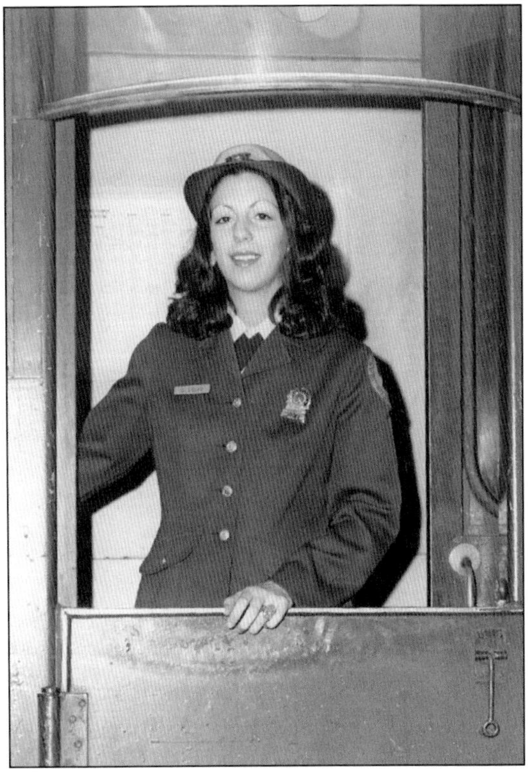

The ranks of personnel manning toll booths along the Garden State Parkway was expanded after 20 years. Donna Celfo was one of the first five female toll collectors hired in 1975. Toll collectors were often called on for driving directions and advice to travelers.

Pete Pruchnicki, one of the toll collectors, got into the spirit of the 1962 winter season at the New Gretna Toll Plaza in Bass River Township, Burlington County, and painted this decoration. For many New Jersey Highway Authority employees, the job entailed more than clocking their time. Extra effort was encouraged and acknowledged.

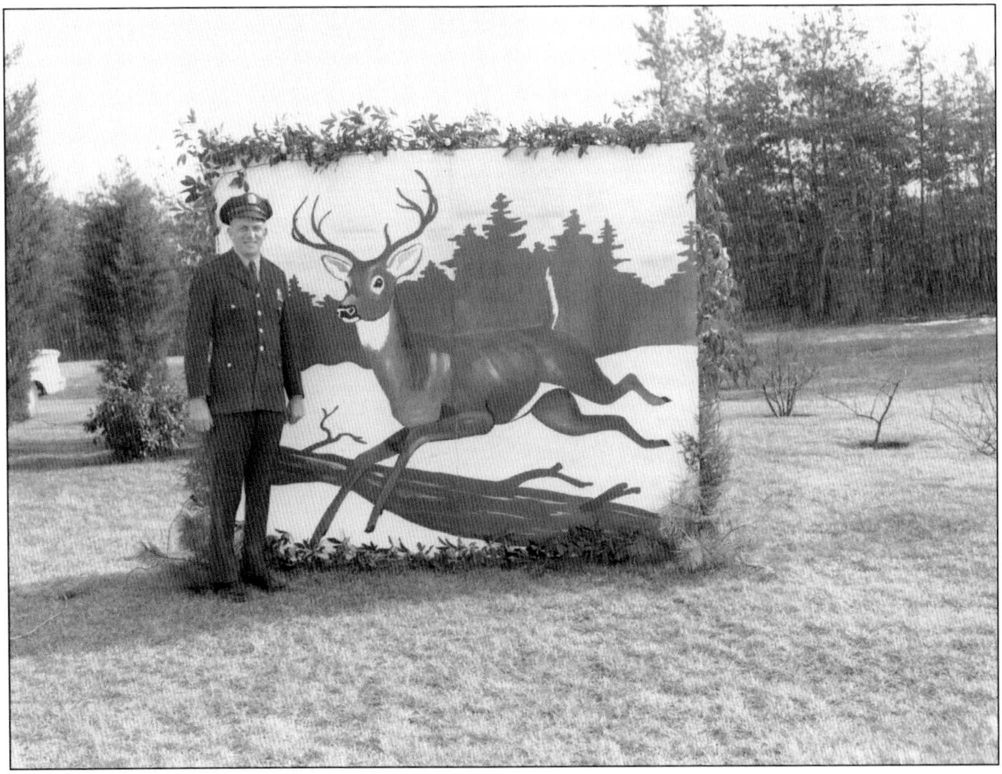

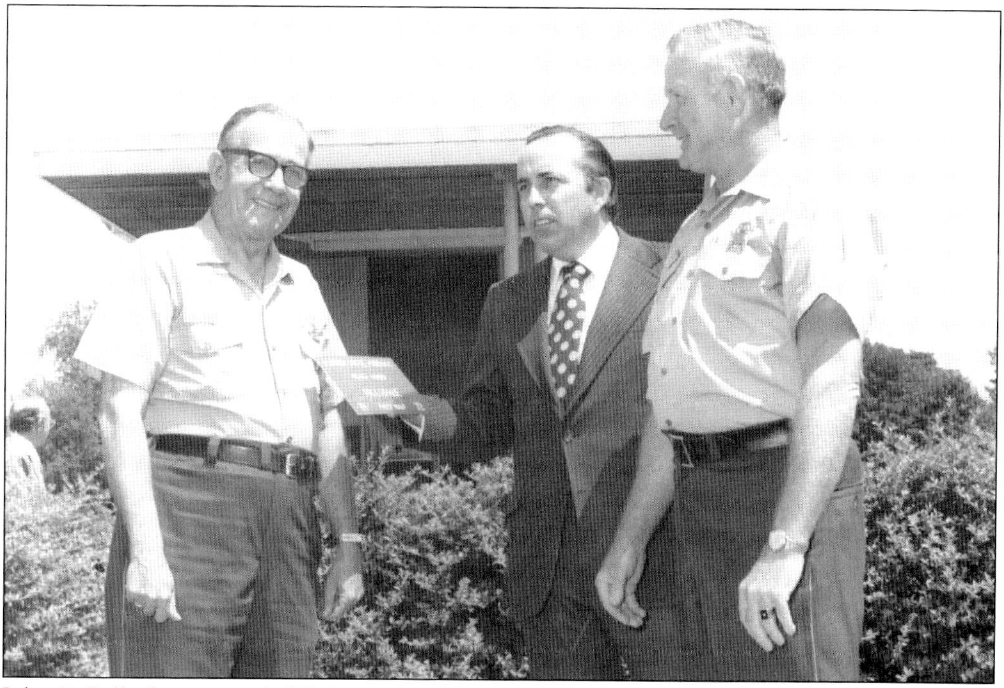

John P. Gallagher succeeded D. Louis Tonti as executive director, holding the position from 1972 to 1976. He is shown here in 1972 presenting a plaza award to the Hillsdale plaza. Accepting the plaque are toll collectors J. Risko (left) and J. Donohue (right).

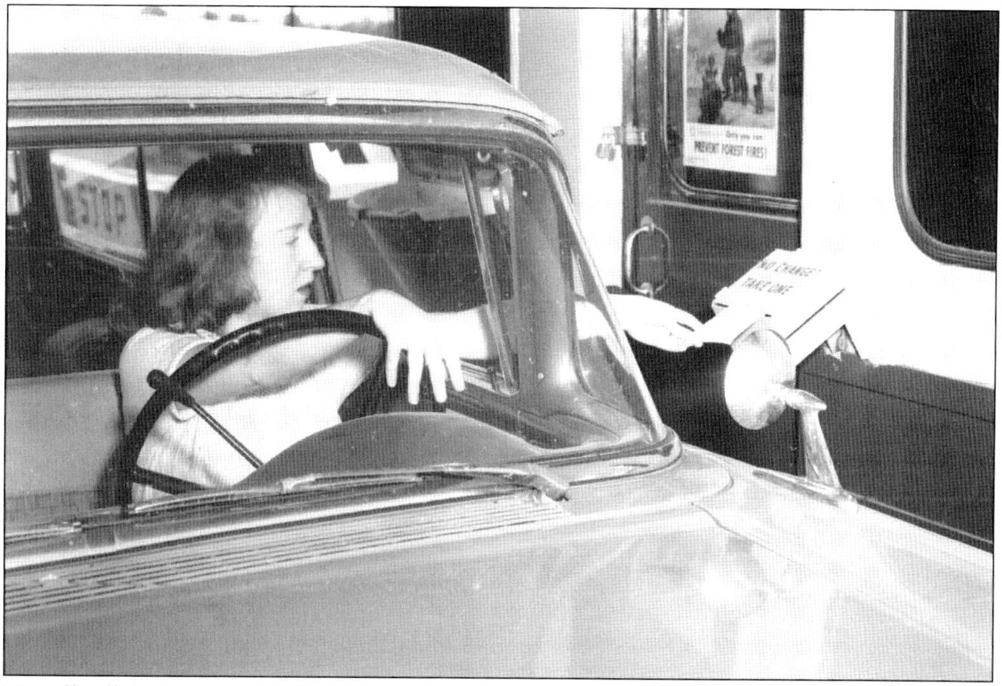

Not all toll facilities could afford to be manned. Automatic toll machines first operated on the honor system, and motorists who did not have enough change could pick up envelopes to mail in their tolls.

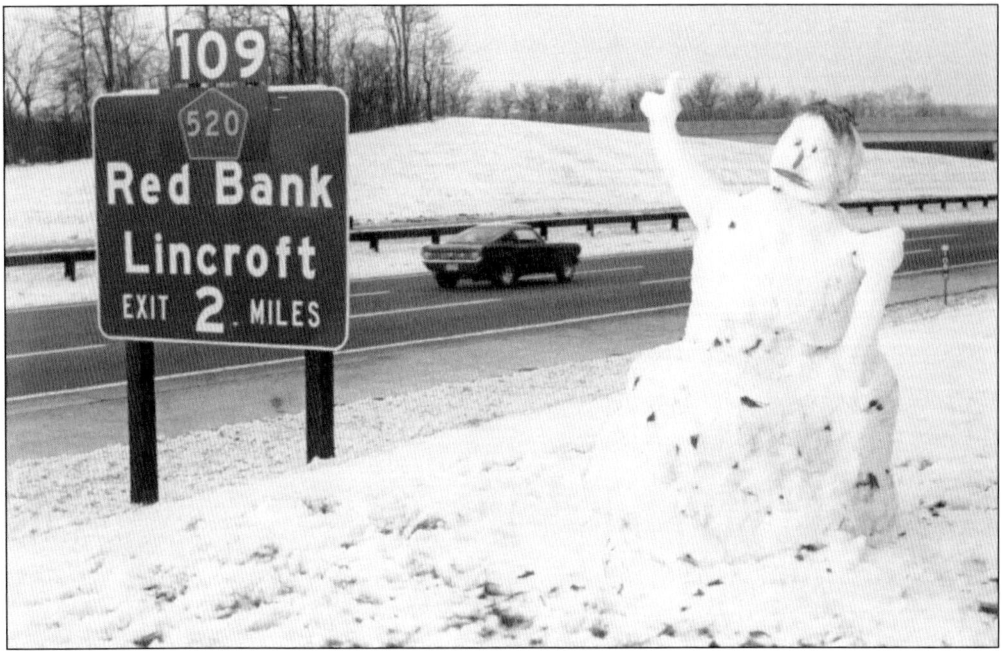

Human hitchhiking is usually frowned upon for safety reasons, but some of the maintenance personnel figured it was safer for snowmen. Keeping the Garden State Parkway open during most weather events requires a diligent and dedicated staff. Once the work is done, there is still some time to have fun.

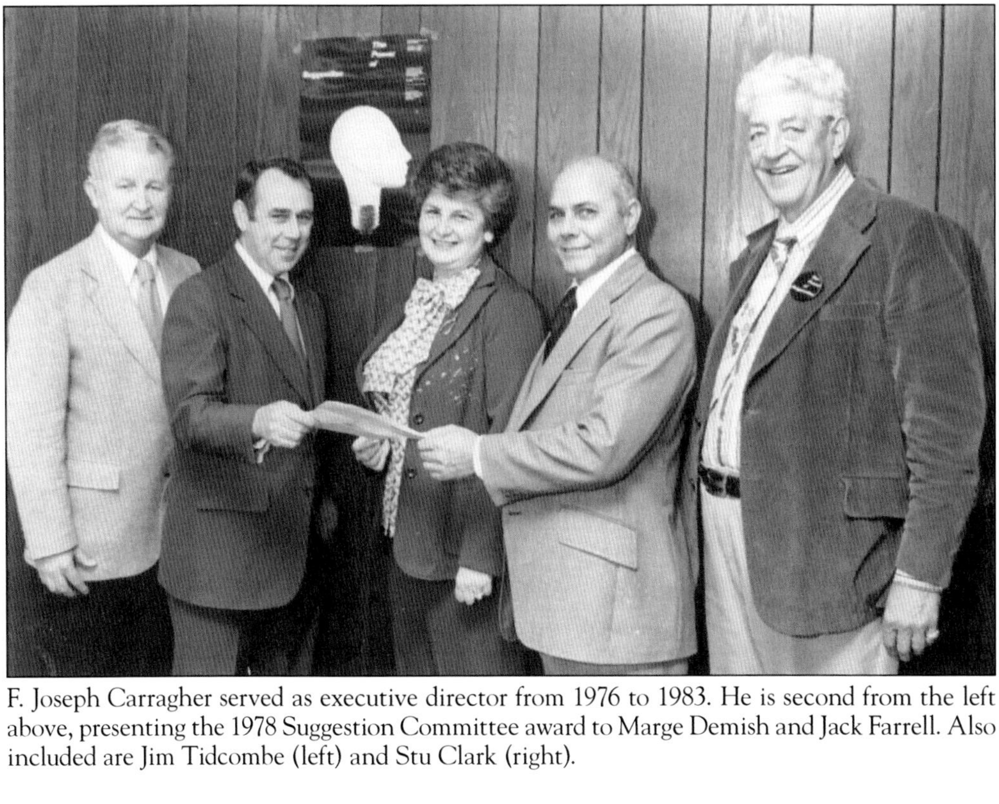

F. Joseph Carragher served as executive director from 1976 to 1983. He is second from the left above, presenting the 1978 Suggestion Committee award to Marge Demish and Jack Farrell. Also included are Jim Tidcombe (left) and Stu Clark (right).

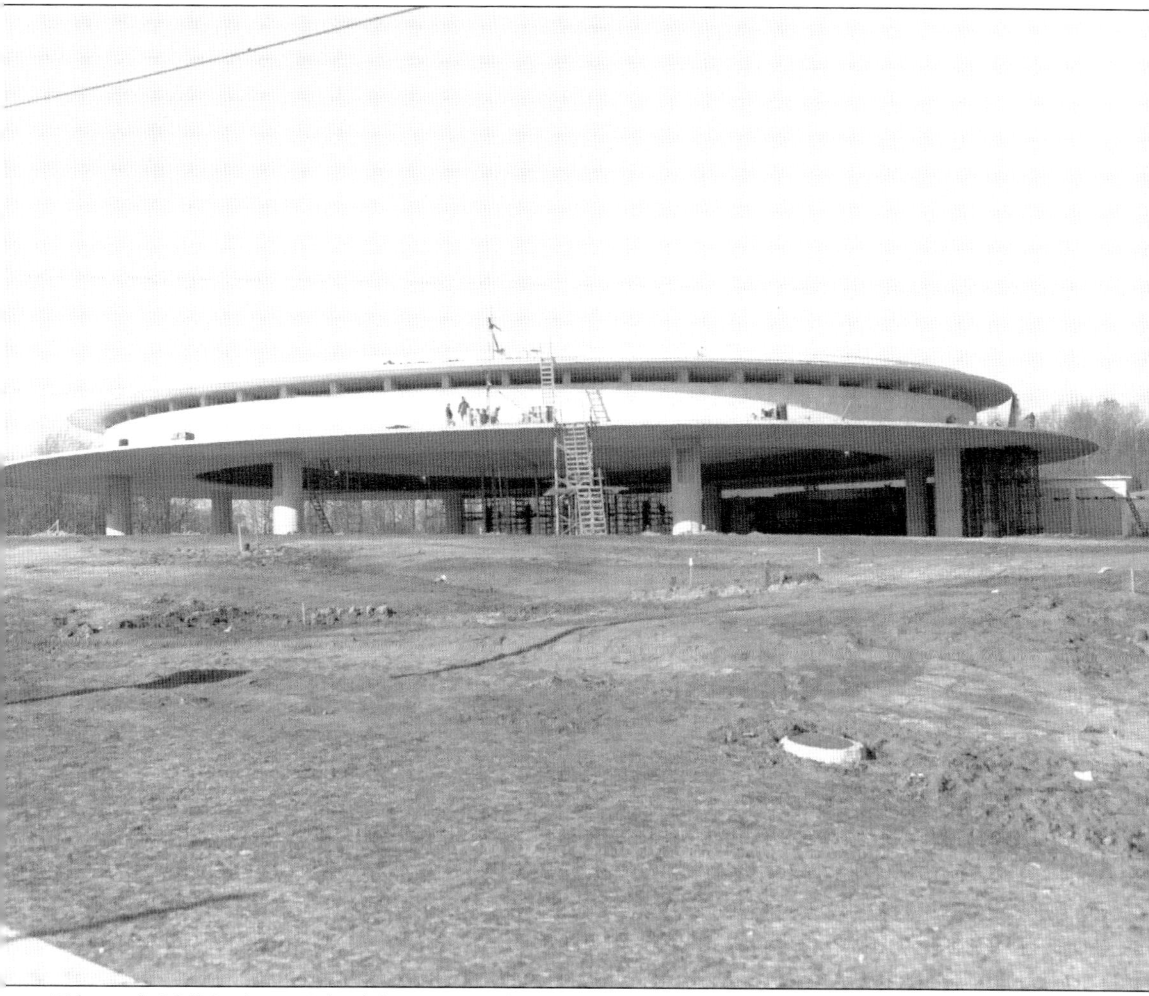

Telegraph Hill Park in Holmdel, Monmouth County, became home to the Garden State Arts Center, now known as the PNC Arts Center. The New Jersey Highway Authority purchased approximately 400 acres at this location for multiple uses. The area surrounds a small patch of 1,209 square feet, which contains the Crawford family cemetery. In 1953, the New Jersey Highway Authority purchased 53 acres from John and Matilda Holmes as part of the parklands. John Holmes was the great-nephew of the cemetery's last internment, Elizabeth Crawford in 1923. The purchase agreement stipulated that the land transfer did not include the cemetery within the property, but that the New Jersey Highway Authority would maintain access for family members. The earliest dates noted in the cemetery are from the 1830s, including John Crawford who was buried in 1834 at the age of 77. At least three generations of the family are present in the cemetery.

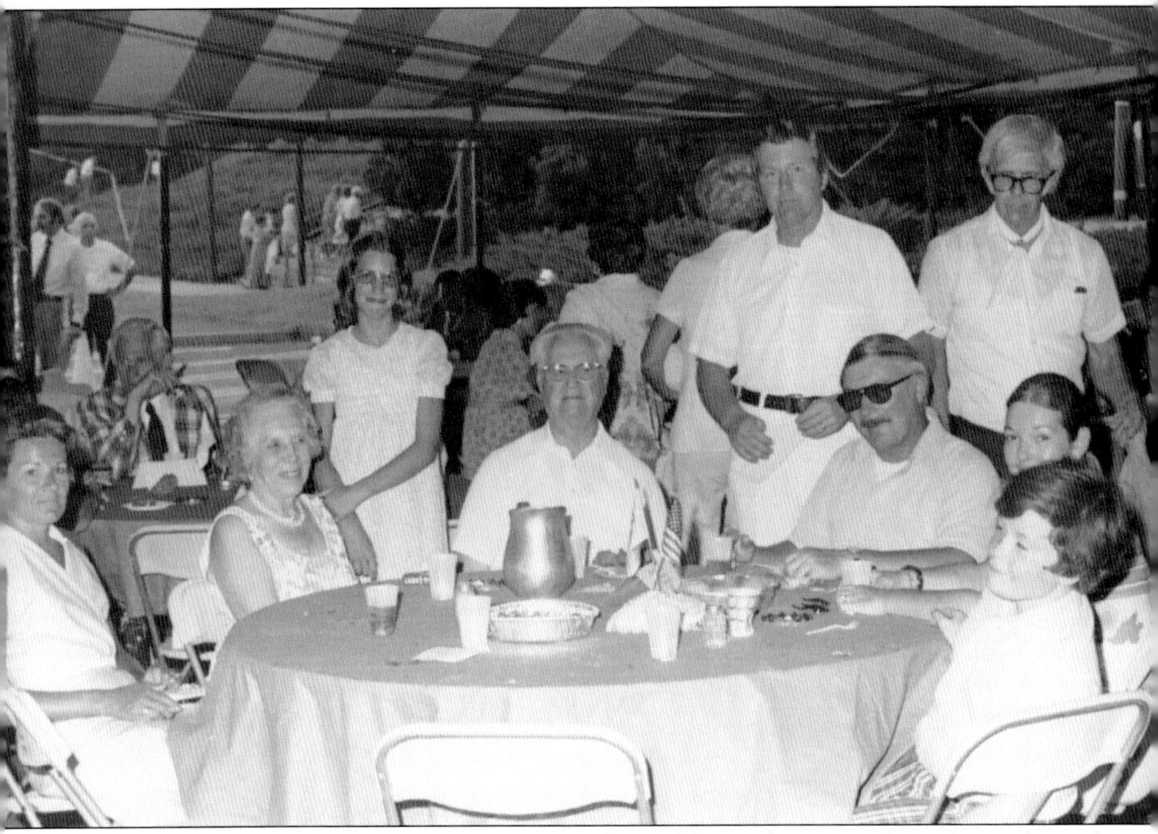

The concert season lasted from June to September and featured country, classical, popular, and rock music and free parking. Under special programs, schoolchildren, the disabled, seniors, and the disadvantaged enjoyed free daytime programs sponsored by the Garden State Cultural Center Fund. The fund also held ethnic heritage festivals, stage shows, and a talent show for teenagers. A number of special events were conducted all year, including a gala benefit performance and a celebrity amateur golf tournament. Here, employees of the arts center, state police, and New Jersey Highway Authority Legal Department relax together at the 1975 employees night. Commissioner Dr. John B. Townsend (behind pitcher) is seated with his son Allan standing to his left.

Four

PARKWAY DESIGN AND SAFETY

Engineers incorporated a number of safety features into the Garden State Parkway design that led to its designation in 1963 as the "safest superhighway in the nation" by the National Safety Council and the American Bridge, Tunnel, and Turnpike Association. Fatalities averaged 0.7 per million miles of travel whereas the national average for roads and turnpikes was 5.4 and 2.4, respectively. Large medians, where possible, served as protection measures in two ways. While the wide median was aesthetically appealing, it served first as a safety feature to lessen the potential for head-on collisions from opposing lanes of traffic. Earthen mounds or swales built inside the medians served as another barrier to crossover accidents. In the second safety feature provided by wide medians, headlights were no longer a distraction to drivers in the opposite lane of travel.

A number of other safety features were designed by the engineers. They created hills and gentle curves to help stymie boredom from a monotonous alignment. The barrier-style toll plazas also served to avert monotony by breaking up travel and forcing drivers to change speed. Interchanges with intersecting roads were minimized as the grade-separated parkway traveled over and under them, providing both an uninterrupted corridor and a safe environment that reduced interaction with other lanes of traffic.

Attention to detail did not stop with roadway design. Planners kept in mind the need to make the Garden State Parkway a pleasurable drive for motorists with signs, service areas, gas stations, picnic areas, and even attractive toll administration buildings. With 173 miles of road, plus the exit ramps, the Parkway needed many standardized signs. Service areas, picnic areas, and service stations also featured signs detailing attractions and towns at each exit. Entrance signs sported a unique trapezoidal shape to differentiate the Parkway ramps from other highways. Timber light posts complementing the pastoral signs dotted the landscape at service areas and later the Garden State Arts Center.

Singing shoulders were included by chief engineer Harold W. Giffin. These consisted of cuts in the shoulder pavement that would "sing" to alert drivers who drifted off the road. Where shoulders were unpaved, the area was stabilized so drivers could pull off the road in relative safety.

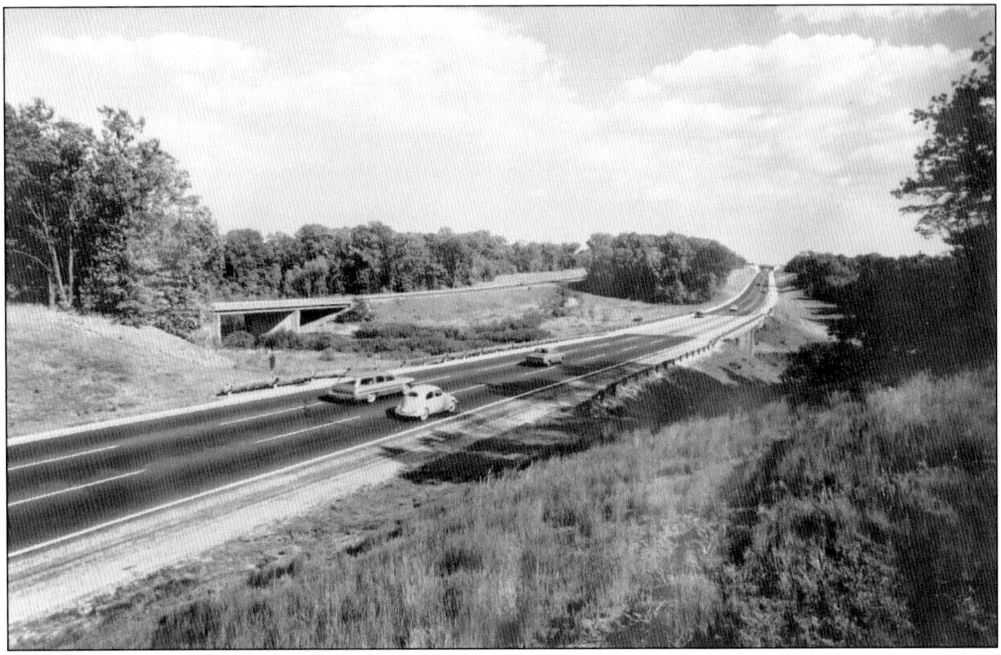

The Tinton Falls section in Monmouth County exemplifies three characteristics of the Garden State Parkway. The first is a wide median supporting vegetation and artificial berms. The second is the pastoral setting. Third is the effort to create two separate roadways, one for each direction of traffic. Here, the northbound and southbound lanes of travel are separated by the large median that includes stands of mature trees.

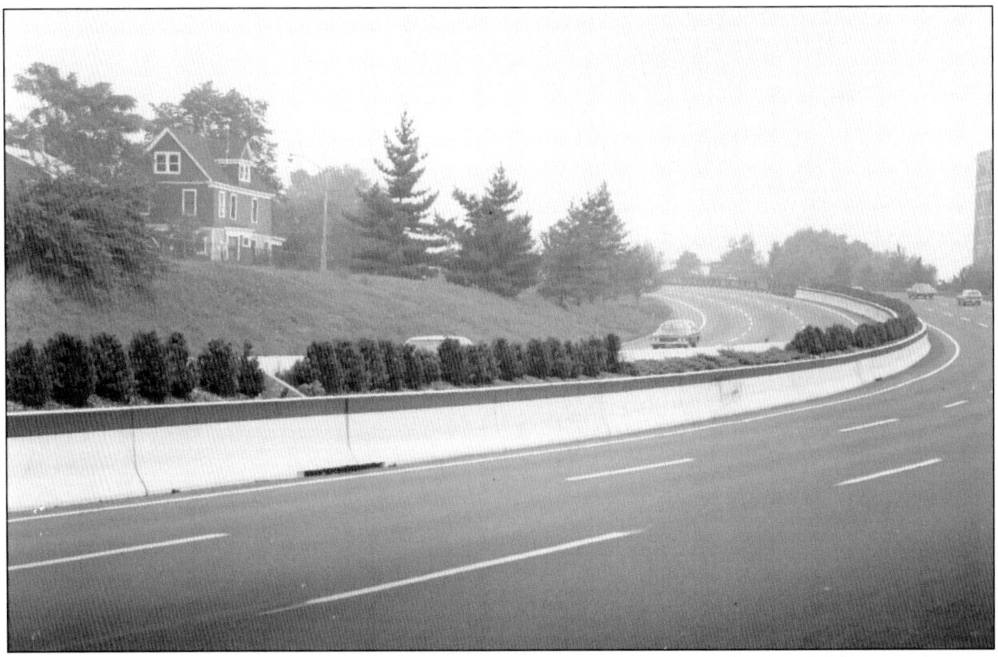

On the other hand, the median consists of concrete barriers where the available corridor was narrow, such as in the Essex County area. Where possible, vegetation was planted on the barriers to soften the appearance and provide screening from headlight glare.

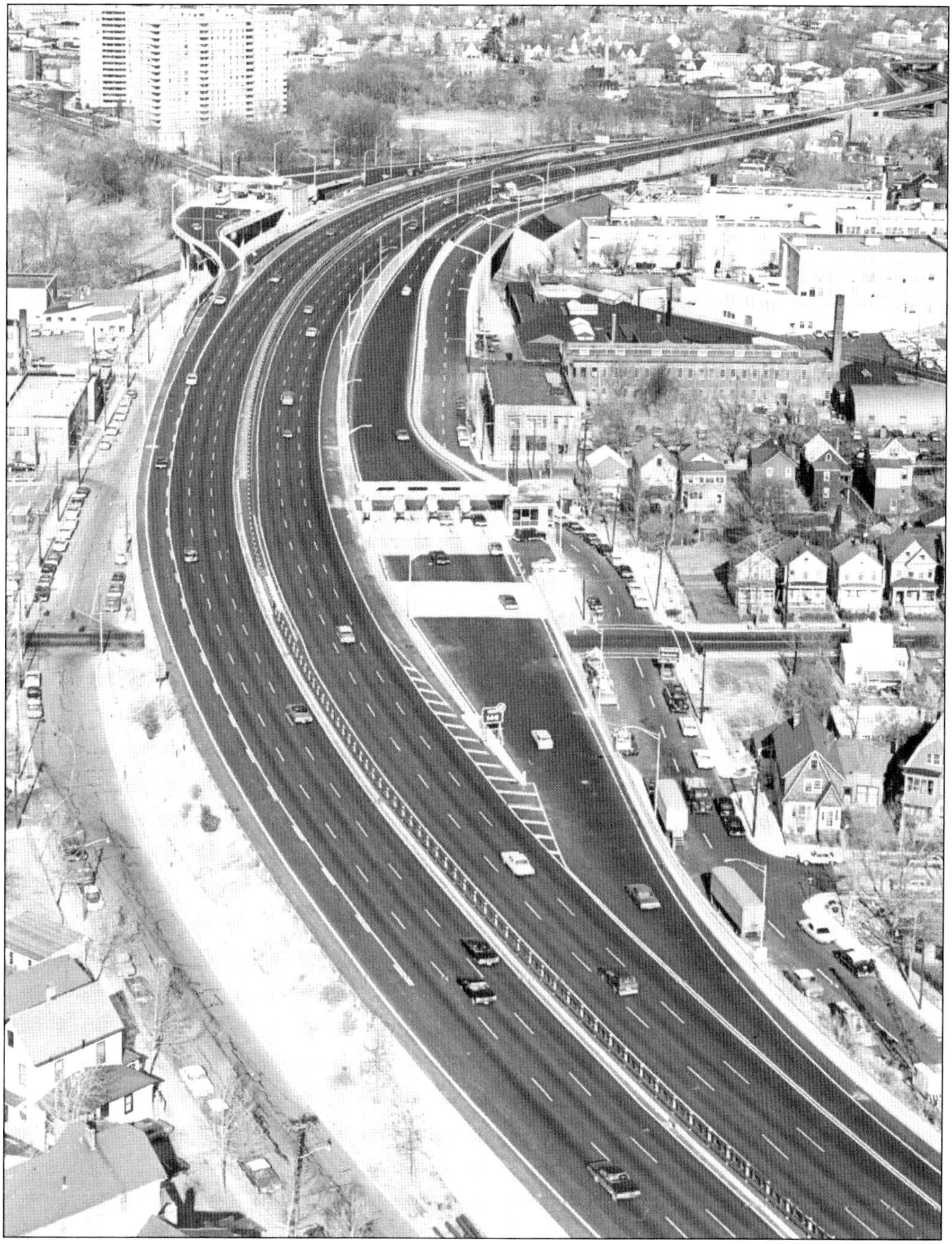

In urban areas, the Garden State Parkway engineers instead chose a relatively new design. The highway was constructed in the middle of the urban area, limiting disruption to the cross street traffic by elevating the Parkway above it. Medians are narrow rather than wide and scenic in order to limit the impact of the roadway on the neighboring community. Other characteristic safety features were maintained where possible to ensure the motorists' safety, such as the gentle curve shown above. Although the purpose of the Parkway is to carry traffic through the downtown area, the intermittent access also reduced traffic on local roads by providing an alternate direct route between points of interest within the city along its path.

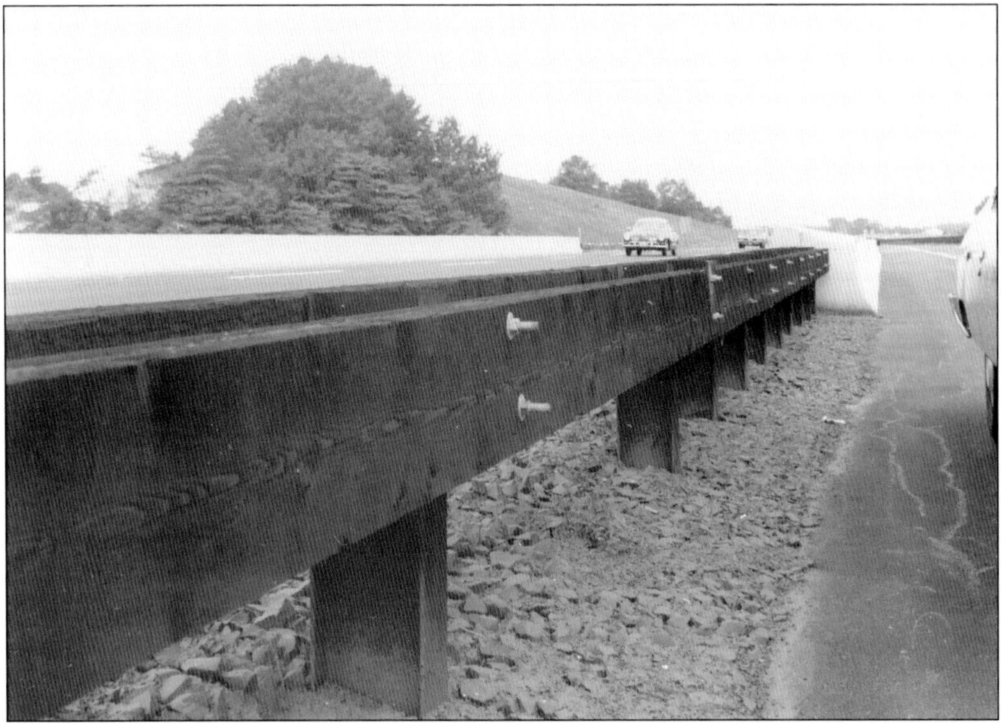

The first guiderails and barriers were constructed of wooden beams anchored by concrete posts. Although aesthetically pleasing, they were later replaced by more modern crash-tested metal beam guiderail to assure that maximum safety was provided for the motorist. Now the wooden beams are dispersed throughout the Garden State Parkway in locations where they do not interact with highway traffic, such as in picnic areas and pathways.

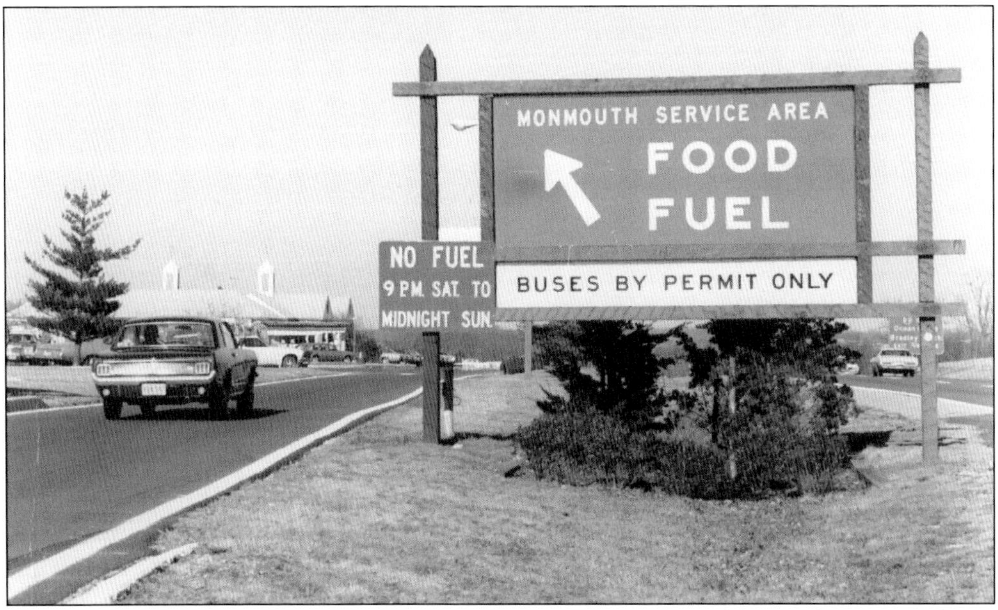

The original wooden posts on the sign contributed to the rustic feeling of the Garden State Parkway. However, over time, like the guiderails, they have been replaced with more modern materials.

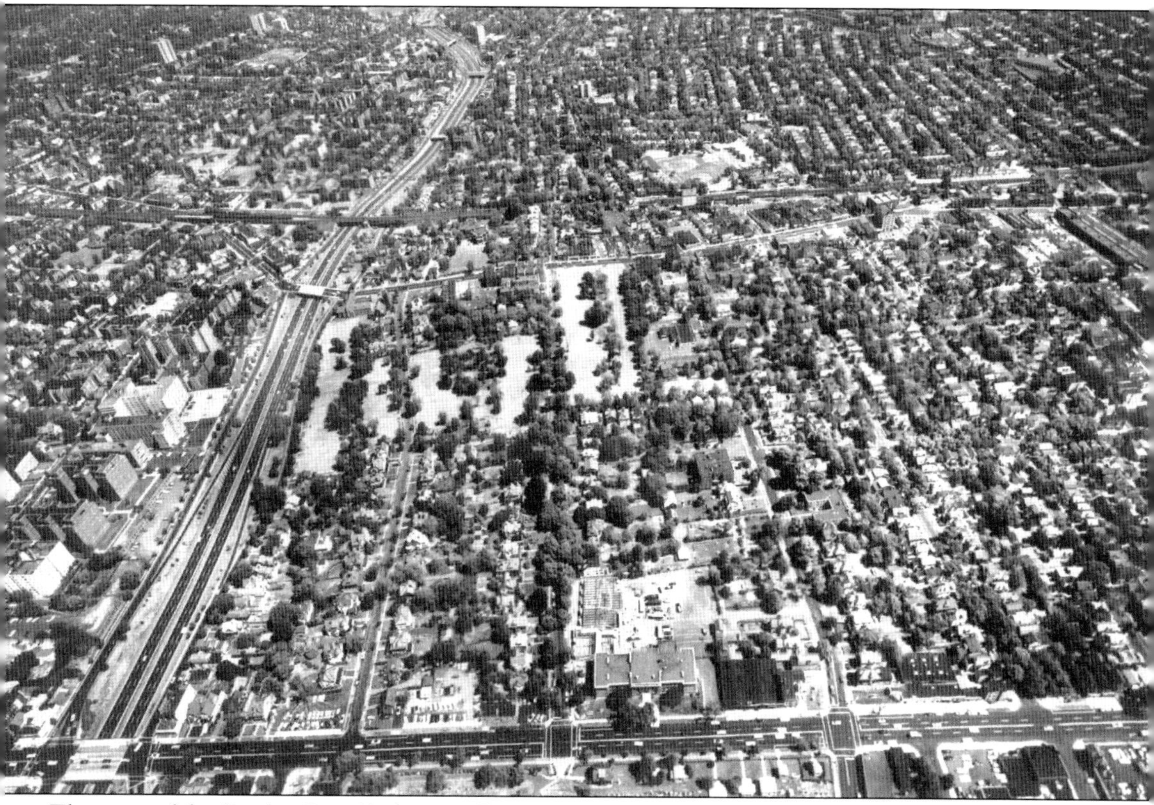

This view of the Garden State Parkway in Essex County exhibits the tight spaces engineers had to accommodate during the design phase. Controlled access to the Parkway resulted in less interaction with merging traffic, which helped improve traffic flow. The Parkway design embraced a new attitude in highway planning. Previous highway construction positioned the roadways outside of urban areas to help decrease property acquisition costs. The result was that traffic along local roads increased as commuters tried to access the highway. By embracing this new design concept, Parkway engineers sought to avoid a situation in which streets designed only for local traffic were overwhelmed by car, bus, and truck traffic seeking highway access.

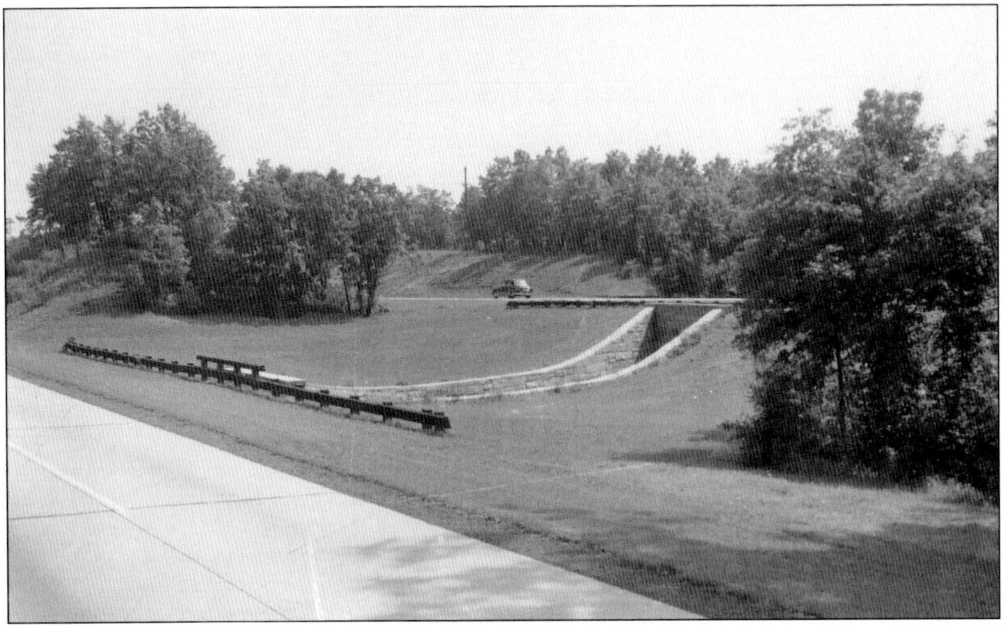

The natural topography was incorporated into the design and utilized for separation of the travel lanes, as shown here. In some locations, however, artificial berms were constructed within the medians to increase the separation of the two roadways. When planted with native vegetation, they enhanced the rural nature of the Garden State Parkway.

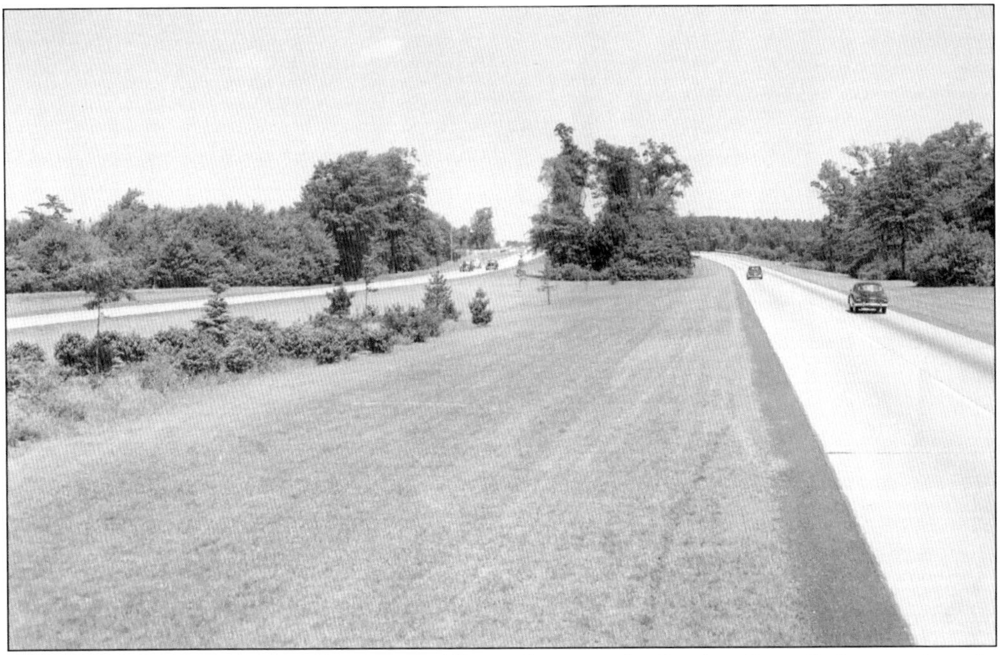

In flat, rural settings, such as here in Middlesex County, the Garden State Parkway primarily uses the existing vegetation to create the parklike setting. Newly planted native vegetation will help to fill in the median and provide the visual separation of the northbound and southbound travel lanes. This portion was constructed by the State Highway Department, which established many of the design parameters for the road.

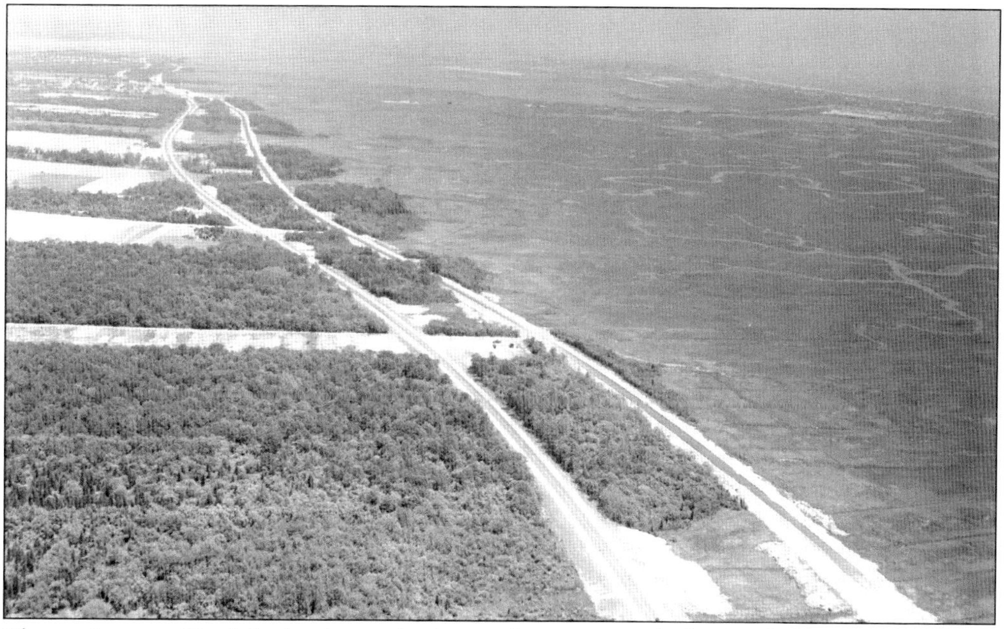

The engineers utilized the landscape in the gently curving path for the Garden State Parkway. Along the scenic Marmora Flats in the Marmora section of Cape May County, the road follows the edges of the marsh, slicing through the edge of the pine forests. In southern New Jersey, the Parkway not only directs tourists to the shore but also provides a firebreak in the forests and an evacuation route for shore dwellers in the event of natural disasters.

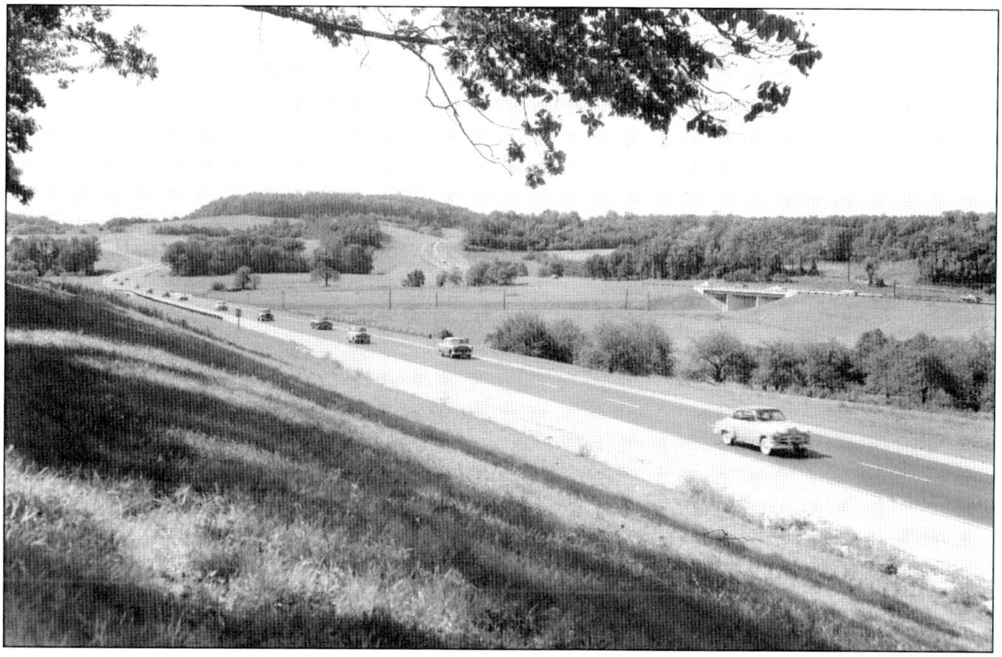

In contrast to the portion of the Garden State Parkway that passed through the New Jersey Pinelands, this stretch in Monmouth County passed through rolling topography that provided views of open space. The Parkway design allowed for areas of scenic driving separated from views of development, including billboards.

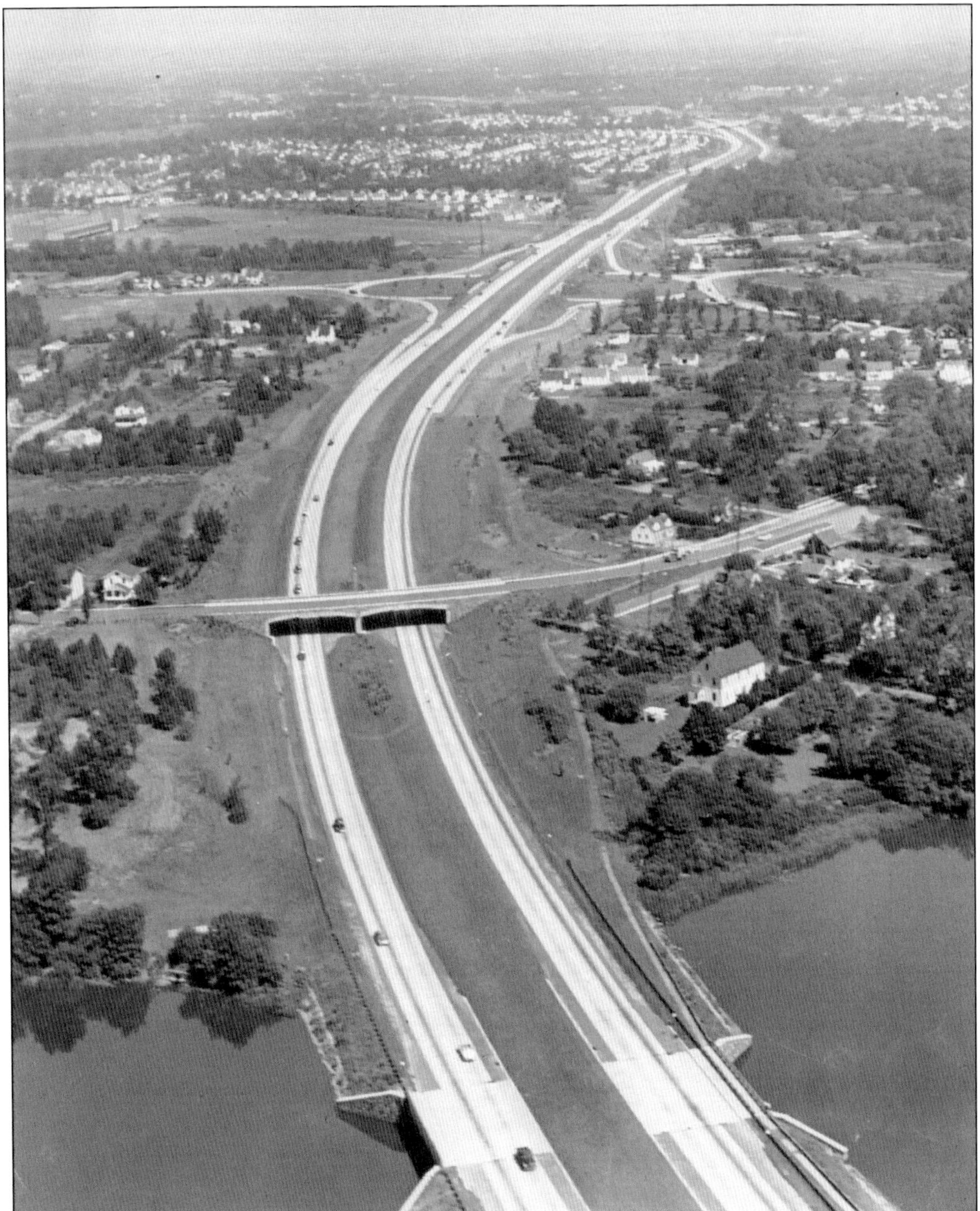

This section of the Garden State Parkway in Union County exemplified a number of typical design features. The median separating the northbound and southbound lanes is wide, but not as wide as in southern portions because of the need to accommodate the interchange. Safety was not compromised due to an increased center swale, which creates grade separation and serves to impede cars from crossing over. In many cases, the Parkway was lowered at intersecting roadways in order to accommodate nearby development, as shown here.

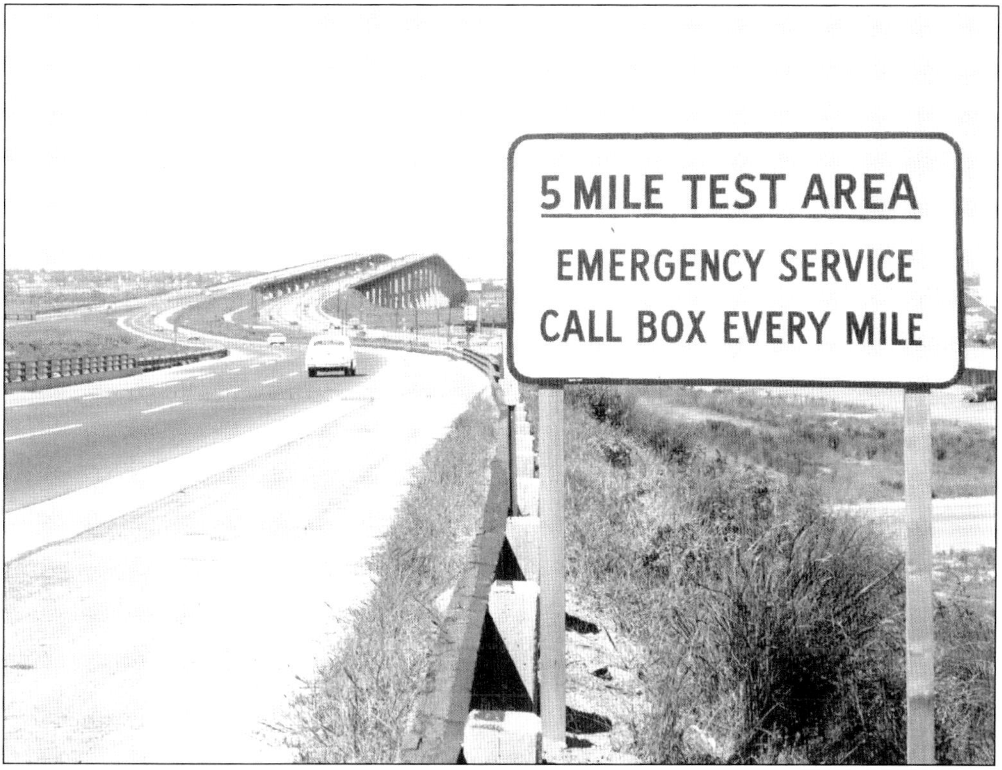

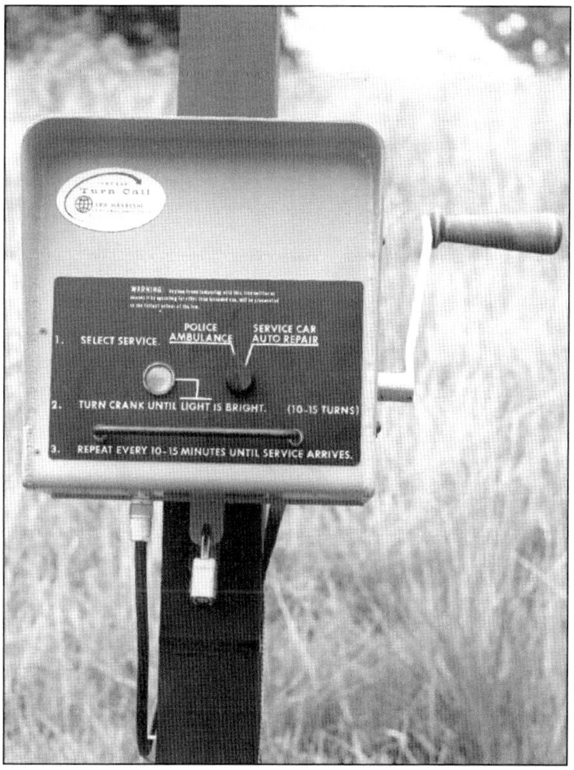

Long before the advent of cell phones, the New Jersey Highway Authority sought ways to improve the means to communicate incidents such as accidents or breakdowns to appropriate personnel. To facilitate this, call boxes were installed in 1962 between Mileposts 125 and 130 in Middlesex County in order to mitigate major traffic backups at the highly travelled Raritan River Bridge.

The emergency call box system was the first of its kind, allowing motorists to contact the New Jersey State Police or call for vehicle assistance. They were never expanded beyond the original test location but were replaced with a combination of pay telephones and an improved maintenance radio system, which allowed New Jersey Highway Authority workers to report incidents with more detailed information.

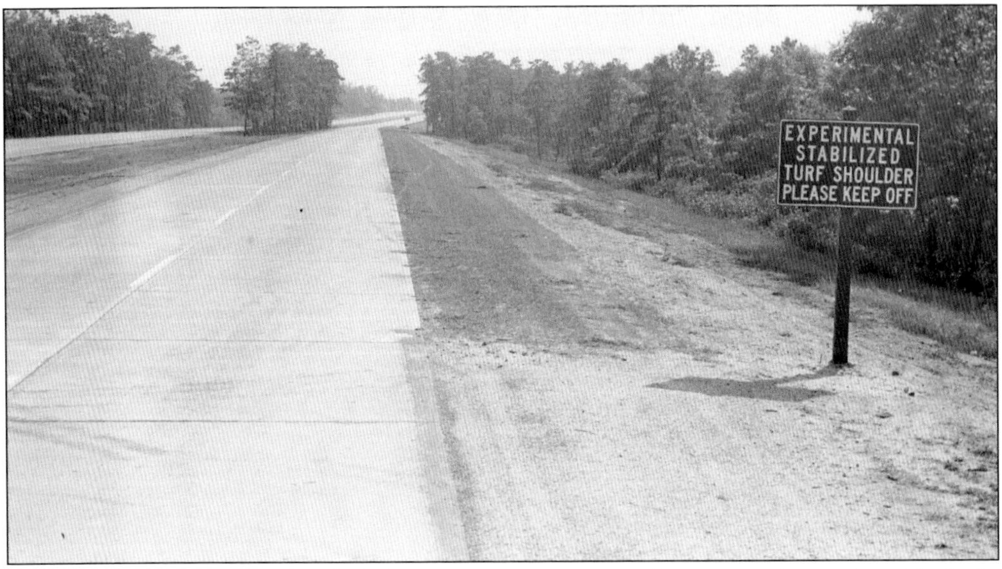

The Garden State Parkway included numerous innovations when it was designed and built. In place of pavement, some portions feature turf shoulders that were stabilized so drivers could pull off the road in relative safety. The turf provides more landscaped area right up to the edge of the travel lanes.

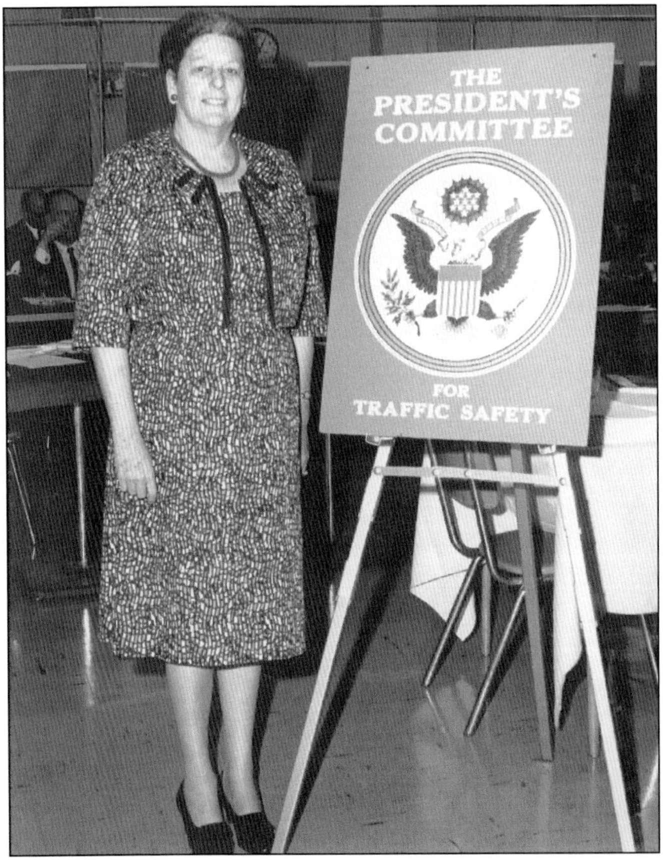

Chairman Katharine E. White hosted a meeting of the president's committee on traffic safety at the administration headquarters in Woodbridge, Middlesex County. President Kennedy appointed her to the committee in 1961, another accomplishment in her distinguished career. By this time, the safety record of the Garden State Parkway had already become well known.

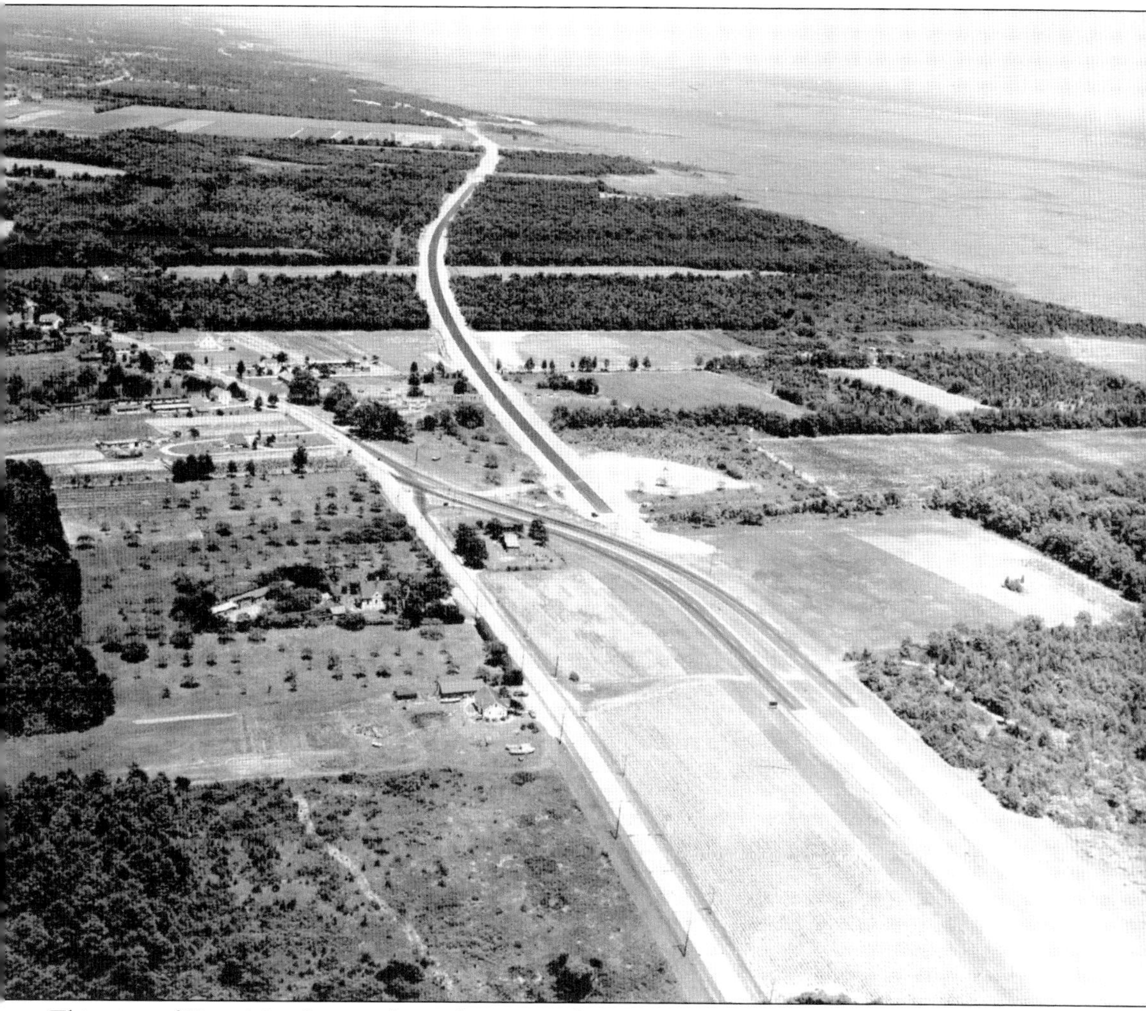

This view of Cape May County shows the area at the merge between the Garden State Parkway project to the north and the US Route 9 bypass for Cape May Courthouse to the south. The Route 9 bypass was built by the New Jersey State Highway Department as a dualized highway and maintained access to the original US Route 9 through multiple at-grade crossings. When this section became part of the Parkway in 1987, the only crossings that were maintained were the three original signalized intersections at Shell Bay Boulevard/Interchange 9, Stone Harbor Boulevard/Interchange 10, and Crest Haven Road/Interchange 11. All other areas of the Parkway to the north were restricted to non-signalized interchanges, which improved safety and convenience. As the Parkway stretched farther north, the designers could also incorporate both a woodland buffer between the Parkway and development and gentle curves, which added to the scenery and experience.

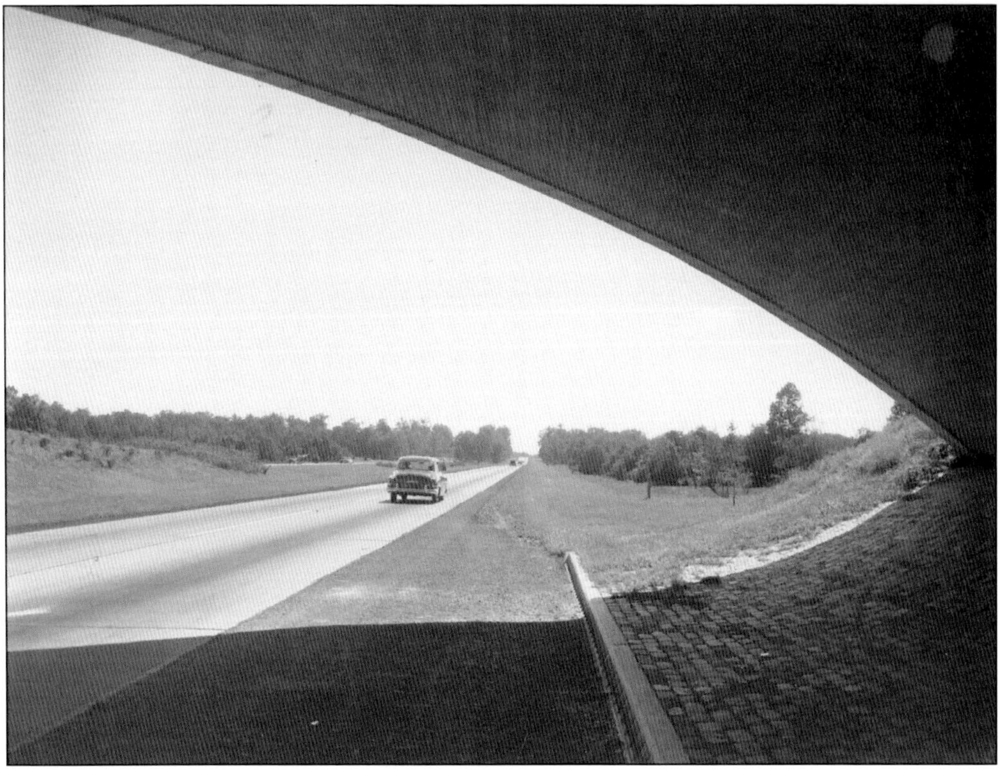

This shot shows the state-constructed section of the Garden State Parkway in Middlesex County in 1953. Note the wide median with an artificial berm. This safety feature protected drivers from the glare of oncoming headlights as well as from head-on collisions.

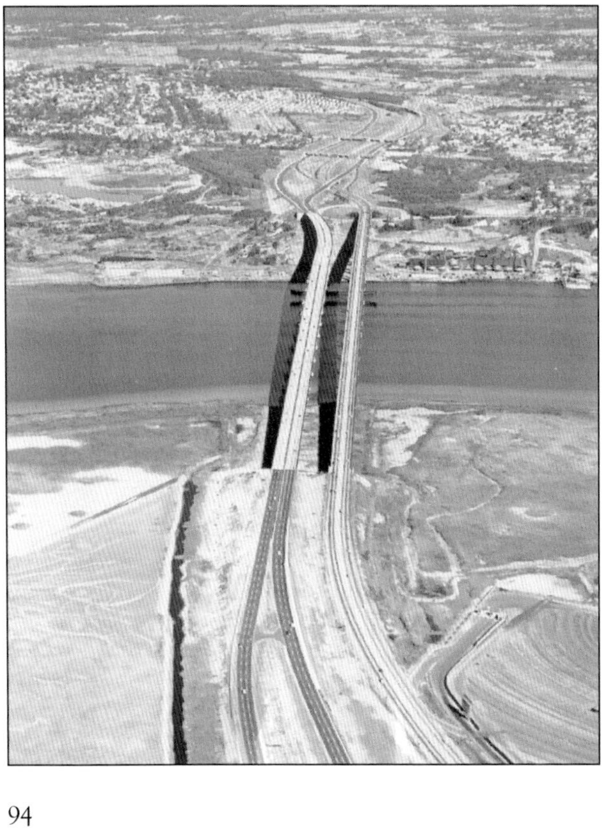

The Driscoll Bridge, shown here to the left of the Edison Bridge carrying New Jersey Route 9, shows the complexity of constructing the Garden State Parkway in developed areas that already contained road network. In addition to the Parkway considering the incorporation of existing roadways into the design and flow of vehicular traffic, it considered navigable waterways and the needed clearance over shipping channels to accommodate boat traffic.

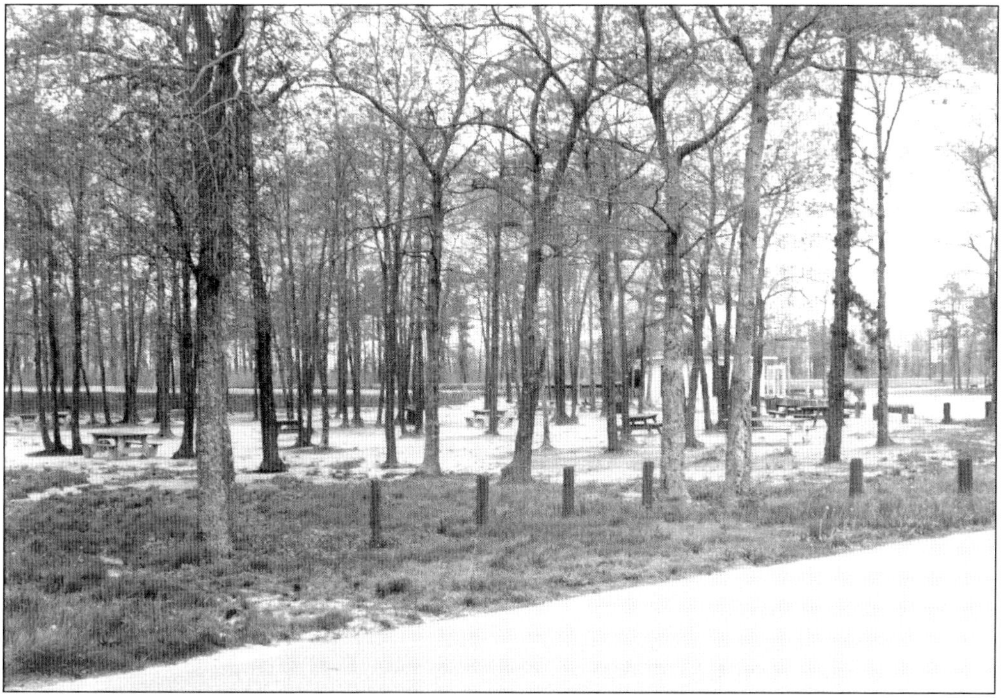

Picnic areas, such as Stafford Forge picnic area in Little Egg Harbor in Ocean County (above) and Shoemaker Holly picnic area in Cape May County (below) offered picnic tables, a loop road, running water, limited bathroom facilities, and grills. Many of the original picnic areas are closed since the service areas are more equipped to handle the needs of modern motorists.

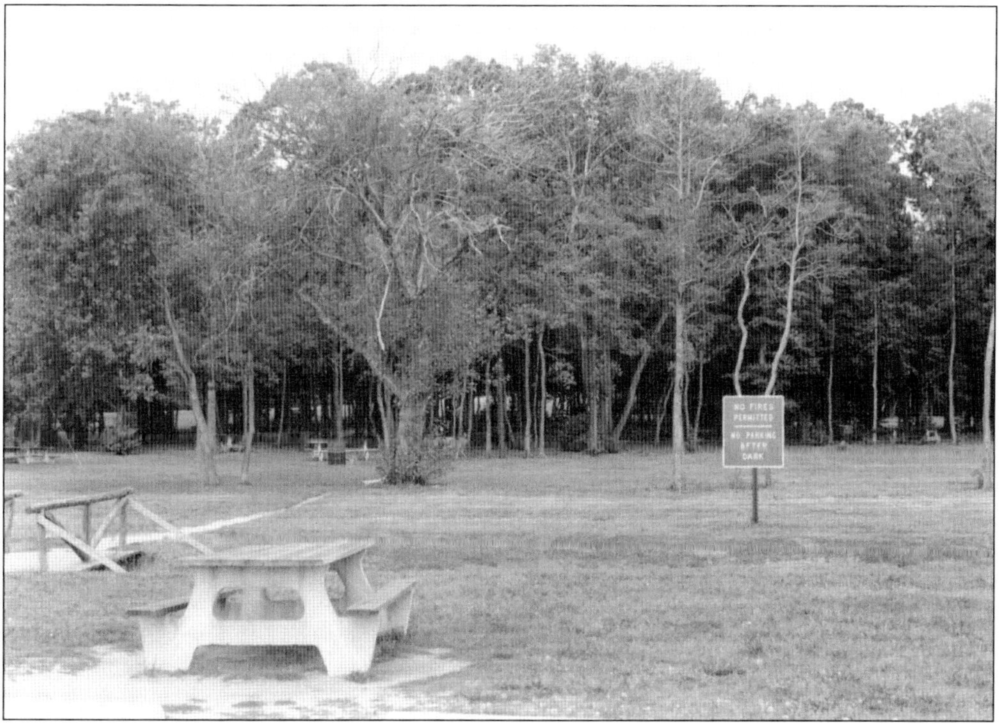

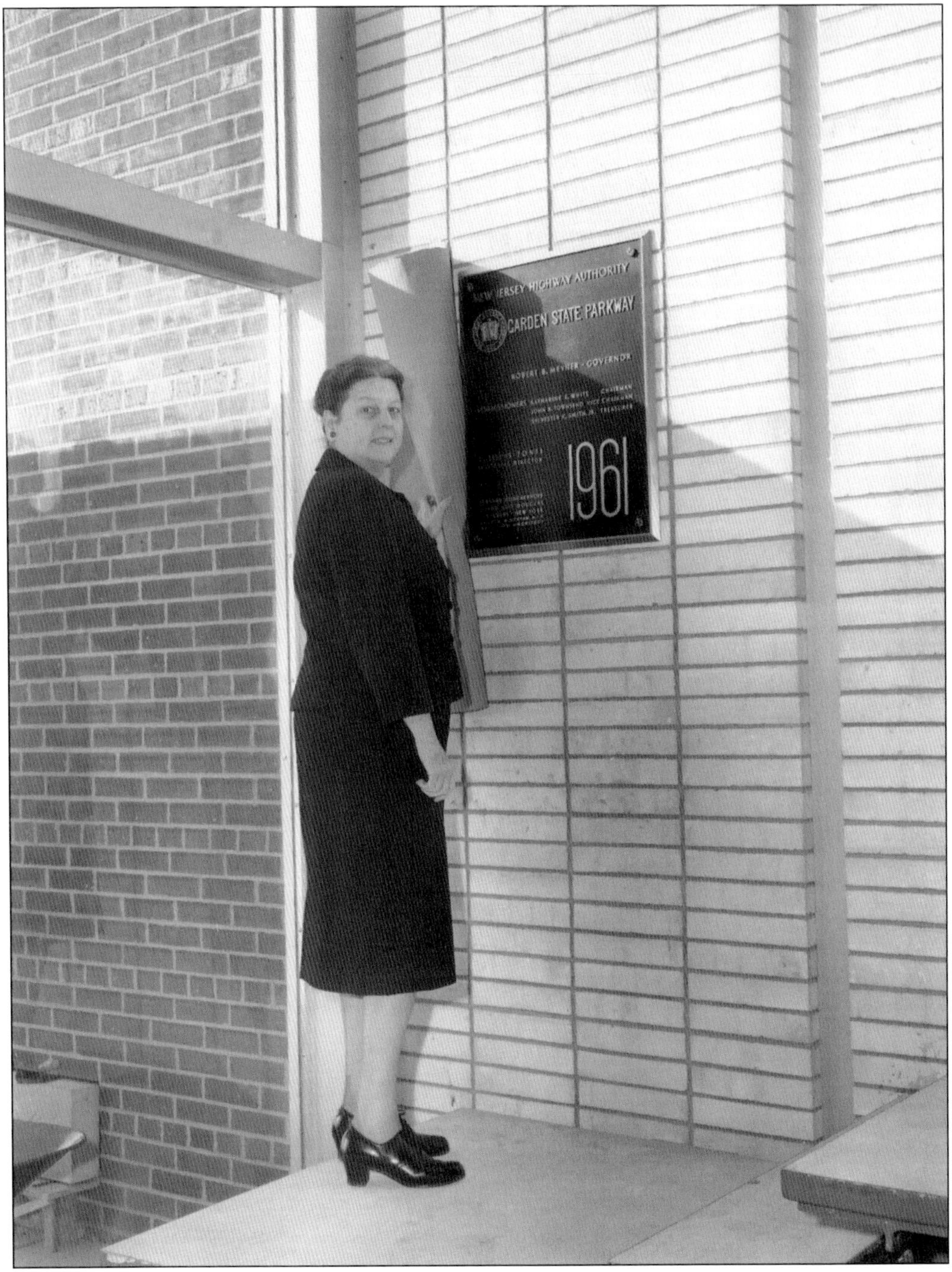

In 1961, chairman Katharine E. White participated in an administration building/cornerstone placement ceremony, here unveiling the dedication plaque. The brick exterior of this structure is a common material for buildings associated with the Garden State Parkway. Prior to the construction of this facility, the New Jersey Highway Authority operated out a former farmhouse near Red Bank, New Jersey.

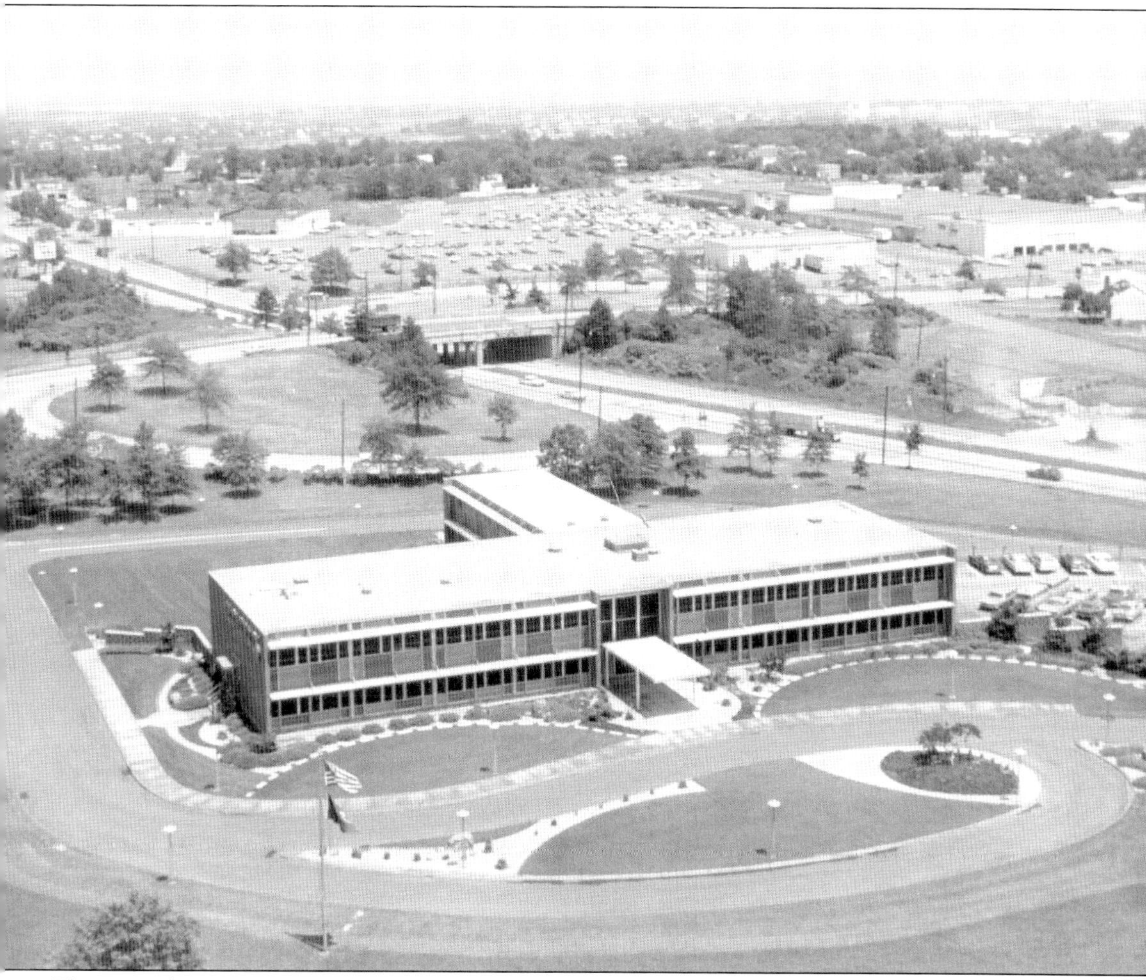

The new administration building was freshly landscaped by John Halleck in 1961 following its completion. This building would serve as the headquarters for the New Jersey Highway Authority until 2003, when it merged with the New Jersey Turnpike Authority. The original building shown here was expanded two times and currently houses the operations, maintenance, and integrated technology services departments of the New Jersey Turnpike Authority. In 2008, the John Cifelli Statewide Traffic Management Center was added adjacent to the building.

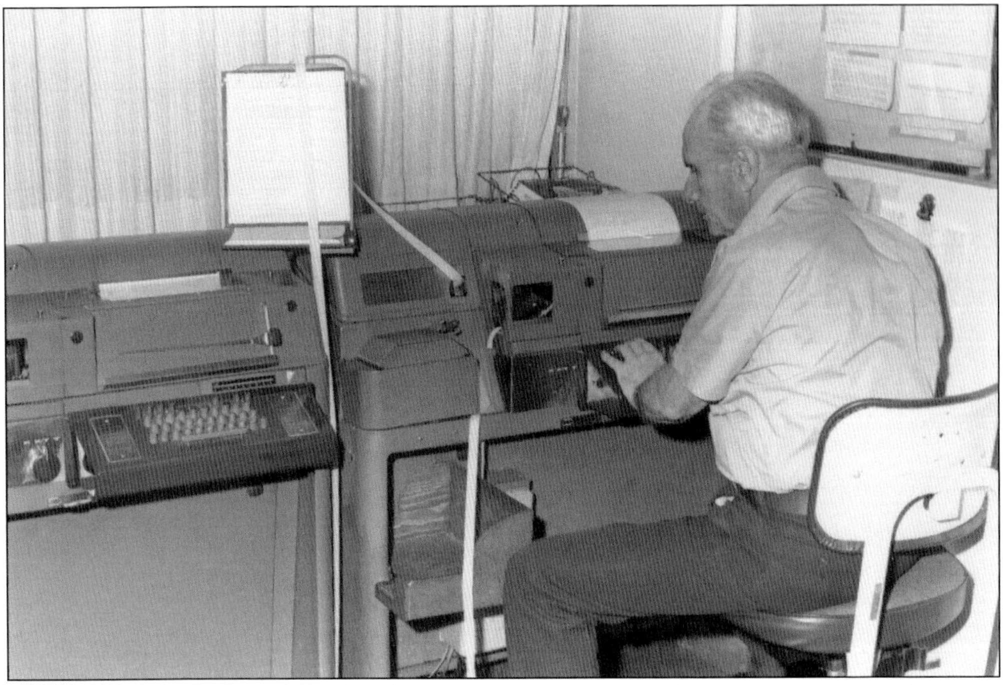

The information network utilized by the New Jersey Highway Authority was incorporated from its earliest days. This dispatcher was responsible for sending out parkway information on a teletype to media and agencies.

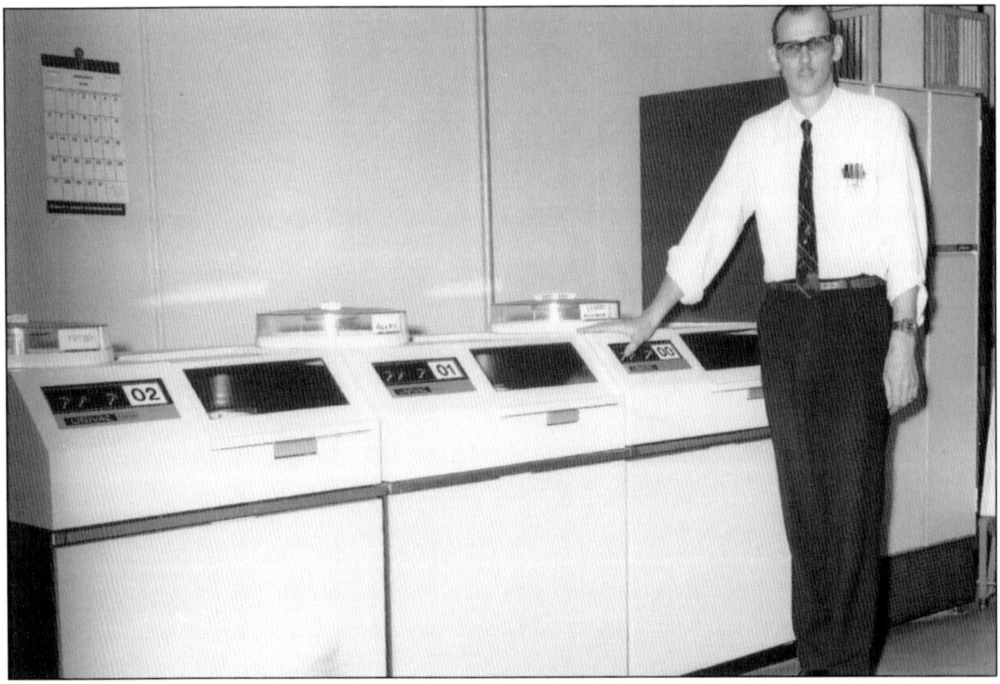

The New Jersey Highway Authority took advantage of new technology as soon as possible. Employee V. Boyce presented the computer room in the 1973 annual report. The New Jersey Highway Authority could track road and toll usage as well as costs and personnel use.

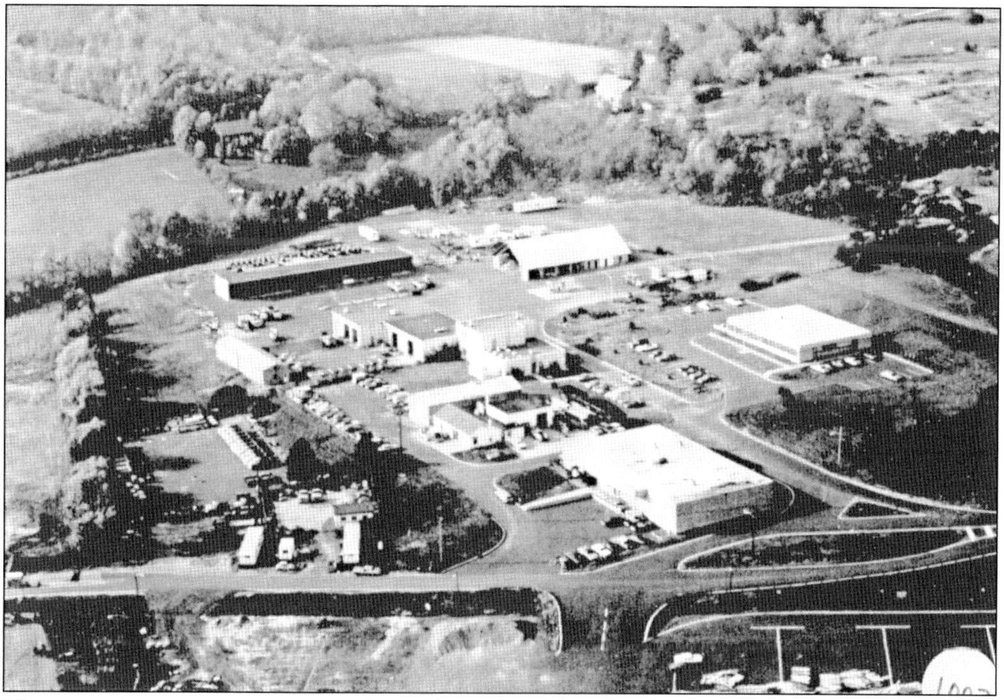

The central maintenance area was housed at Telegraph Hill in Monmouth County in 1974. The New Jersey Highway Authority was responsible for all maintenance and operations of the Garden State Parkway. This central yard was supported by smaller district facilities along the Parkway.

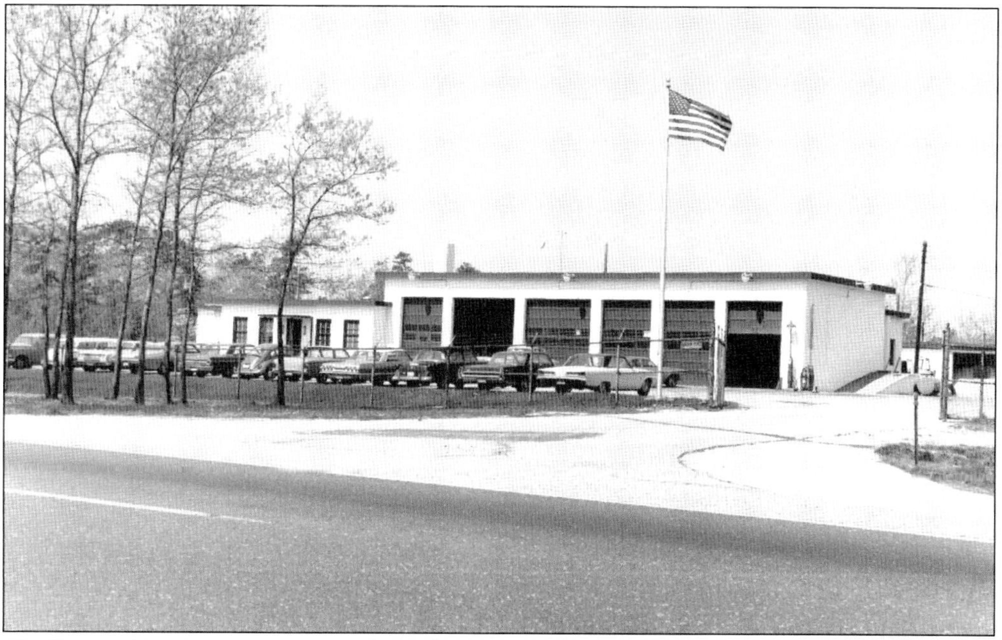

The District No. 6 maintenance yard, also known as Whitehorse, is located in Galloway Township, Atlantic County. It is one of nine along the Garden State Parkway. Originally, a garage, shed, nursery area, and an office building comprised each maintenance district yard. The garages were usually one-story, concrete block structures, as pictured here.

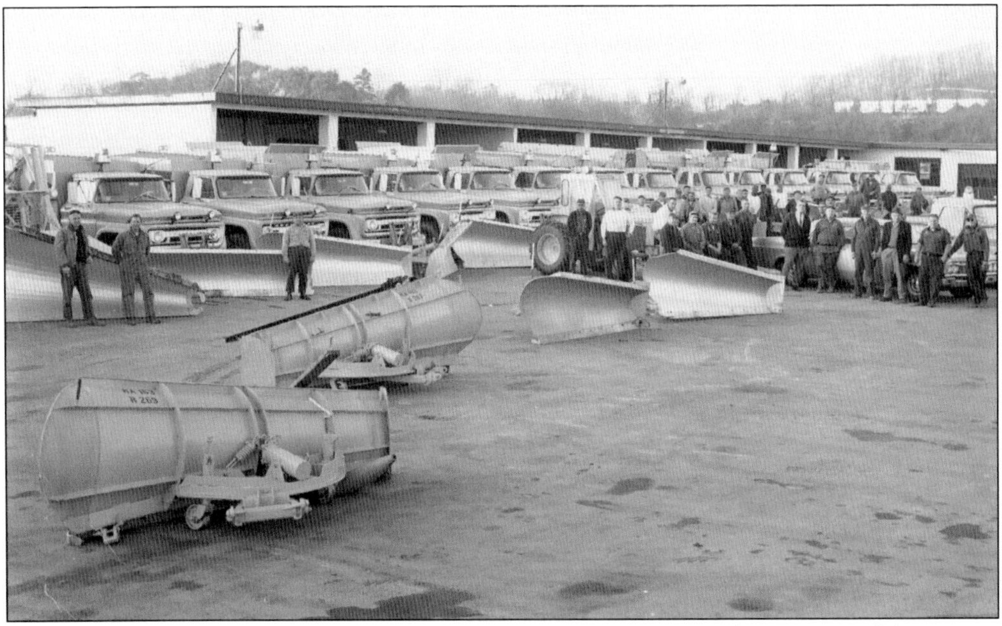

These maintenance workers at the Telegraph Hill maintenance yard are prepared for winter. Crews, if needed, worked around the clock to keep the Garden State Parkway open for the motoring public.

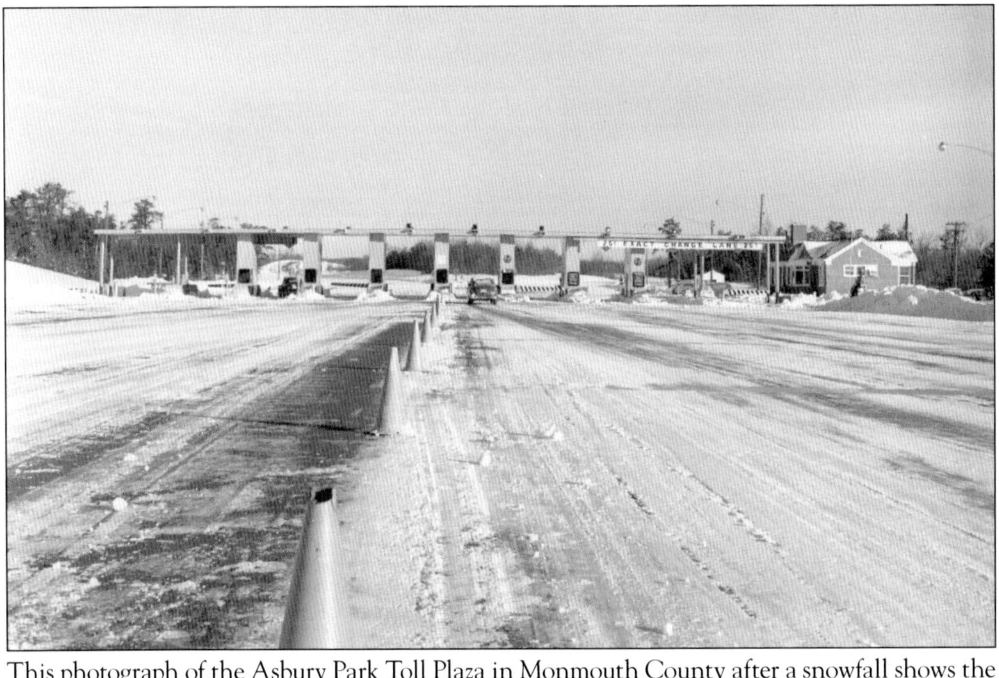

This photograph of the Asbury Park Toll Plaza in Monmouth County after a snowfall shows the efforts resulting from maintaining the road under all conditions. One of the reasons barrier toll plazas were implemented was to ensure adequate collection of tolls, especially in areas near the un-tolled State Highway Department–constructed portions. Early in the road's history it was noted that many drivers were avoiding tolls and depressing the expected revenue. Therefore, it was important for safety and toll collection to maintain the lanes at the plazas.

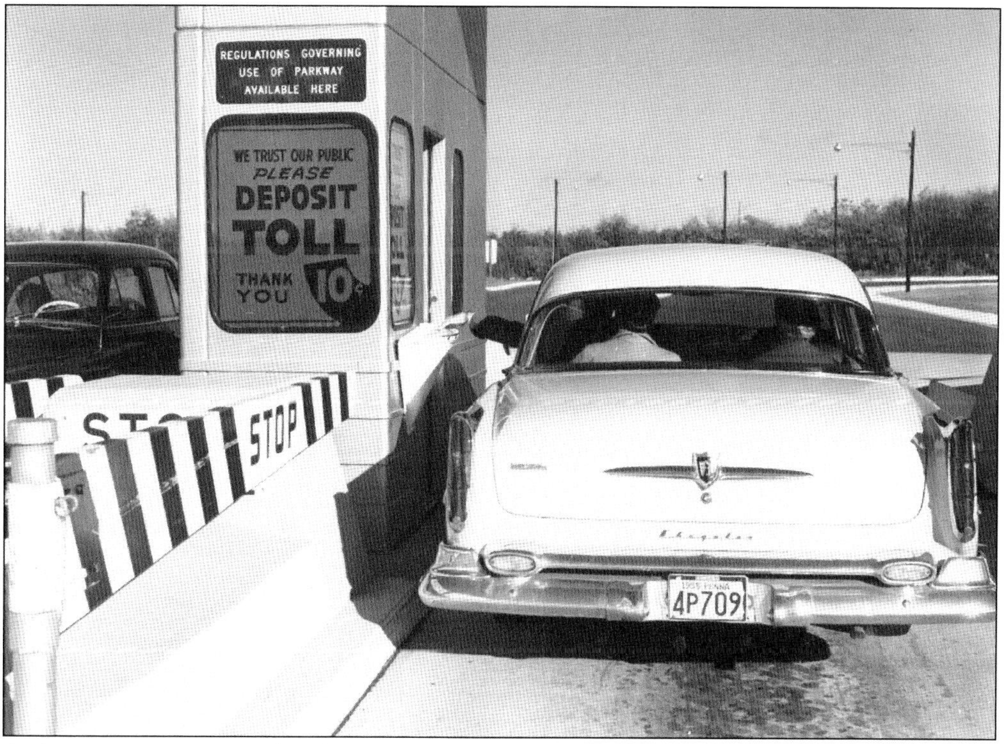

At first, operators manned each booth, but beginning in 1955, some of the toll collectors were replaced by baskets, which allowed drivers to toss in exact change and save time. Later, automatic machines became standard at most toll plazas.

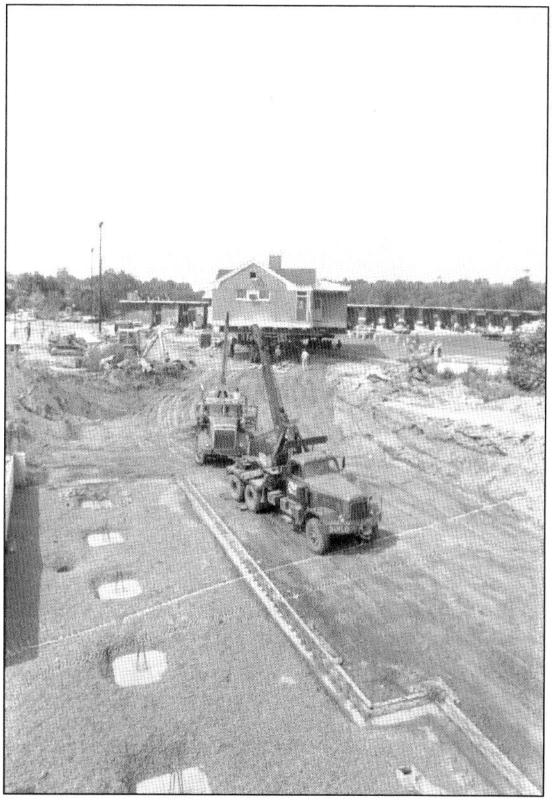

Designers created two types of tollbooths, the designs of which have changed over the years but consistently involved booths covered with a flat roof. The administration buildings, off to the sides of the booths, showed a design similar to the service areas and state police barracks and reflected the Colonial Revival motif. The single-story, brick buildings had painted white trim and wood shutters. Here, the original Union Plaza administration building was moved to be reused in a maintenance district.

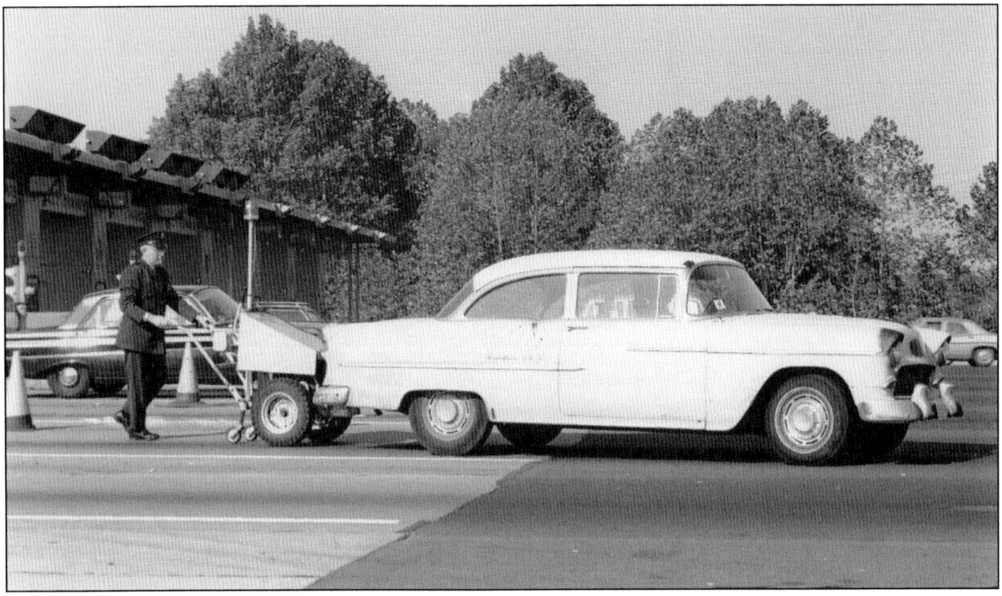

As part of the safety and efficiencies of the Garden State Parkway, tollbooths even stocked equipment to push stalled cars out of the way as shown in 1968 at the Essex Toll Plaza in Bloomfield, Essex County.

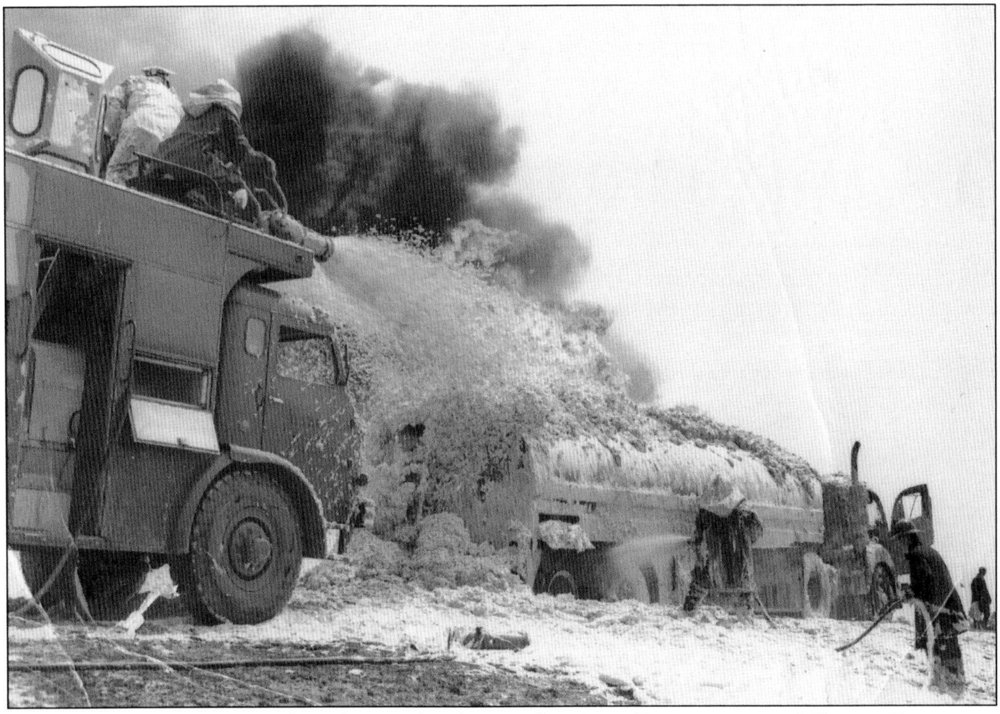

Parkway equipment assisted in this tanker fire in the Toms River section of Ocean County in 1960. All maintenance matters and some emergency situations were handled by the New Jersey Highway Authority rather than by state or local governments. This independence allowed for the New Jersey Highway Authority to operate in an efficient manner and ensure that needs were met as quickly as possible.

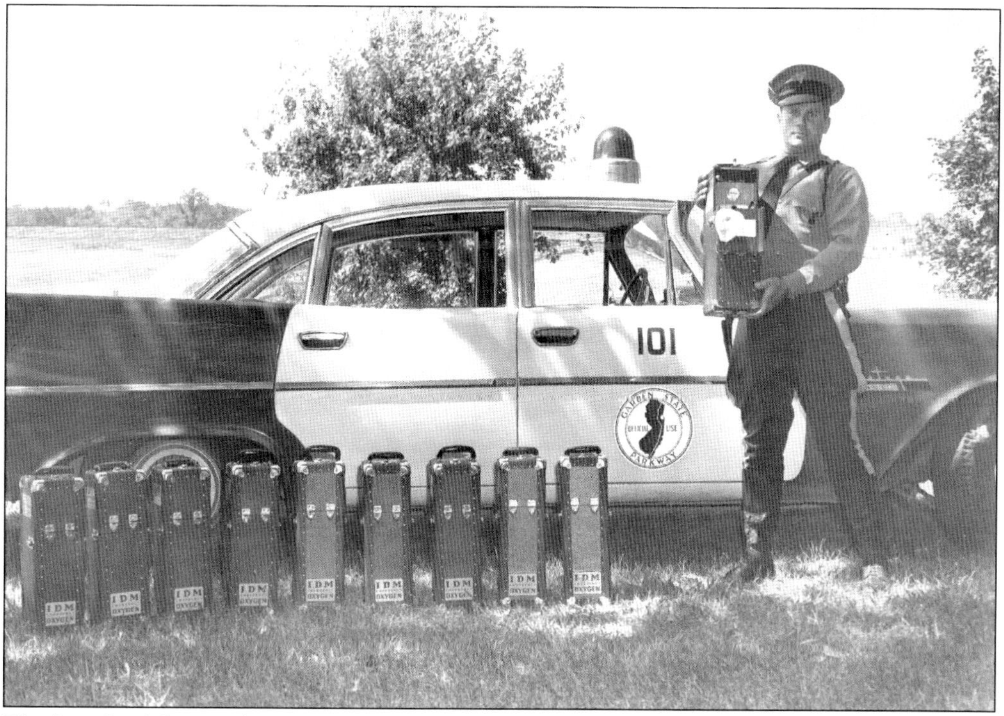

The length of the Garden State Parkway is patrolled by New Jersey State Police, who maintain a constant presence. Many have noted that several police cars were observed during each commute. The New Jersey Highway Authority paid for all of the operating costs and salaries of troops associated with the Parkway. As this photograph shows, the state troopers were well prepared for emergencies and carried portable oxygen inhalators.

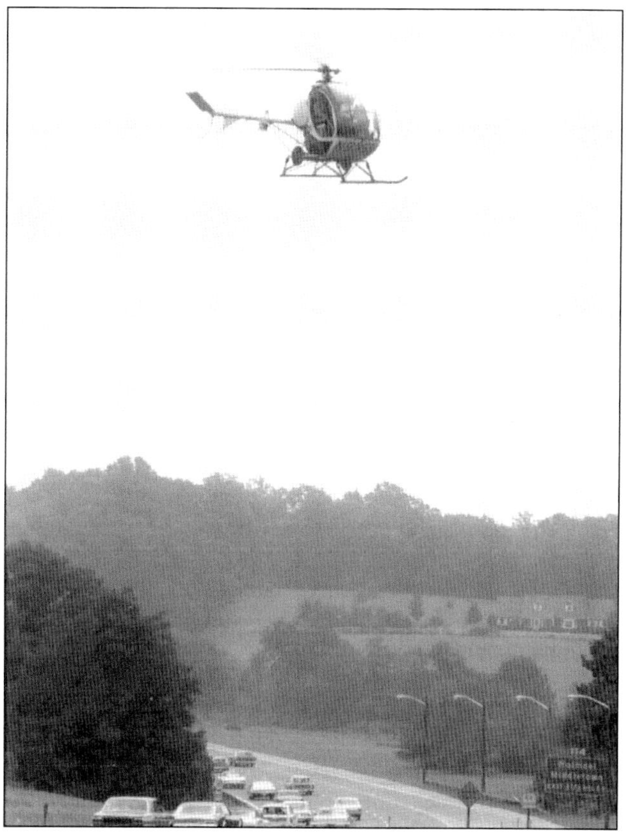

State police used a helicopter to patrol heavy traffic during peak travel times in the summer. Consolidated in 2011, Troop D and E of the New Jersey State Police patrols the Garden State Parkway and the New Jersey Turnpike. This helicopter was assigned to the Parkway in 1962.

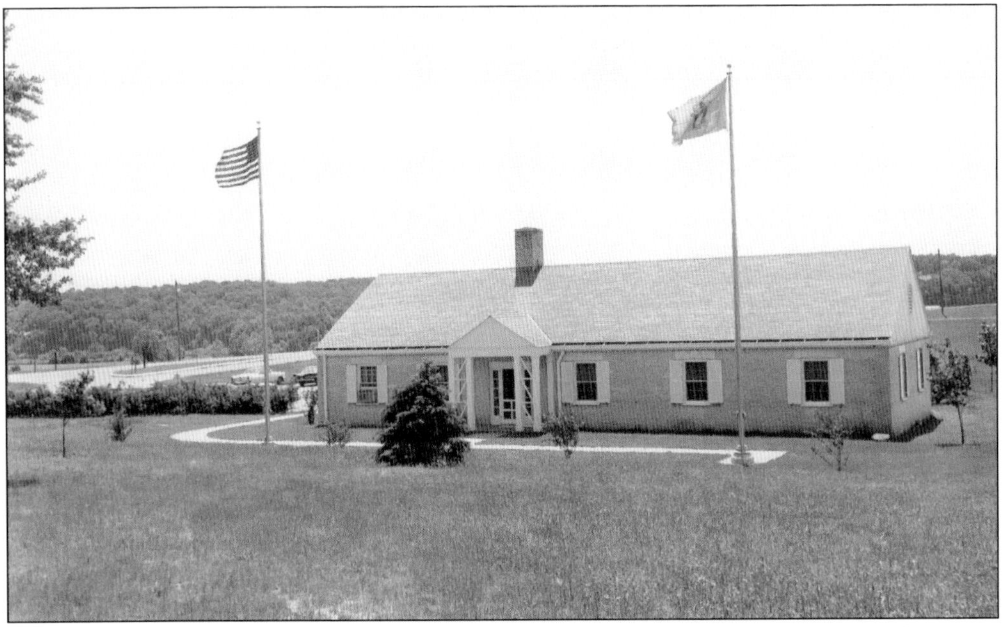

The state police barracks in Holmdel, Monmouth County, exhibited the Colonial architecture style prevalent throughout the Garden State Parkway as well. Consistent architectural components link the Parkway from New York to Cape May.

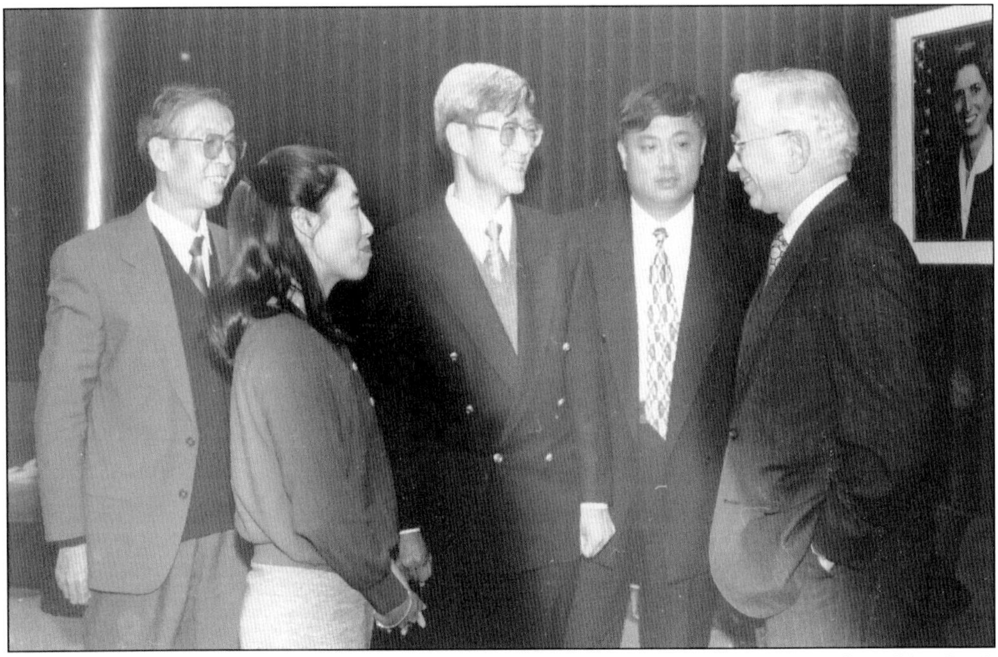

The notoriety and importance of the Garden State Parkway has been recognized worldwide. A delegation from China is given a briefing by executive director Lewis B. Thurston III in 1995. While the original planners and engineers worked to create a special roadway, few could have imagined the iconic status the Parkway would achieve. The Chinese visitors were here to study the Parkway and its operations because of how successful it has been. Delegates from China have come back to New Jersey as recently as 2012 for the same reason.

Five

Always Planning and Moving Forward

The Garden State Parkway design was guided by several major principles intended to promote safety, functionality, and the unique aesthetic of the roadway. There was no at-grade cross traffic for almost its entire length with the exception of three intersections near the southern end, and access was restricted to non-signalized ramps. Roadside commercial and residential advertising was prohibited, and billboards were barred from the roadside area. Opposing lanes of traffic were separated by a wide median with high artificial berms and foliage. Horizontal curves were superelevated, and steep grades and vertical curves were essentially eliminated to contribute to more efficient driving. Finally, engineers endeavored to eliminate monotonous elements in the design.

Less than a year from the official opening of the Parkway, expansion became necessary. In 1955, additional northbound and southbound lanes were added to the 52 miles between the Paterson interchange and the Asbury Park Toll Plaza. As urban populations grew, more people moved to central and southern sections of New Jersey made more accessible by the Parkway. New communities sprang up in less populated areas of the state near the shore towns. The shore towns experienced construction booms as they created the support systems needed to supply services to larger populations. Shopping centers and commercial development opened as the Parkway provided a route for some of those residents to commute for work. As these new population centers grew, congestion became more of a problem and increased pressure on the Parkway. Its ability to efficiently carry traffic was strained, necessitating even more new construction.

It is a difficult balancing act to provide safe transportation and reduce congestion, yet maintain the parklike setting of the road. In 2003, through an act of the legislature, the New Jersey Highway Authority was consolidated with the New Jersey Turnpike Authority. The New Jersey Turnpike Authority continues to retain the Parkway's defining characteristics as per the historic district determination of 2000. This is evident in maintenance operations that replace existing features whenever possible. With public and official participation and support, the Parkway can retain its historic characteristics. The public, which voted the Garden State Parkway into life in 1952, will help control its future.

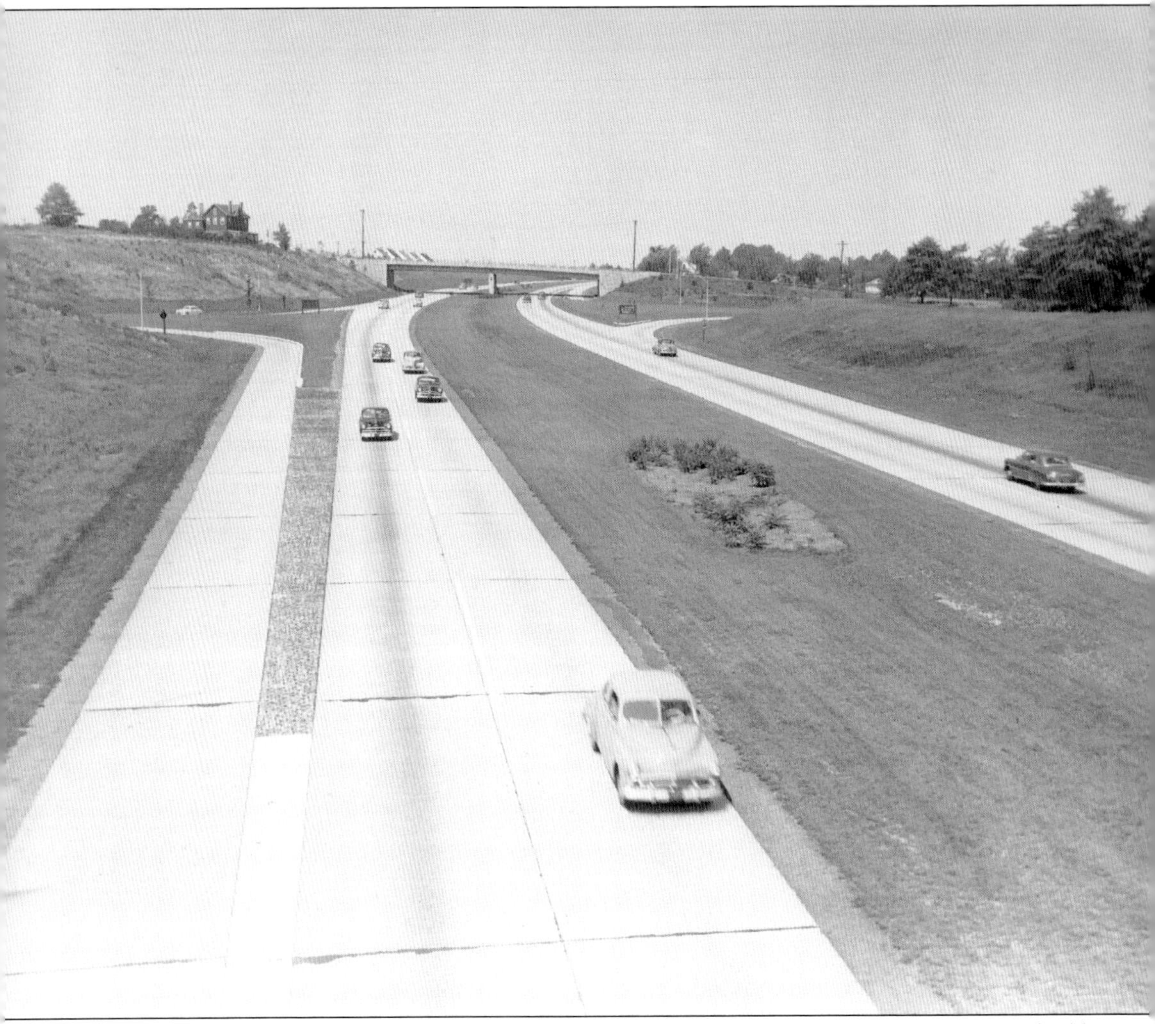

The New Jersey Historic Preservation Office has evaluated the Garden State Parkway as eligible for listing in the National Register of Historic Places. A resource is considered eligible for listing if it has historical significance and it maintains original integrity. The Parkway is considered eligible because of its impact on the economy of New Jersey and the development of the shore region and for its design, which combined the elements of early-20th-century parkways with high-speed highways. This section of the Parkway built by the State Highway Department in Union County shows that even in the more developed northeastern section of New Jersey, the Parkway provided a modern, spacious road that presented travelers with a pleasurable experience. Much of the original fabric of the roadway has been preserved and, with careful planning and design, will be maintained or replicated.

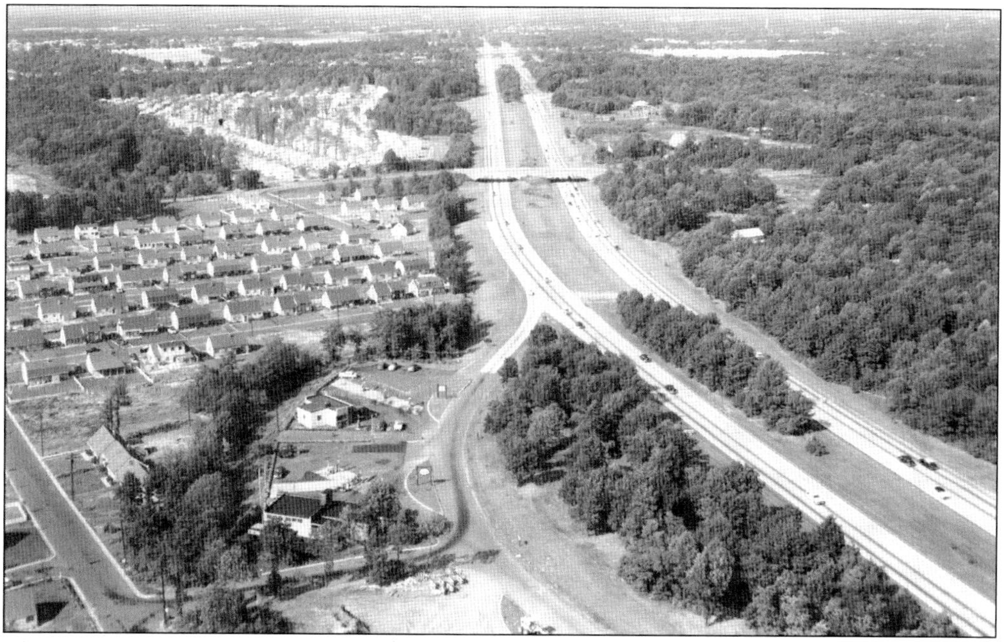

This view of the largely original roadway in Middlesex County in 1961 looks north with New Dover Road crossing over the Garden State Parkway. This illustrates the vegetation that lines the Parkway, providing screening for the residential developments that abut the right-of-way. Mature trees in the infield are utilized to separate the service area from the roadway.

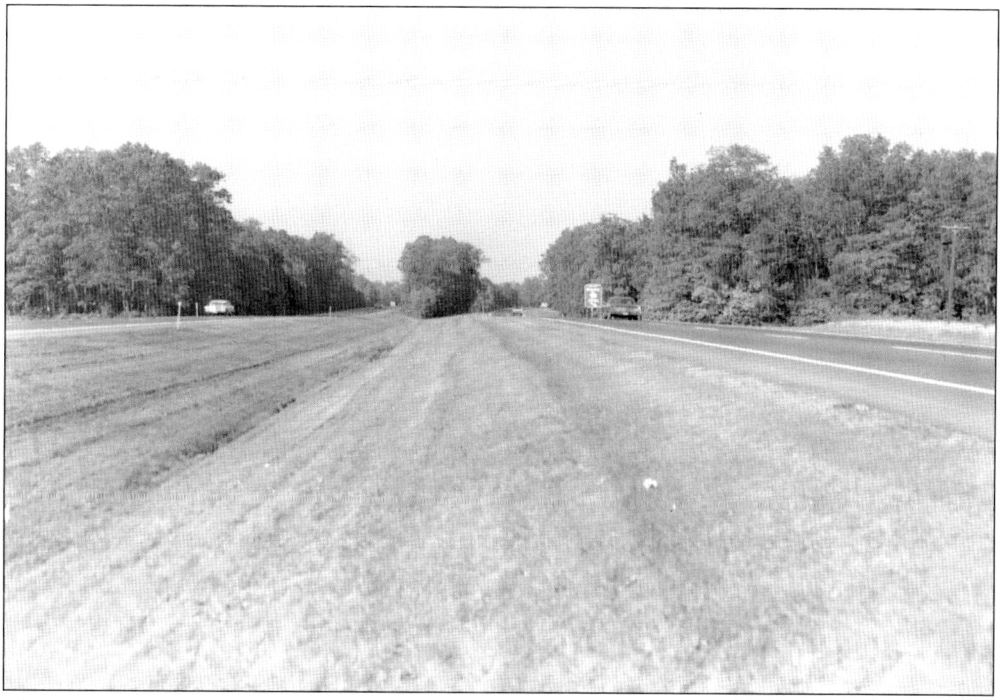

This scenic photograph illustrates the country feel landscape architects designed, particularly evident in the southern sections of the state, which were not urbanized. This location in Ocean County is near the Polhemus Picnic Area in Toms River.

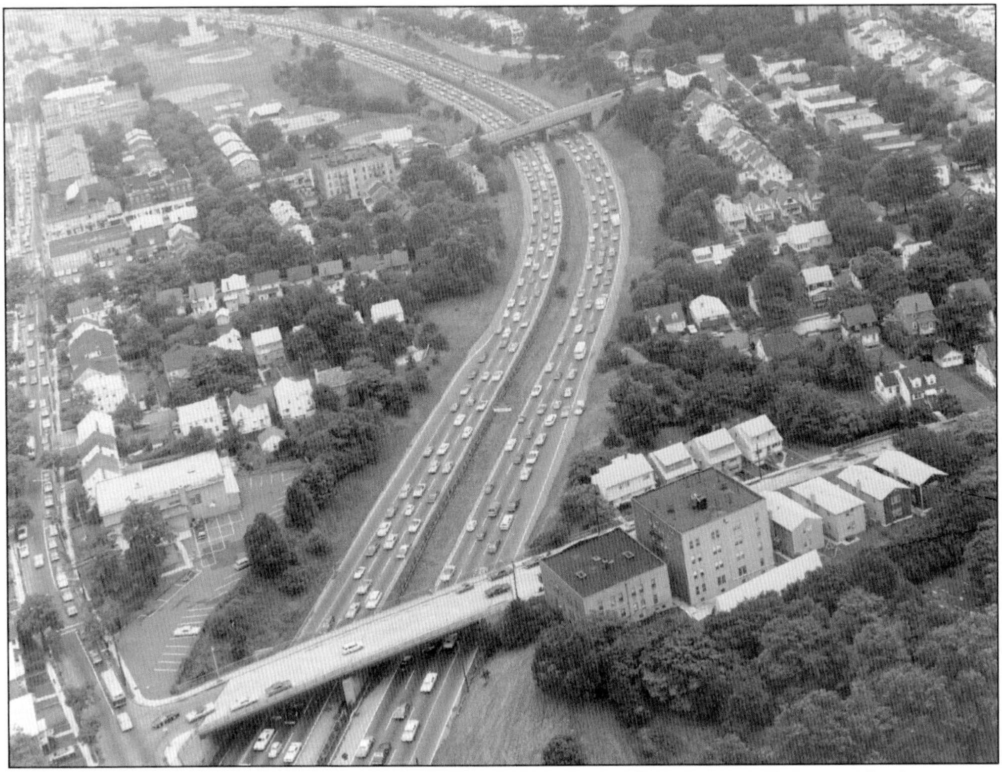

Even by 1961, the success and popularity of the six-lane Garden State Parkway in the Irvington section of Essex County led to it being near capacity. The heavy use of the Parkway exhibited the cycle of better roads increasing residential development, which in turned created higher traffic volumes that necessitated road improvements.

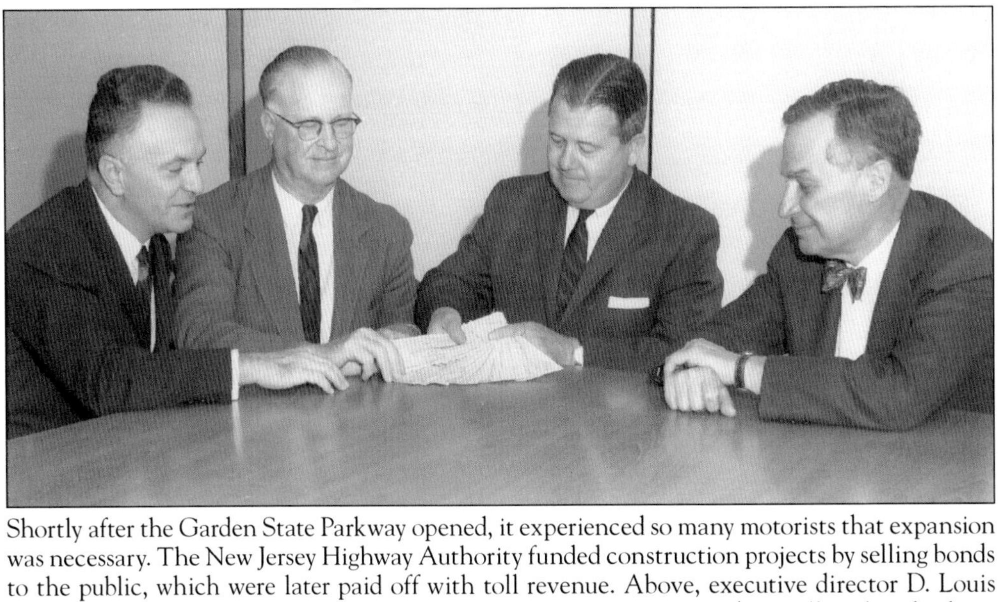

Shortly after the Garden State Parkway opened, it experienced so many motorists that expansion was necessary. The New Jersey Highway Authority funded construction projects by selling bonds to the public, which were later paid off with toll revenue. Above, executive director D. Louis Tonti and Commissioner John B. Townsend attend the closing of a $40-million bond sale in New York City.

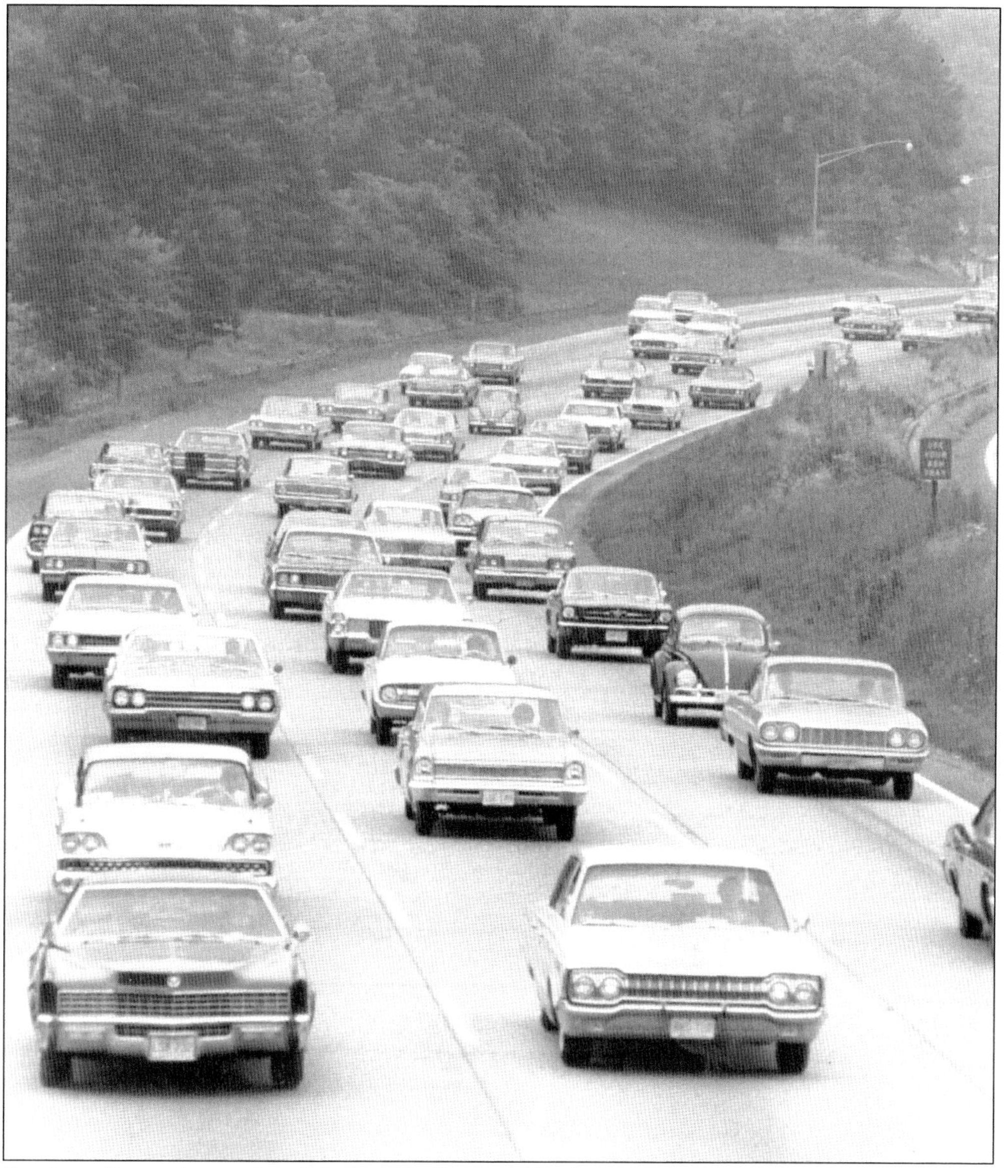

Beach traffic on days such as July 7, 1967, illustrated both the effects of the Garden State Parkway on the shore and the need for more widening projects. The Parkway was important for modifying how New Jersey residents traveled, worked, vacationed, and lived. When the Parkway was extended to the southern terminus of the state, the shore opened up to year-round residents and tourists. Commercial and residential development exploded in shore towns, as more people had access to these locations, stimulating the local and state economies. New residential developments at the shore grew up near the Parkway as it provided commuters with easily accessible transportation routes to work. Ocean County, for instance, saw its population increase almost fivefold between 1950 and 1976. The tourist trade also exploded after the construction of the Parkway. Prior to 1949, resort businesses were suffering from declining revenues. Once the Parkway to Cape May was completed, though, the trend reversed itself. Retail sales between 1954 and 1956 skyrocketed by over $31 million in Monmouth County, $22.5 million in Atlantic County, $38 million in Ocean County, and $22 million in Cape May County.

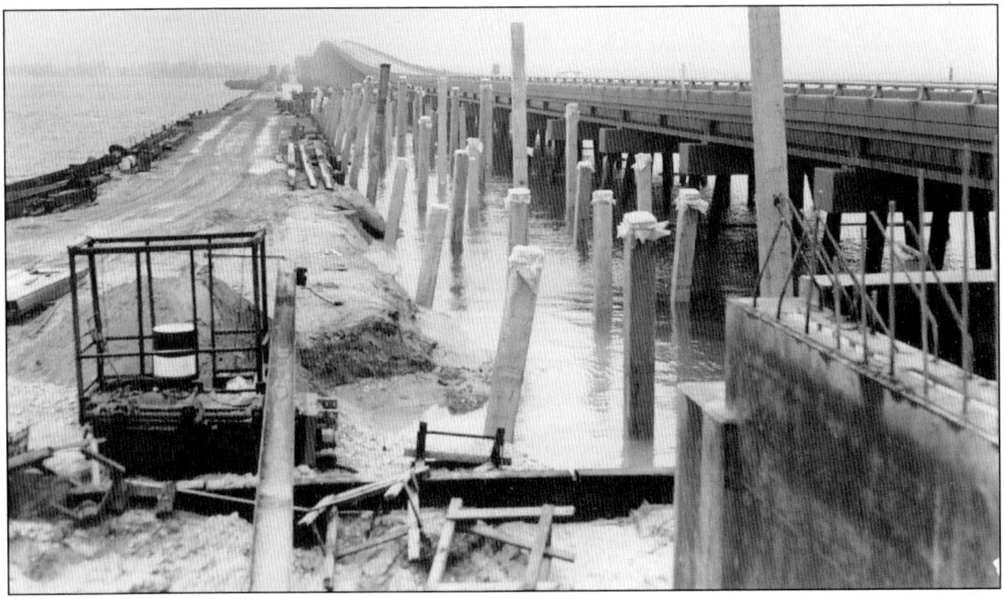

The Great Egg Harbor Bay Bridge was originally only two lanes, which created a bottleneck as traffic levels increased. The bridge was expanded by building another structure of the same size in 1972, immediately adjacent to the original. Above, a temporary road has been constructed behind sheeting to allow equipment access for construction. In 2013, the New Jersey Turnpike Authority will expand at this site once again by constructing a new bridge to carry southbound traffic and rehabilitating the existing bridge to carry the northbound.

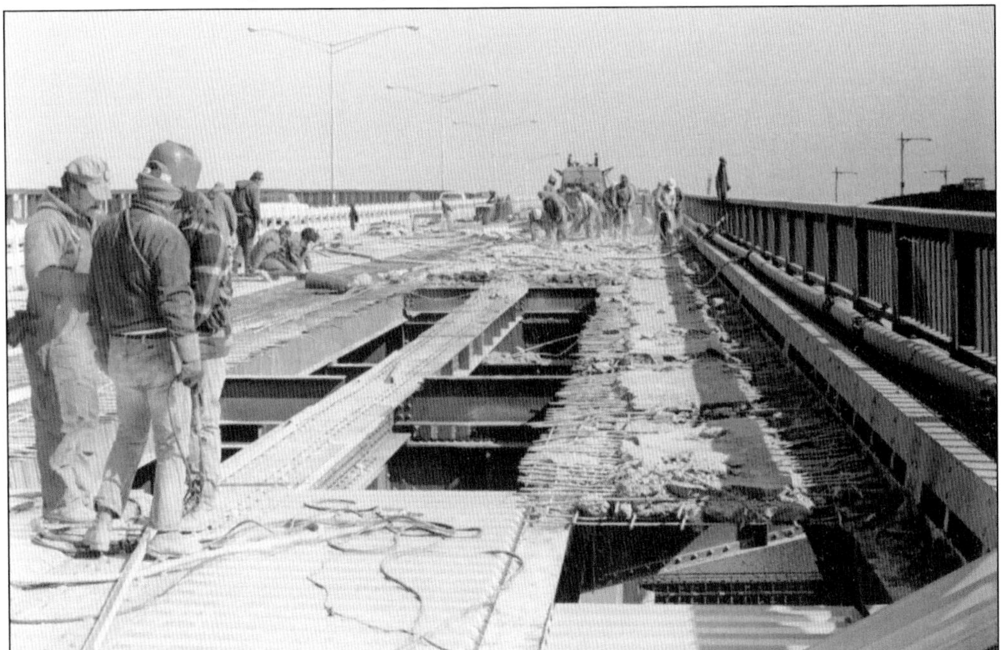

This rehabilitation of the Driscoll Bridge took place in 1972, following the completion of the additional lanes, which allowed for the maintenance of traffic. Such work is an ongoing need for such a heavily used roadway.

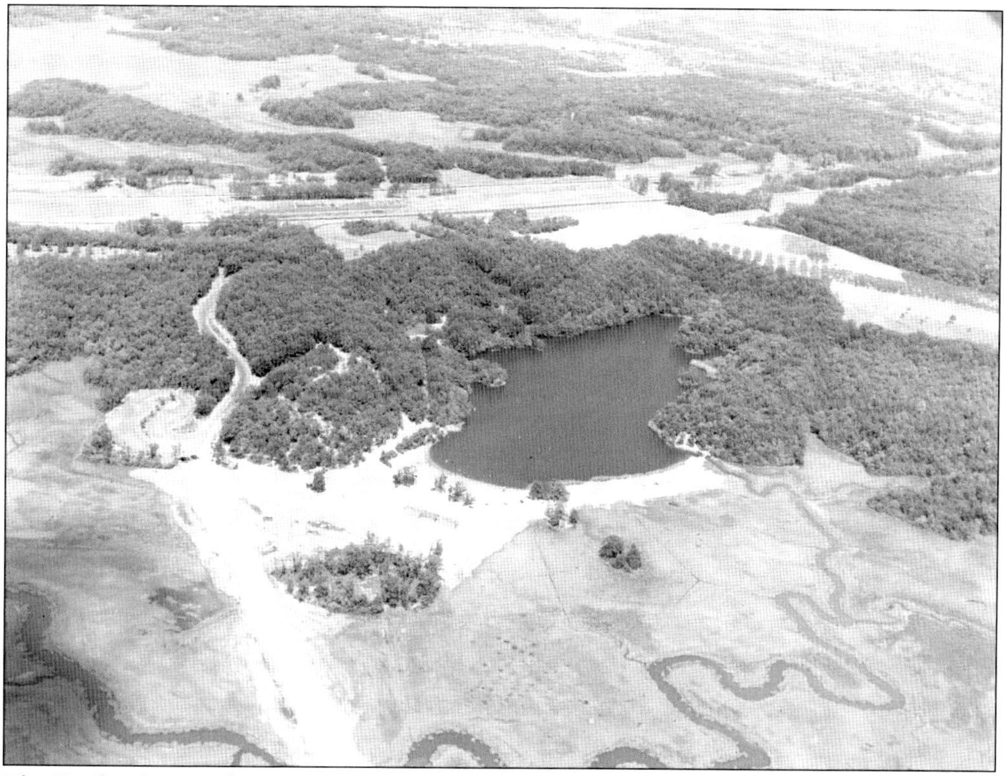

The Garden State Parkway travels through the Cheesequake State Park in the Sayreville section of Middlesex County during its journey through central eastern New Jersey. The Parkway afforded opportunities to access numerous parks and wilderness areas in addition to the Jersey Shore.

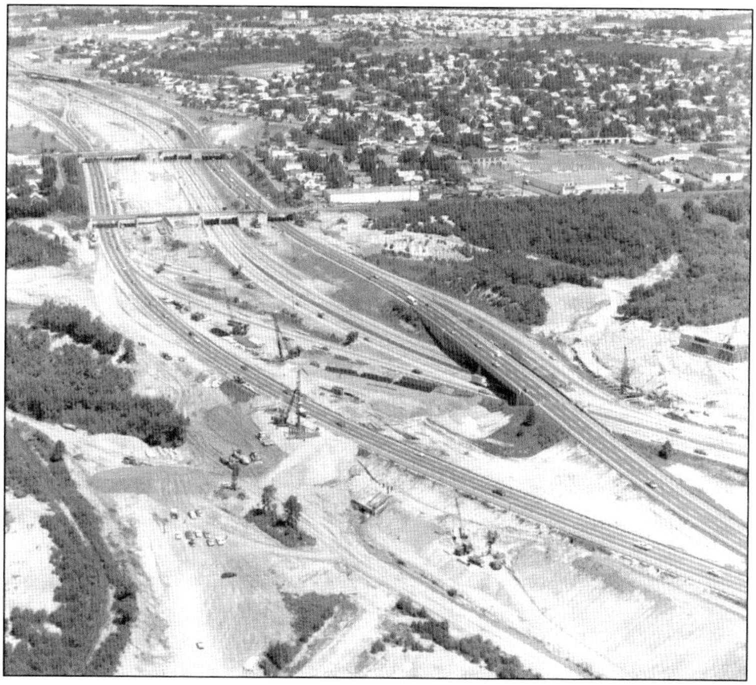

In 1969, the Garden State Parkway linkage with Interstate 287/Route 440 was expanded to meet the growing demands of commuters through Woodbridge. The Parkway has become a vital artery in the regional road network, especially for urban New Jersey and New York City.

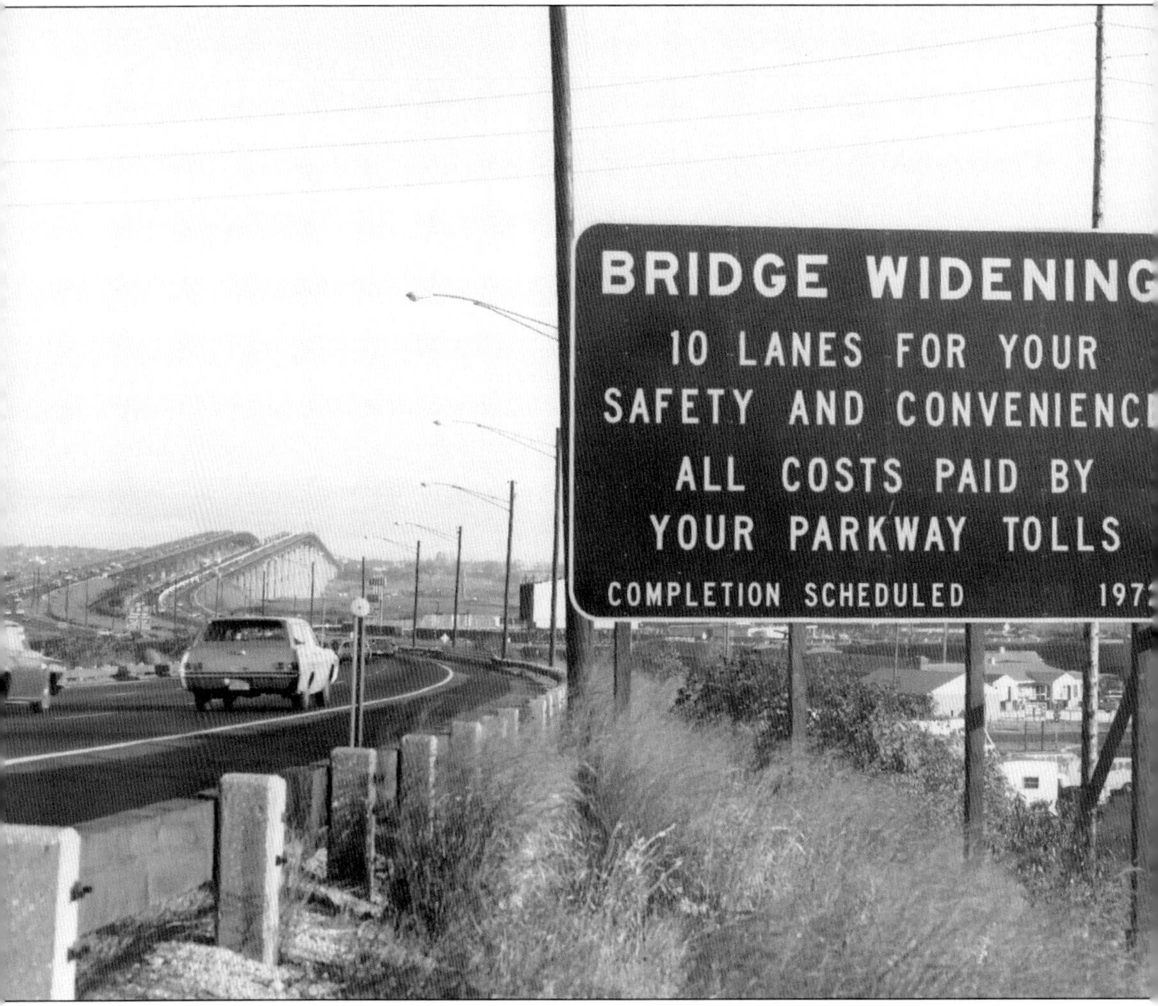

The New Jersey Highway Authority was originally able to operate the Garden State Parkway outside of the vagaries of the New Jersey Legislature and the US Congress. The original funding plan allowed the New Jersey Highway Authority to operate and undertake needed improvements regardless of the election cycle by relying solely on user fees. As traffic continues to grow and congestion creates even larger snarls, the Garden State Parkway may face new pressures that necessitate more changes. In 2010, in fact, 433,412,000 vehicles traveled the Parkway compared to the 39 million when it first opened in 1954. New safety features will be added, resulting in additional changes along the Parkway. That has already occurred with the original guiderails, which have been mostly replaced. Additional traffic will undoubtedly add more lanes in the future. Through it all, changes to the Parkway will be consistent with the original plan and retain some of its design elements to keep them compatible with the original scenic and cohesive design.

The expansion of the Driscoll Bridge in the 1970s was actually planned for in the original design, which included an extra series of foundations. The expansion was accomplished by adding a third set of columns on the unused foundations, increasing the bridge's capacity to 10 lanes. Aside from the extra foundations, the Driscoll Bridge was largely a twin of the Edison Bridge seen in the background, which carries US Route 9 and opened in 1940.

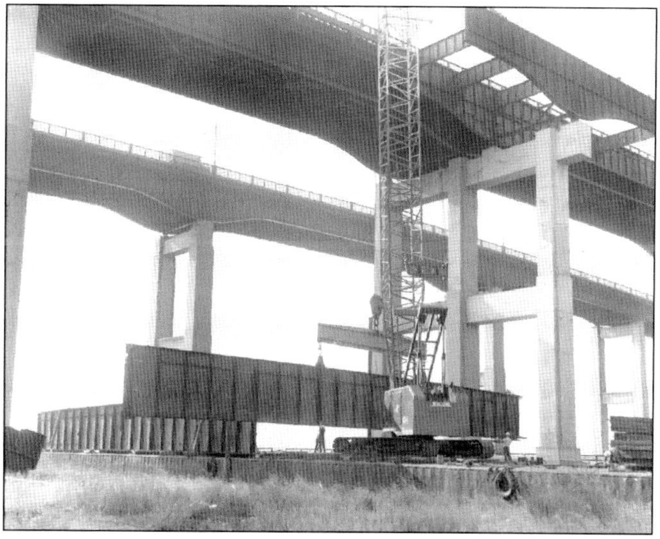

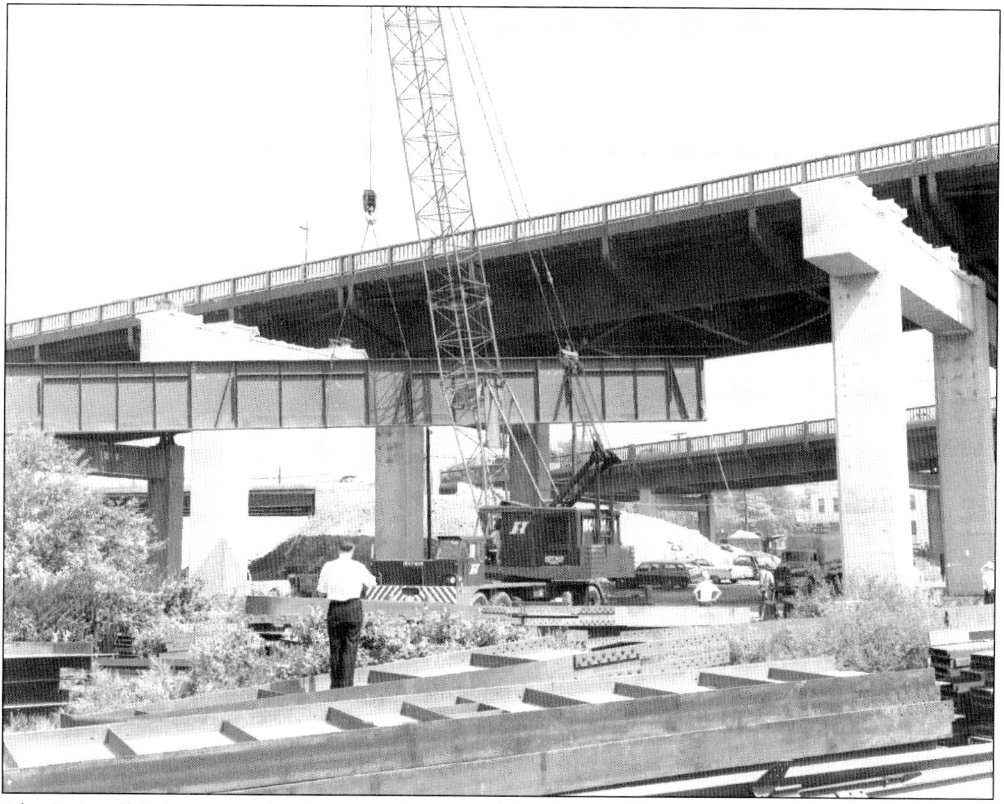

The Driscoll Bridge over the shipping channel of the Raritan River was originally opened in 1954 as a single-span bridge carrying two lanes of traffic each way. In 1957, the lanes were narrowed from 15 to 10 feet wide, allowing room for two additional travel lanes. Above, a girder is lifted into place by a crane in 1970 during a major expansion to the bridge, which was completed in 1972. Modification of the median barrier in 1984 provided room for six lanes in each direction, and another expansion in the first decade of the 21st century increased the capacity to a world record 15 travel lanes.

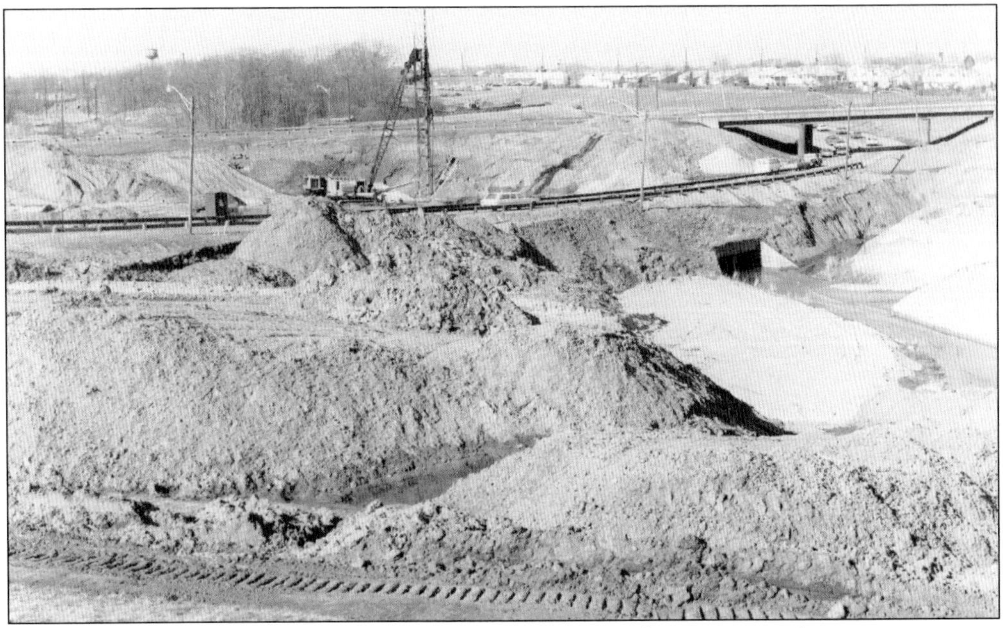

Far from static, the Garden State Parkway has been growing almost constantly since its opening. In concert with the expansion of the Driscoll Bridge, this 1972 expansion of the roadway in Monmouth County added additional travel lanes to the inside of the original traffic lanes.

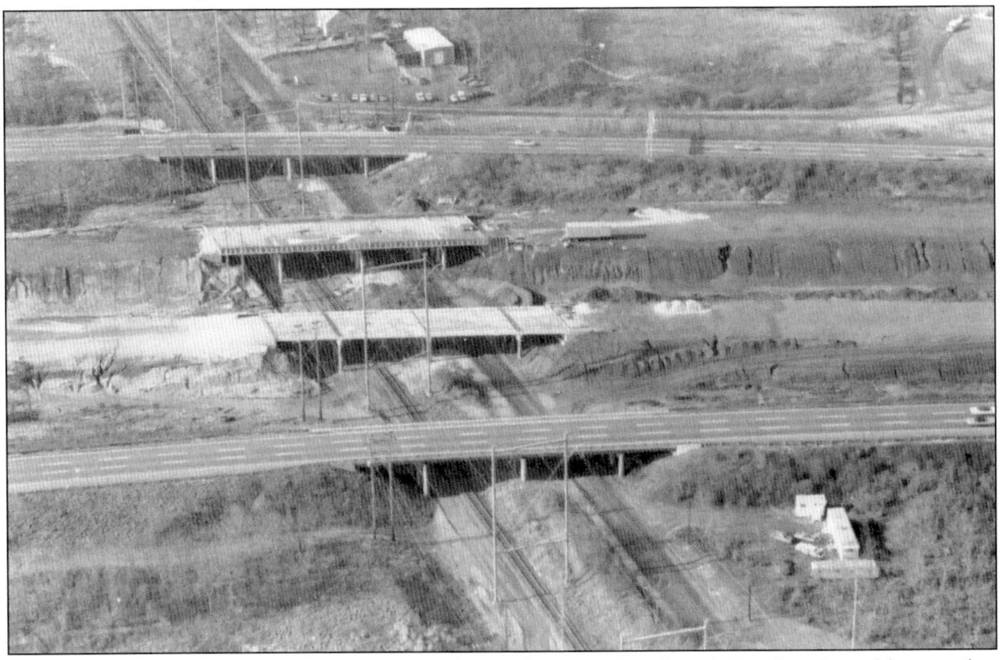

Two inner roadways are constructed within the median over Pinebrook Road and a rail line in this 1972 expansion project in Tinton Falls, Monmouth County. This negated the need to purchase additional right-of-way and expand the Garden State Parkway's footprint. The inner roadways were designed as express lanes extending from south of Interchange 105 for Routes 18 and 36 to south of Interchange 125 for Route 35. The only direct access to exits along the express lanes is at Interchange 105 (southbound only) and Interchange 117.

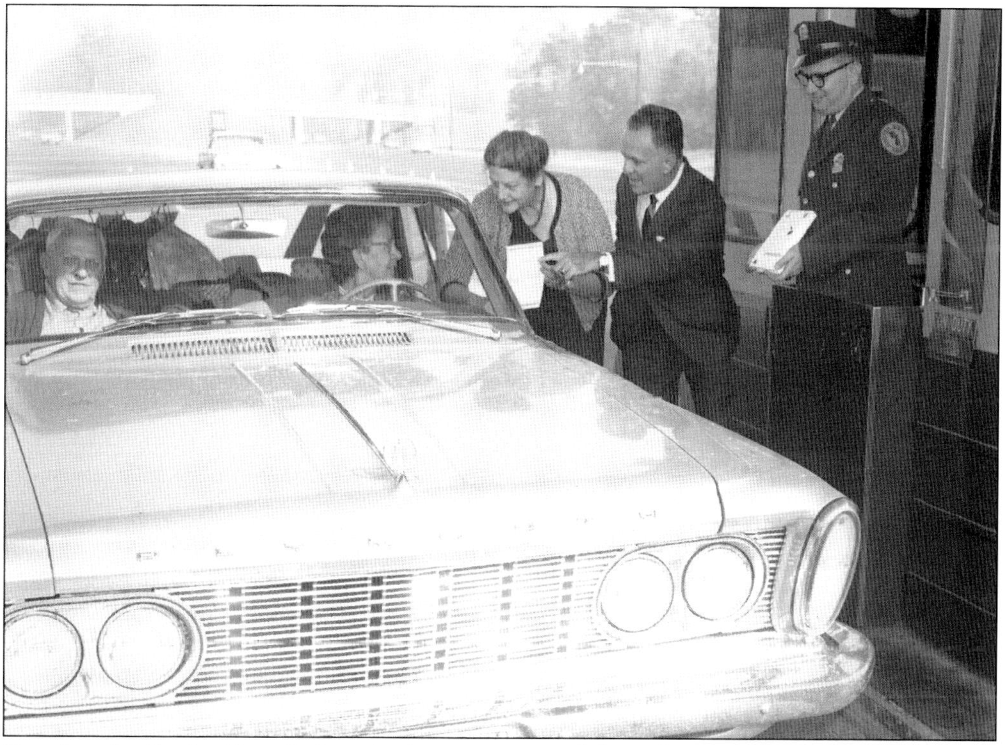

Travel on the Garden State Parkway had an international flavor from very early on. In recognition of the amount of travelers from outside of New Jersey and the country, chairman White and executive director Tonti pass out maps in French at the Hillsdale Toll Plaza (now known as Pascack Valley Toll Plaza) in 1963. Toll collector Nathan Street keeps an eye on the happenings and the new toll workers. Publicity for the road has always been part of the process.

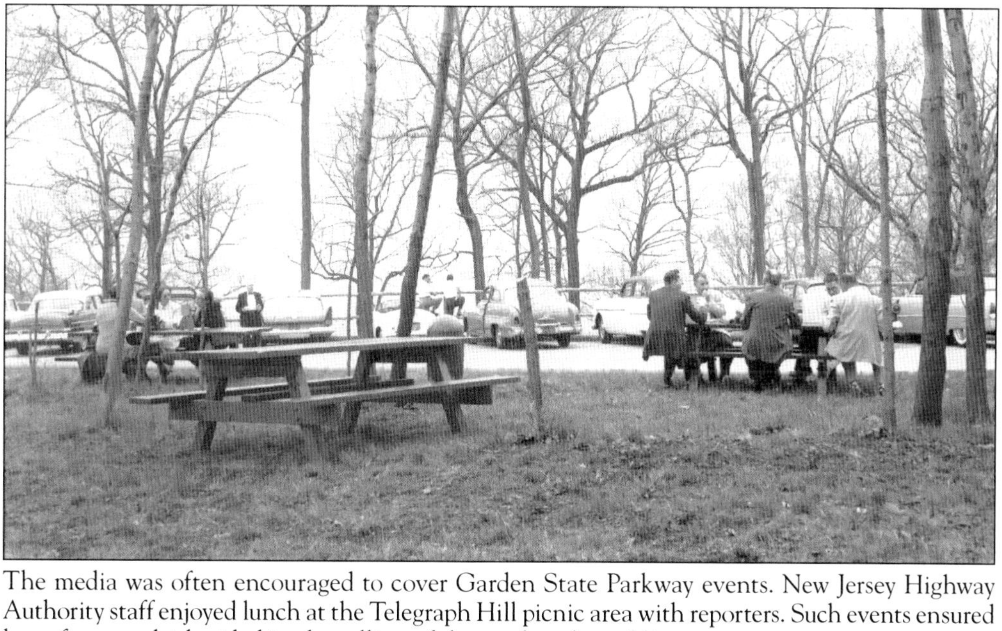

The media was often encouraged to cover Garden State Parkway events. New Jersey Highway Authority staff enjoyed lunch at the Telegraph Hill picnic area with reporters. Such events ensured lots of press, which aided in the selling of the road to the public.

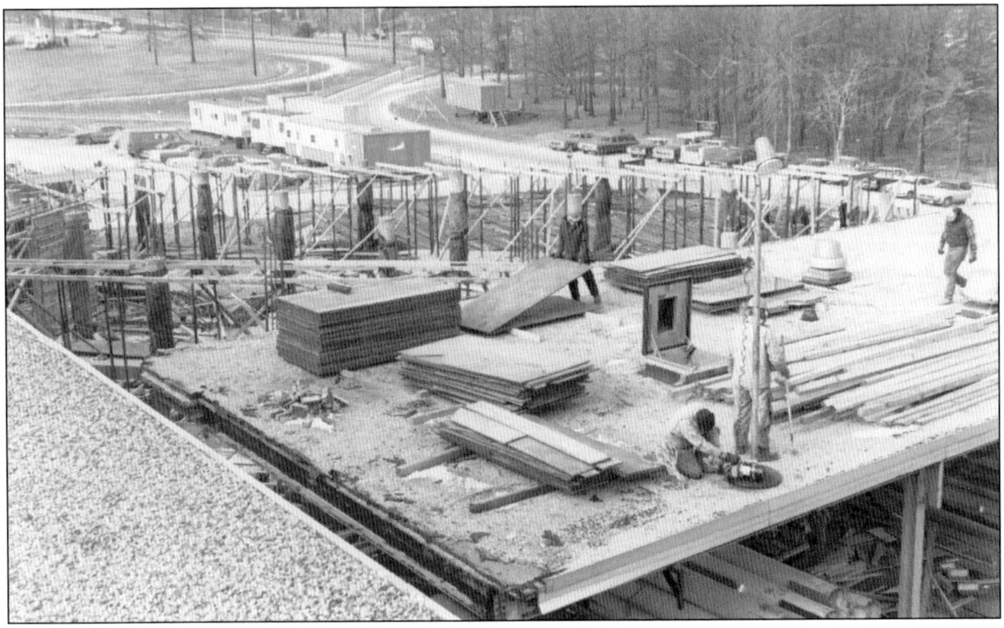

The roadway was not the only facility to expand since original construction. As the Garden State Parkway grew and operating the agency became more complex, more space was needed to house the workforce. Originally occupied in 1962, the Woodbridge Administration Building undertook a major expansion in 1980.

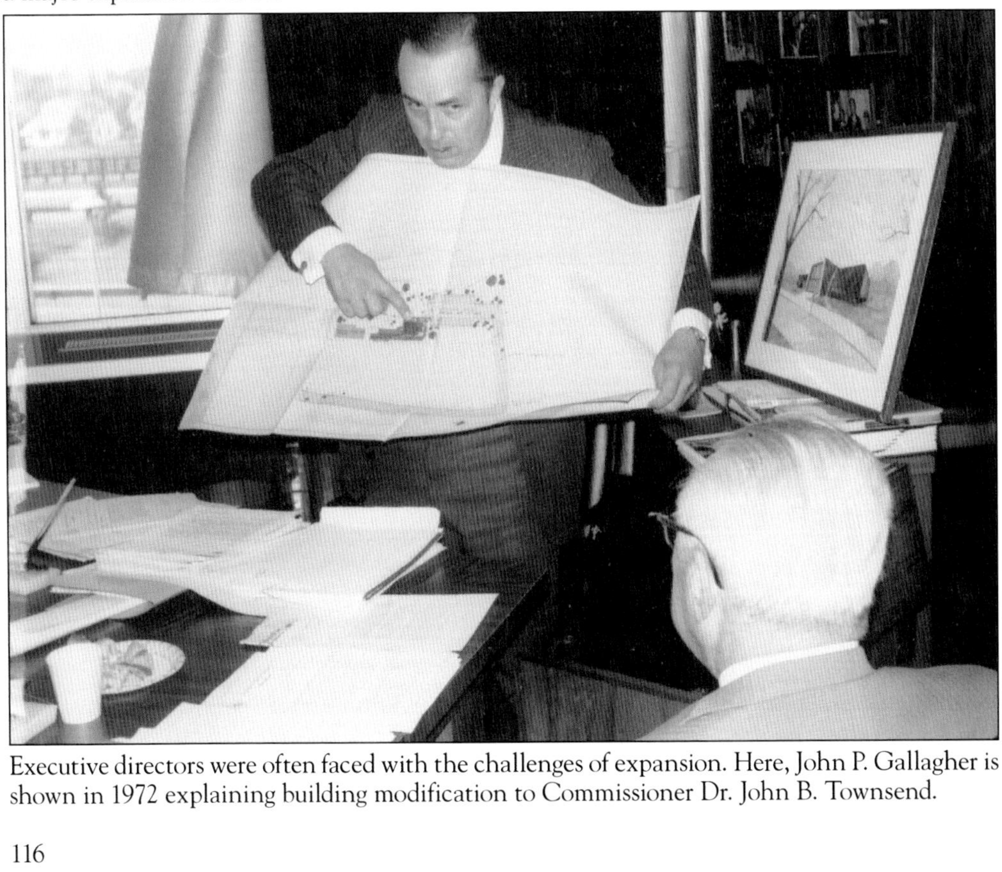

Executive directors were often faced with the challenges of expansion. Here, John P. Gallagher is shown in 1972 explaining building modification to Commissioner Dr. John B. Townsend.

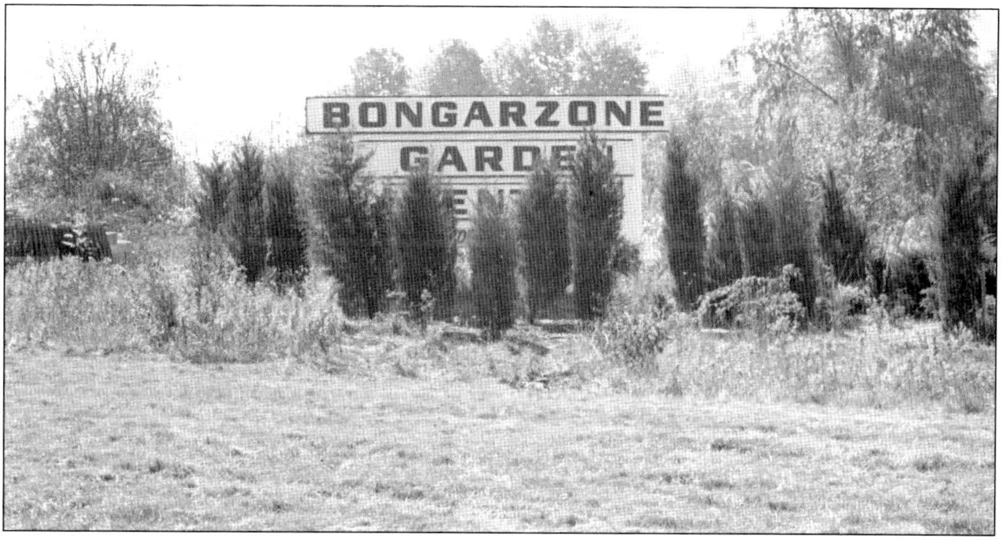

Advertising billboards were prohibited along the Garden State Parkway. Here, trees mask a billboard alongside the Parkway in Tinton Falls, Monmouth County, in 1966. The advent of cell phones has introduced a new element unanticipated for the Parkway. Some towers and their accompanying buildings have been built within the wooded sections of the Parkway and camouflaged or hidden by trees. Others, particularly New Jersey Highway Authority communication towers, have not been disguised at all but rather sit in the median. Their presence is a matter of safety and therefore requires accommodation.

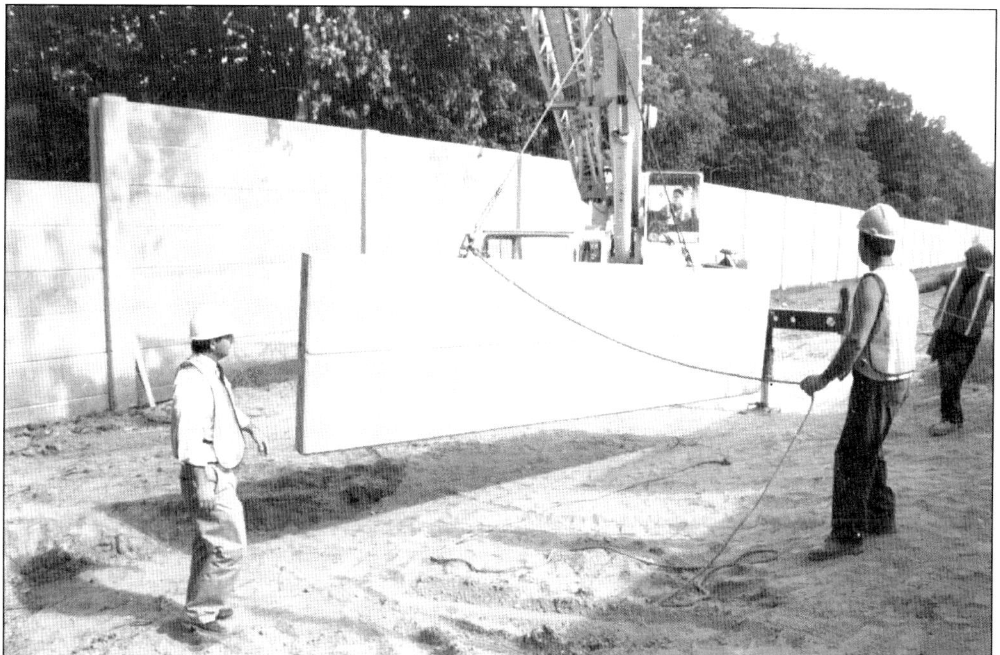

Sound barriers were erected in some areas to reduce noise in nearby communities. This kind of buffer was not the original intent of designers, who relied on the natural landscape to separate the Garden State Parkway from the surrounding community. However, in some locations, encroaching development abuts the Parkway and adaptations have occurred.

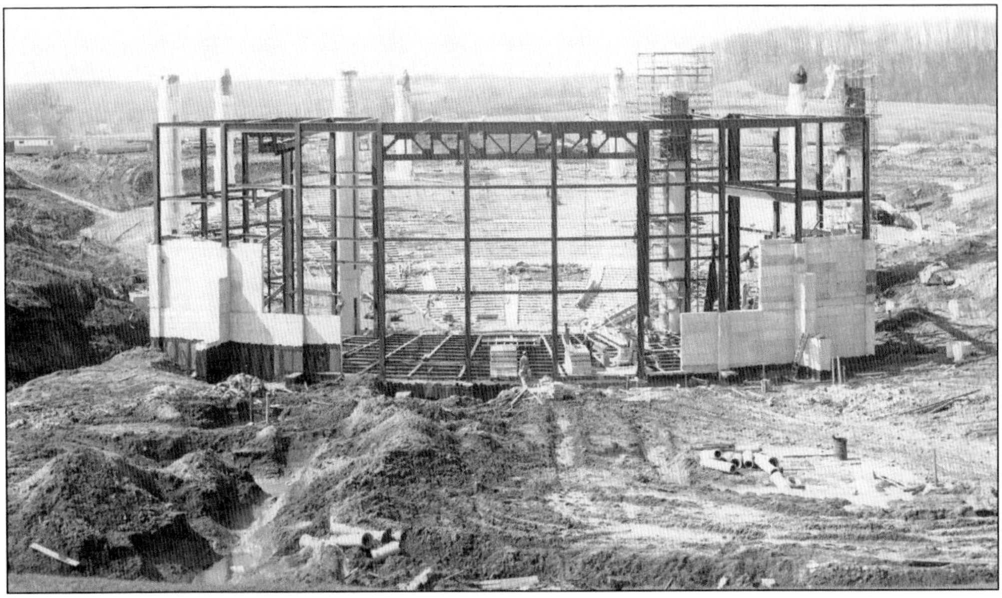

Seen here is the construction of the Garden State Arts Center in Telegraph Hill Park overlooking the Parkway at exit 116 in Holmdel, Monmouth County. The center was designed by Edward Durell Stone, who had a hand in the designs for Radio City Music Hall in New York and the Kennedy Center in Washington, DC. Ground was broken in 1965, and the center opened in 1968 with 5,300 seats beneath the roof of the circular amphitheater and room for 5,500 more on the surrounding lawn.

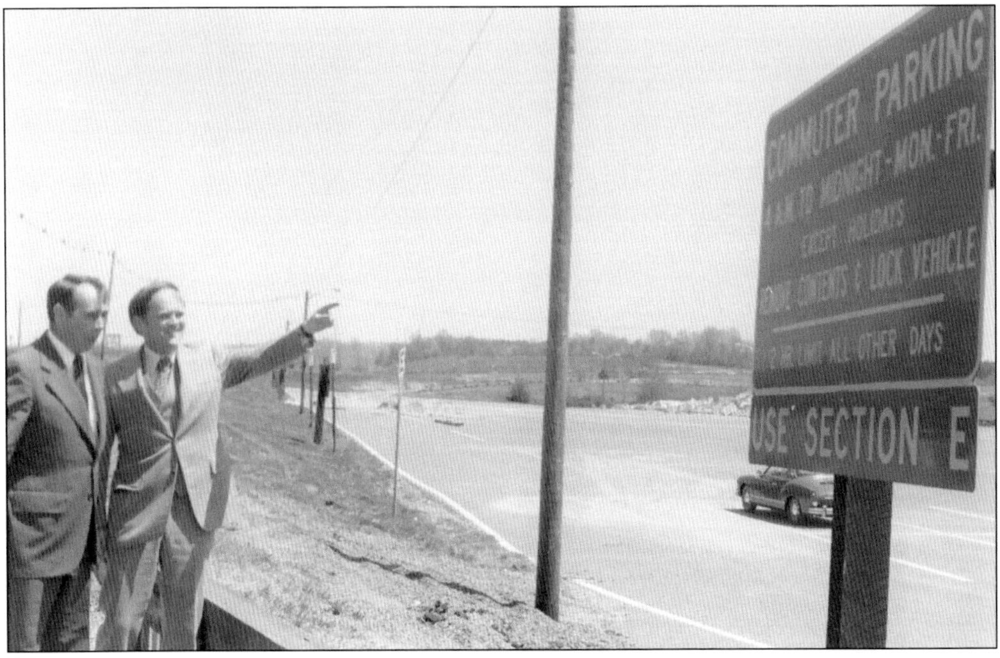

At the opening of the upper lot for commuter parking at the Garden State Arts Center, Commissioner Charles E. Starkey points to the sign while executive director F. Joseph Carragher takes in the view. This expansion in 1978 continued the New Jersey Highway Authority's encouragement for carpooling and mass transit to help reduce traffic levels on the roads.

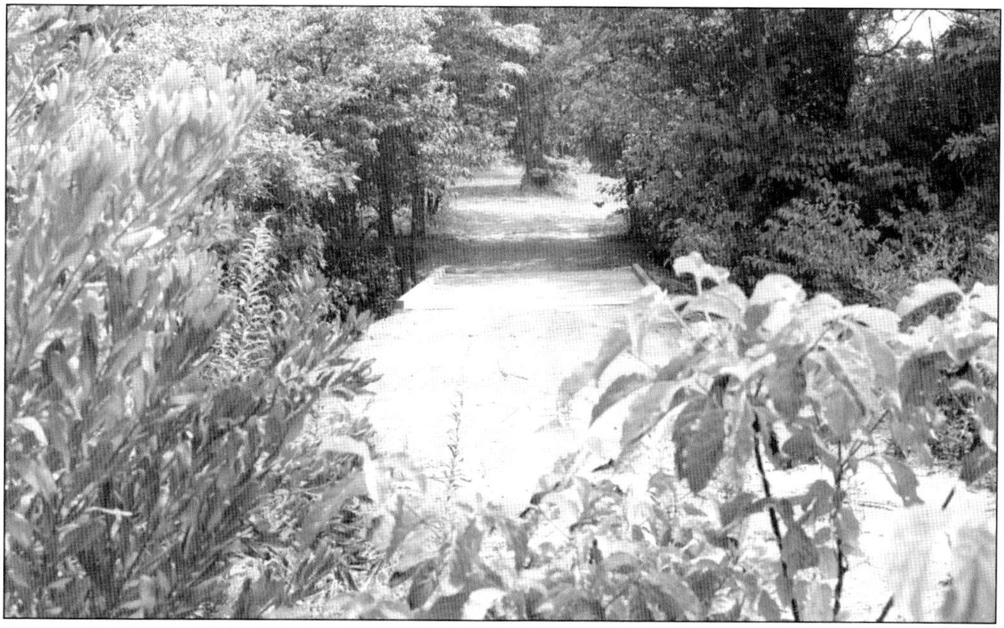

Telegraph Hill in Holmdel was chosen as the site for a cultural and recreational center to be administered by the New Jersey Highway Authority in 1964. Above is a view of the undeveloped park in 1966. In addition to the Garden State Arts Center, which opened in 1968, Telegraph Hill now features nature trails, the New Jersey Vietnam Veterans' Memorial, and the Vietnam Era Museum and Educational Center.

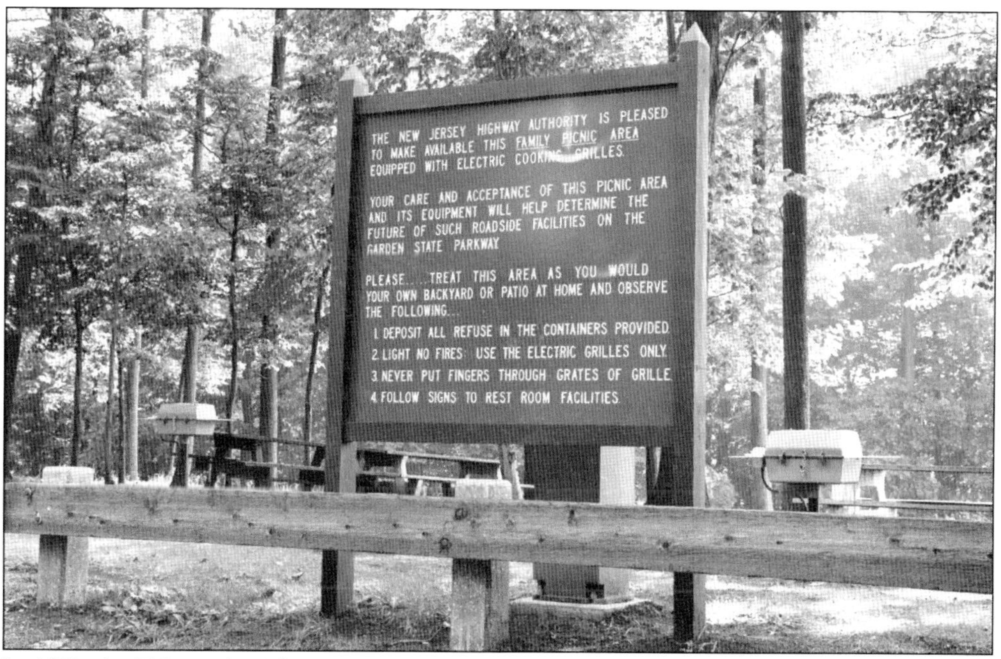

In 1970, the Telegraph Hill Picnic Area was enhanced with electric grills. As travel increased along the length of the Garden State Parkway, amenities were improved to provide a safer and more enjoyable experience. This sort of feature exemplifies the park portion of the Parkway, by giving travelers much more than a road from point A to point B.

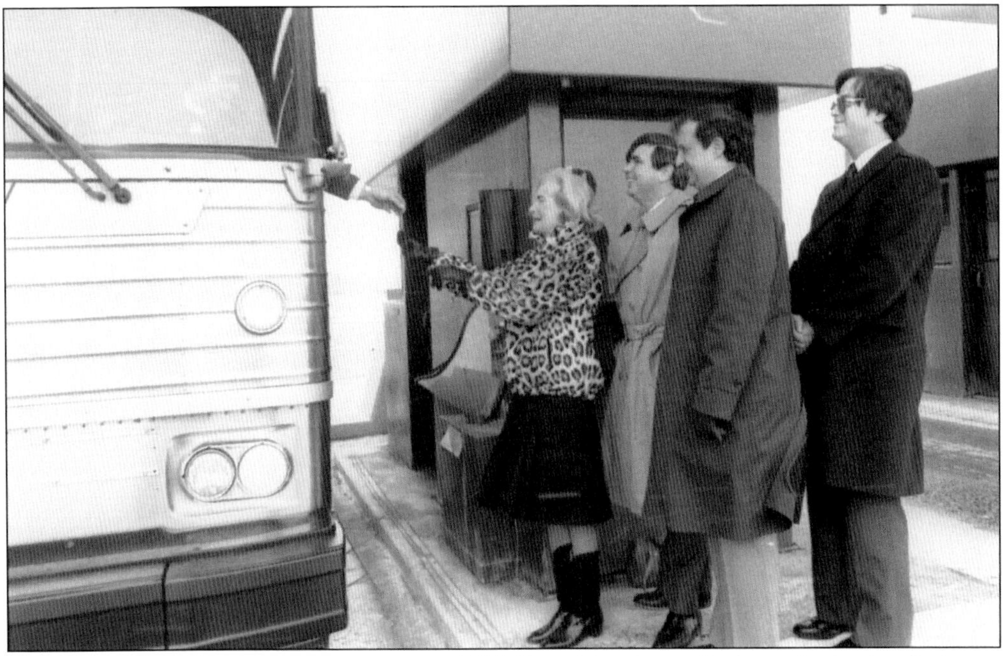

Buses were allowed to use tokens starting in 1985. Here, New Jersey Highway Authority chairman Judith H. Stanley collects the first token. Accompanying her are, from left to right, J. Crawford from the New Jersey Department of Transportation, New Jersey Highway Authority executive director George P. Zilocchi, and B. Feigenbaum from New Jersey Transit.

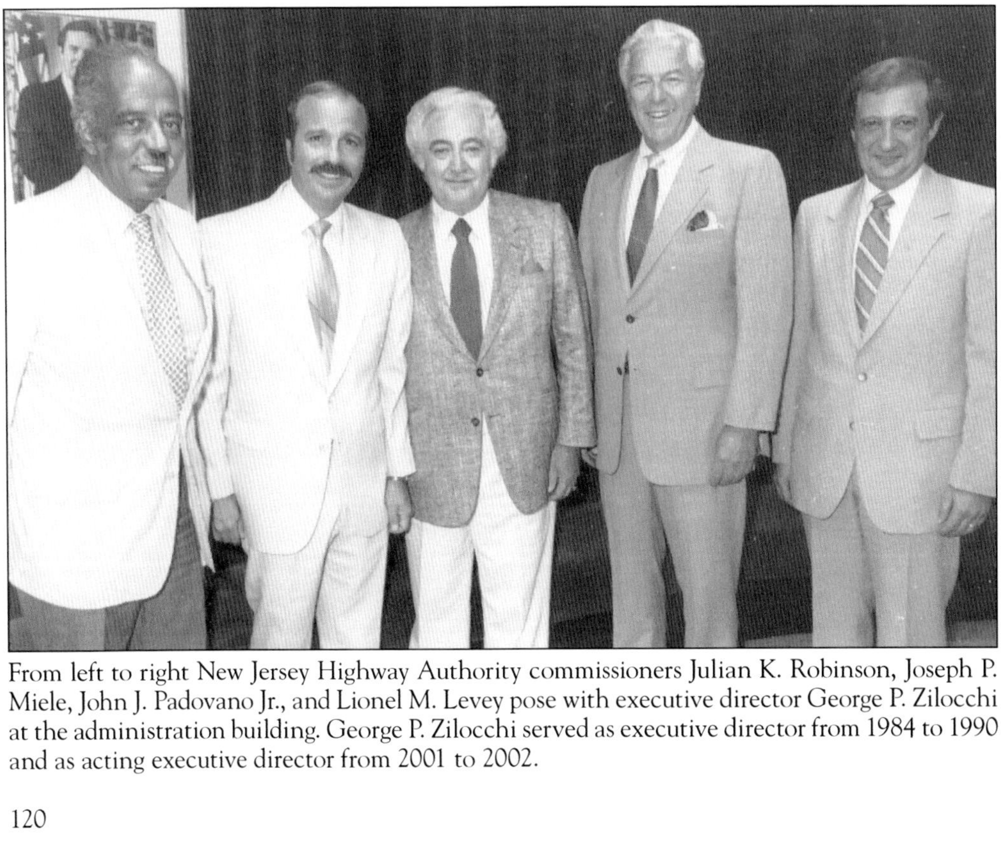

From left to right New Jersey Highway Authority commissioners Julian K. Robinson, Joseph P. Miele, John J. Padovano Jr., and Lionel M. Levey pose with executive director George P. Zilocchi at the administration building. George P. Zilocchi served as executive director from 1984 to 1990 and as acting executive director from 2001 to 2002.

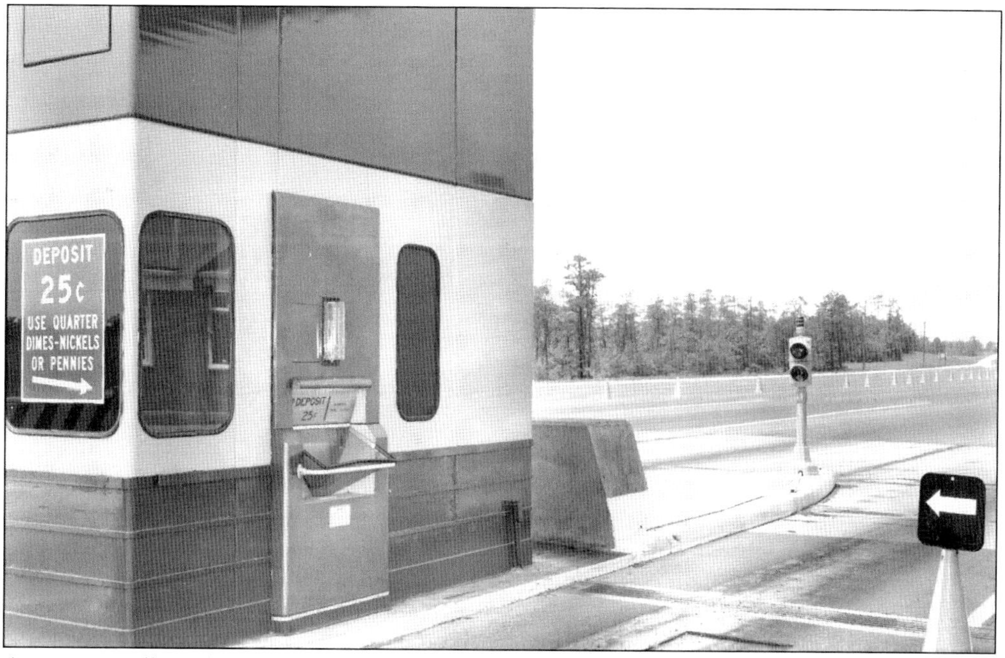

Automatic toll machines at barrier plazas allowed drivers to toss in exact change and save time by bypassing interactions with toll collectors. With the installation of the E-ZPass, motorists can pay toll costs electronically and continue through specially marked lanes at tollbooths without stopping or waiting in line to pay.

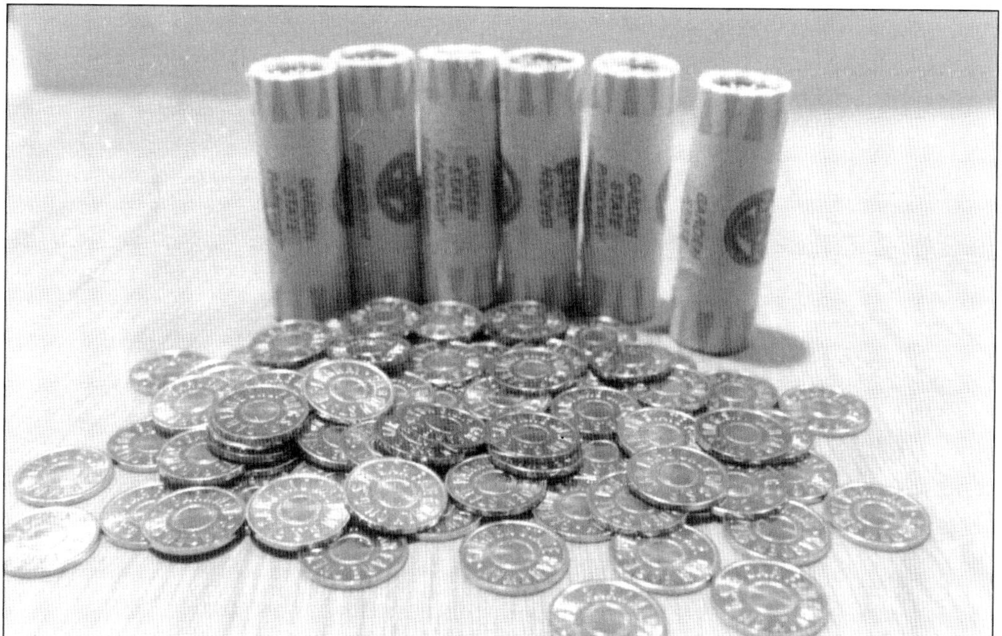

In an effort to both expedite travel and give frequent customers a discount following the first increase in toll amounts in 1988, tokens were introduced at a reduced rate. As a forerunner to E-ZPass, they further reduced the need for toll attendants and eased the traffic slow downs at the barrier tolls. The tokens were retired in December 2008.

New Jersey residents would be in danger of losing a scenic yet efficient and safe drive, the very qualities that made the Garden State Parkway so special in the first place, if it were not for protective measures put in place to preserve its integrity. Some of these measures include consultation with the New Jersey Historic Preservation Office, the New Jersey Turnpike Authority, and other agencies. Structures have been documented in written reports and with photographs. Historical markers and informational signs have been placed within service areas. When bridges must be modified or replaced, designs similar to the original structure have been employed. Landscape plantings have been replaced, such as in this photograph, and a modern variation of the singing shoulder was installed. Even videos and websites showcasing the history of the Parkway have been produced.

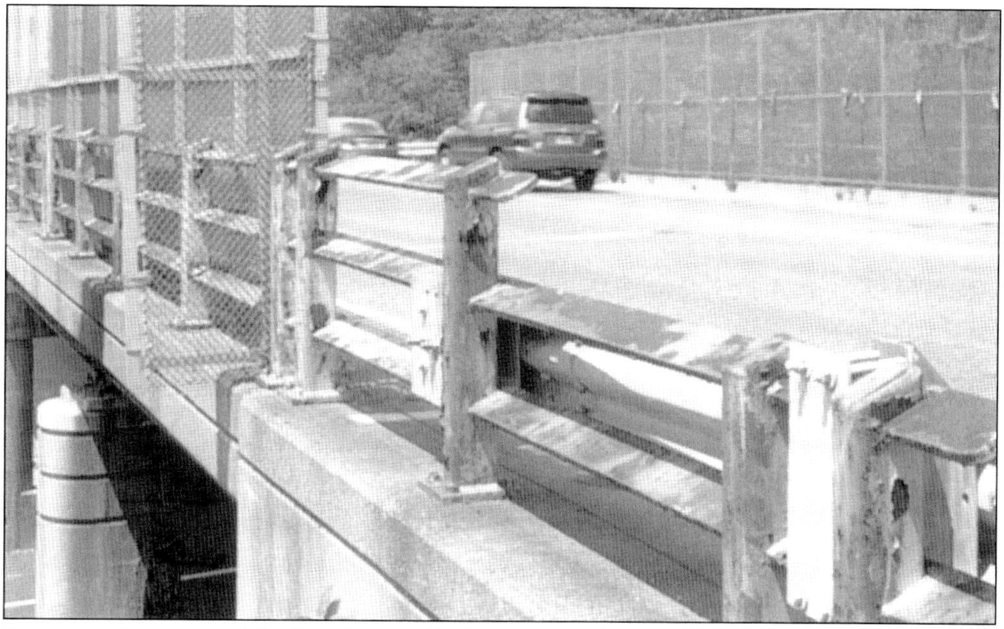

Prior to replacement of the Bay Avenue Bridges at Interchange 67, the original structures were documented to Historic American Engineering Record (HAER) standards using a four-by-five camera. Here, the original tri-rail bridge railing was still in place, though it had been fronted with a chain-link fence over the roadway and tied into steel guiderail.

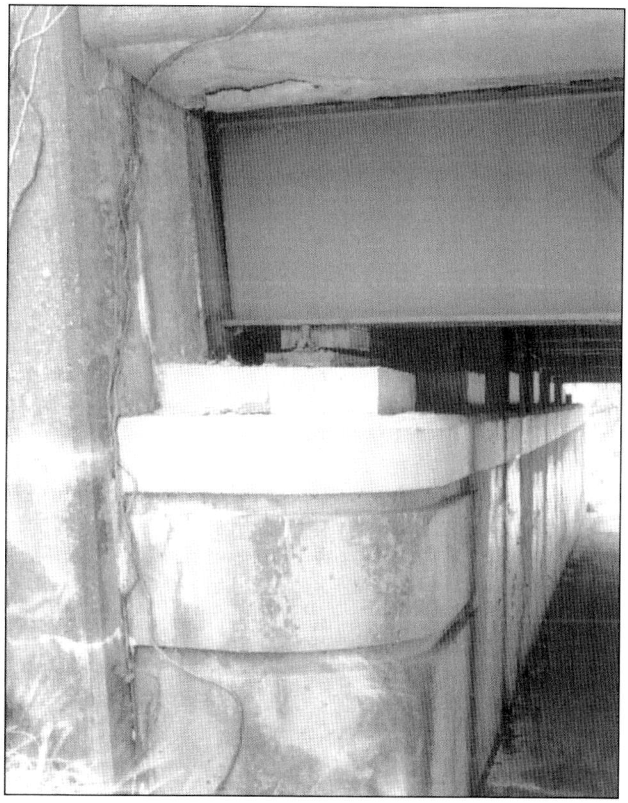

In this close up documentation photograph, the two reveals are shown on the abutments. This detail is being replicated for all the structures that replace the existing concrete structures that were originally given this treatment. In this way, the Garden State Parkway appearance is preserved for future generations of travelers and residents. The center piers have three reveals.

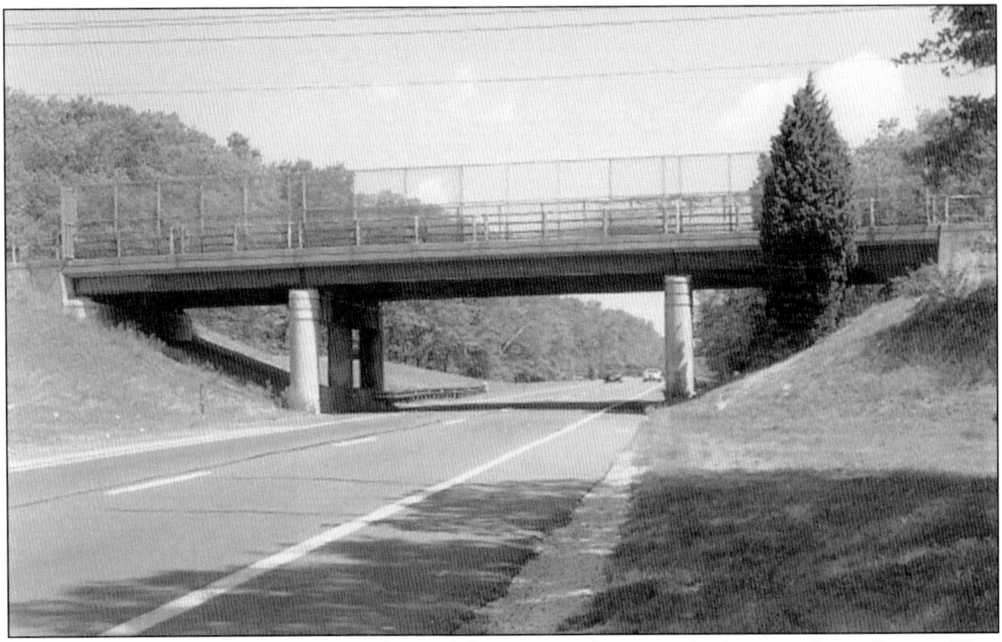

This view of Bay Avenue crossing the southbound Garden State Parkway at Interchange 67 in Ocean County shows the largely intact original structure that was considered a contributing element to the Garden State Parkway Historic District. Improvements were made to Bay Avenue in 2008 that necessitated a replacement of the bridges over the Parkway. At the same time, the replacement structures were lengthened to accommodate three travel lanes and shoulders in advance of the planned expansion for the Parkway from Interchange 30 to Interchange 80. The widening program developed a programmatic agreement to address the necessary impacts to the historic district. In addition to documenting the original structures within the project area, mitigation measures also resulted in the production of this book.

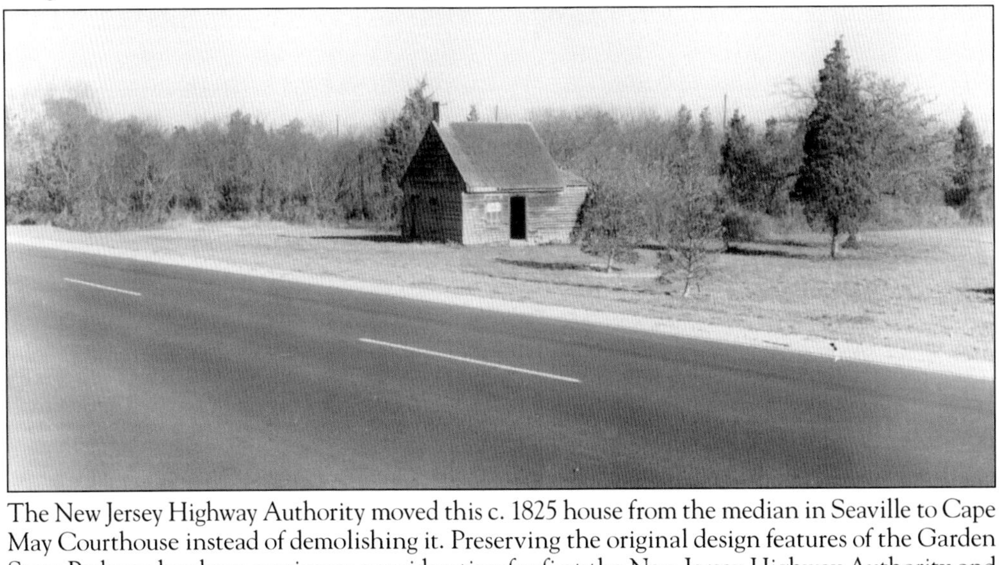

The New Jersey Highway Authority moved this c. 1825 house from the median in Seaville to Cape May Courthouse instead of demolishing it. Preserving the original design features of the Garden State Parkway has been a primary consideration for first the New Jersey Highway Authority and now the Turnpike Authority. It has been a delicate balancing act of maintaining the road with the highest element of safety, but not losing the characteristics of the Garden State Parkway.

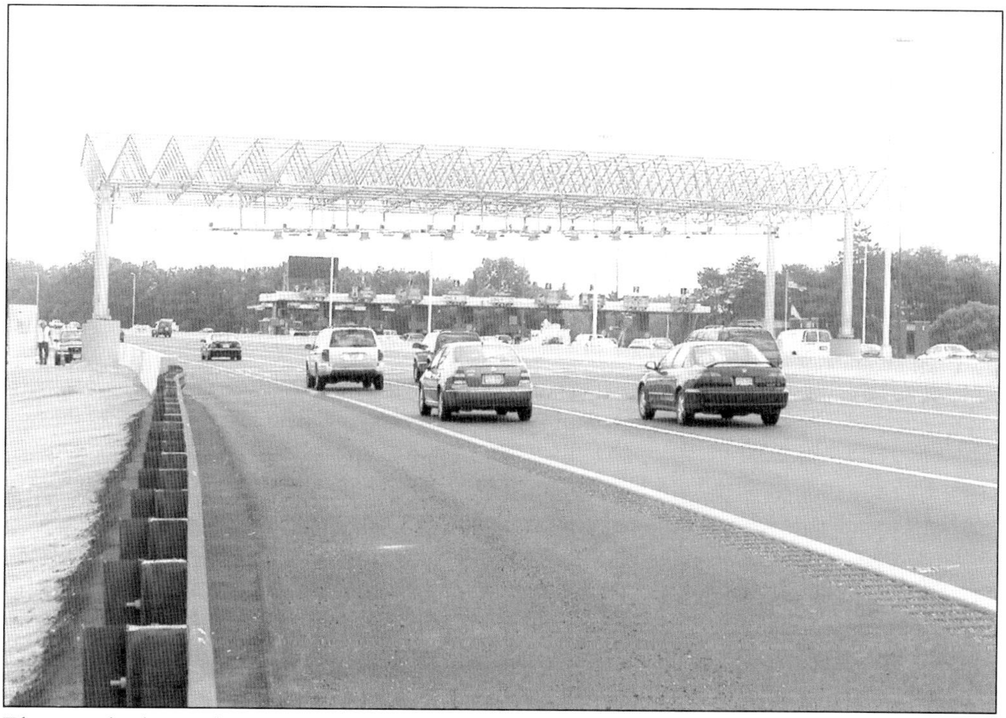

These are high-speed E-ZPass lanes at the Raritan tolls. This version of the system permits drivers to continue at the legal speed limit when paying tolls along the Garden State Parkway.

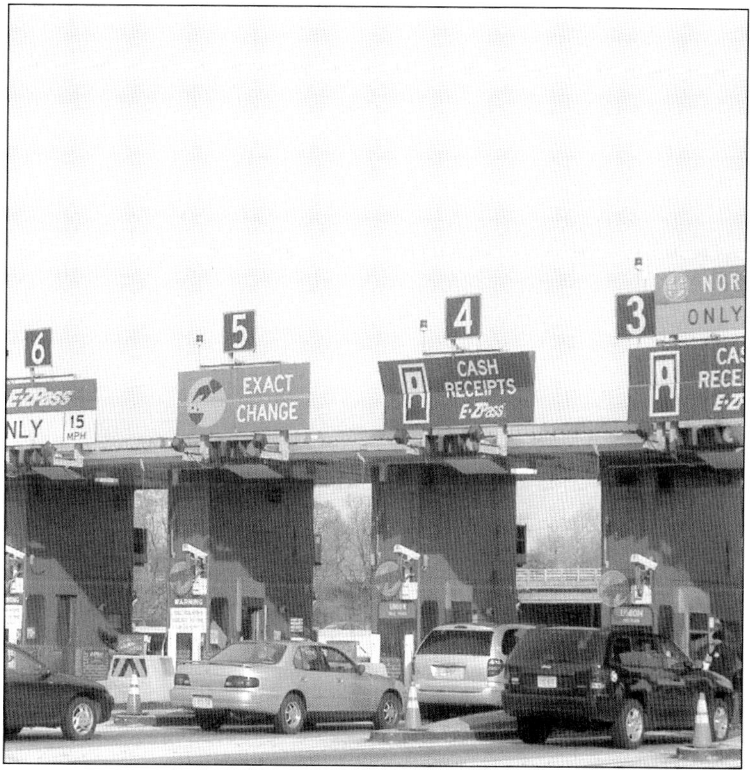

The E-ZPass system has increased the efficiency of travel along the Garden State Parkway. Barrier tolls such as these in Union have been integrated with multiple means of toll collections spread across the plaza in order to allow for drivers to access the payment type necessary.

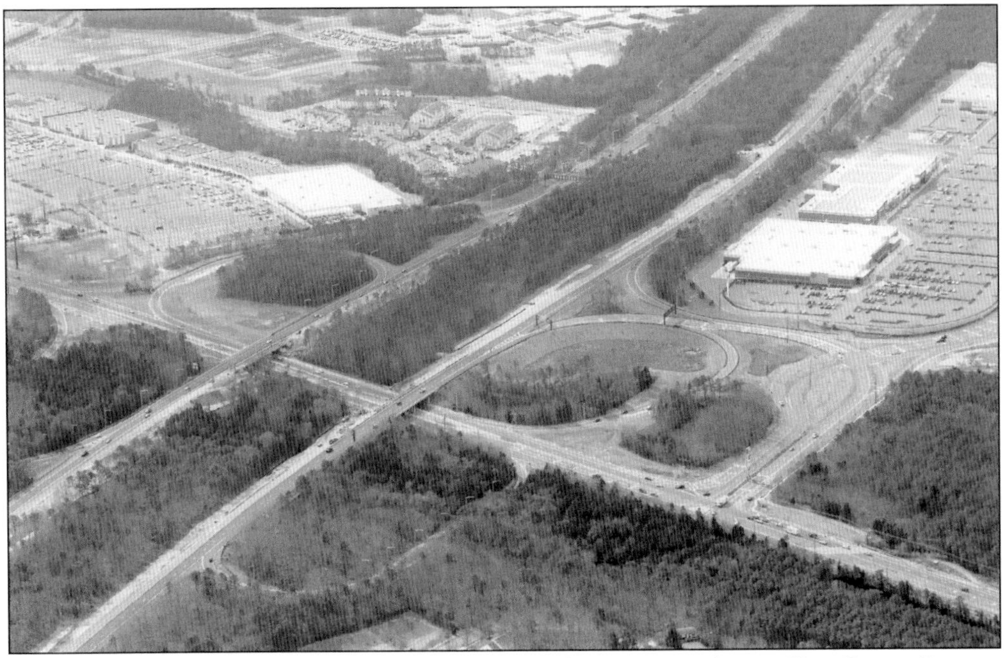

This view shows the widening of the Garden State Parkway at Interchange 63 in Ocean County. A small portion of the median is utilized for the addition of a third travel lane in each direction. The broad right-of-way of the Parkway allows for such expansions without needing additional land or severely impacting the original design concept.

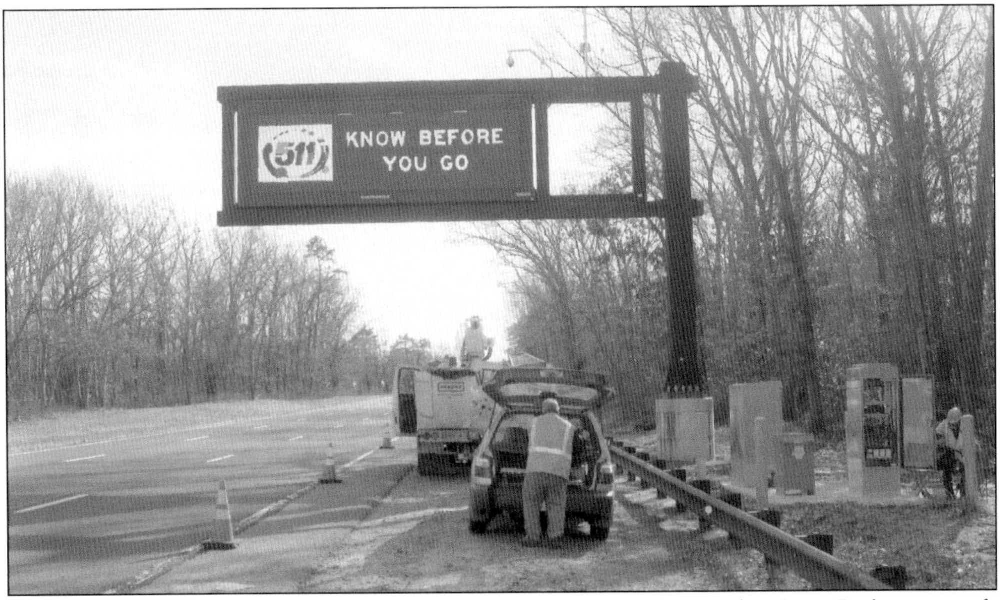

As part of the advancements and use of technologies to keep the Garden State Parkway as safe as possible, electronic variable message signs have been installed along the road to alert travelers of changing conditions along the way. Cameras are also installed to remotely monitor traffic and road conditions. The 511 system provides traffic information via telephone. This modern technology was developed to mimic signage used historically on the roadway through the use of vierendeel trusses and weathering steel supports.

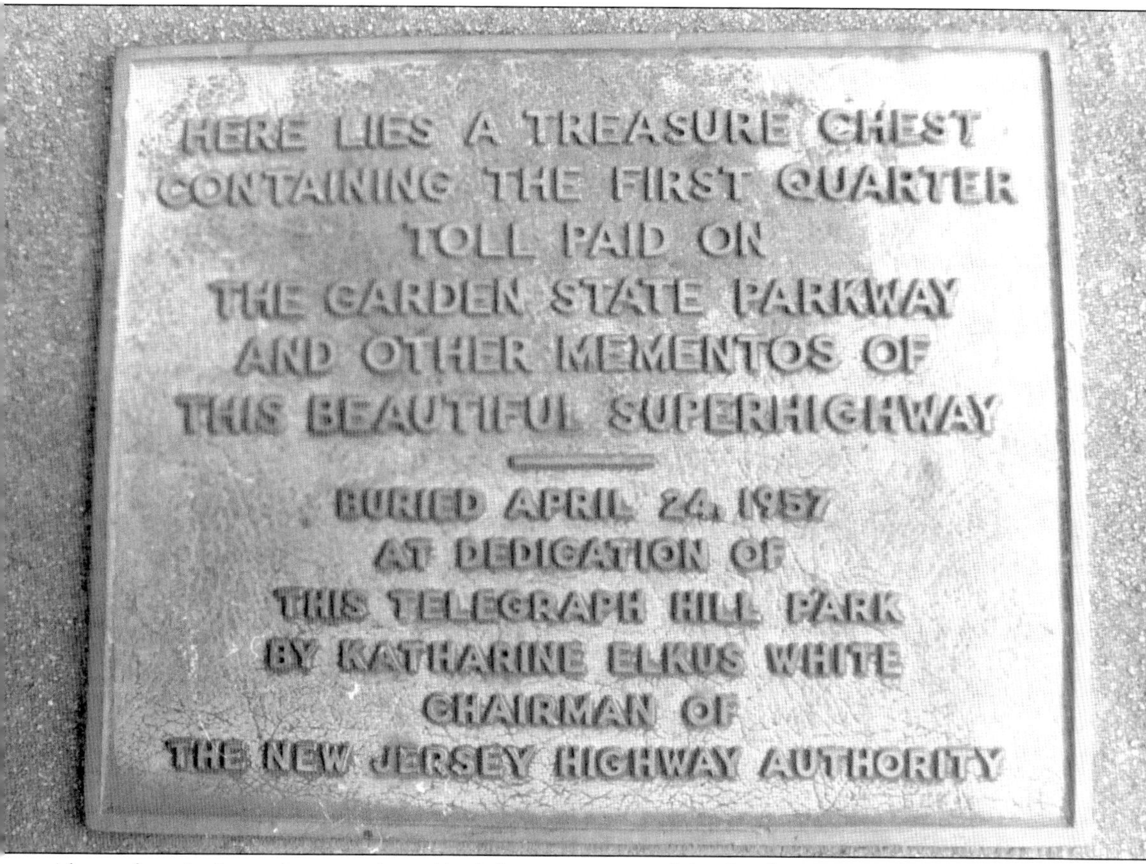

Almost from its inception, people realized the importance of the Garden State Parkway and the impact it would have. The Parkway was envisioned as the country's first high-speed toll road, which incorporated a parklike aesthetic in its design and is significant for its engineering, architecture, and landscape architecture. It stands as an elegant compromise between the Sunday drive and the commute, the desire for a pleasurable drive and the need for a direct route. The Parkway further significantly contributes to "the second toll road era," when roadways were desperately needed to relieve traffic congestion after World War II but governments lacked the funds to pay for them. For a short period of time, state authorities were created to build these highways. Revenue bonds were sold to finance highway construction and tolls were collected to repay those bonds. Once the Federal-Aid Highway Act was signed in 1956, though, federal funds began flowing into state treasuries, and states no longer needed to find ways to finance additional highways on their own. Toll road construction was no longer necessary. New federally funded highways generally have been built with cheaper utilitarian designs, further enhancing the importance of the Garden State Parkway and the legacy of the former New Jersey Highway Authority.